Information Technology and LIBRARIES

Dr. Amjad Ali

Deputy Librarian

Aligarh Muslim University, Aligarh

Ess Ess Publications

4837/24, Ansari Road, Darya Ganj,
New Delhi-110002
✆ : 23260807
Fax : 23274173
E-mail: info@essessreference.com
url:http://www.essessreference.com

First Published 2004

ISBN : 81-7000-390-3

Price : Rs. 925/-

Published by :

Ess Ess Publications

4837/24, Ansari Road, Darya Ganj,
New Delhi - 110 002
Phone : 23260807
Fax : 23274173
E-mail : essess@del3.vsnl.net.in

Printed at :
Print Line

Dedicated to

My Parents

Preface

The role of IT in collection, storage and dissemination of information is now widely recognized all over the world. The impact is visible on all disciplines of study in the educational institutions. More evidently, the syllabi of courses have been revised to accommodate recent developments, specially, the components of IT.

Libraries are directly involved in the business of information. As a result, they respond to the changes brough out by IT earlier than any other field of education and training. During the last one decade or so the names of almost all departments of 'library scince' have been changed to 'library and information science'. Some new courses have also been introduced reflecting a wider component of IT within them.

This book is an attempt to bridge the gap between the traditional librarianship and the modern library and information science of today. The organization of the contents of the book reflects a desire on my part to provide the students of library and information science and other readers with a thorough understanding of the fundamentals of InformationTechnology as applicable to libraries, so that at the end they will be well prepared for carrying out the work in a better way. It is also intended to meet the requirements of working librarians, information professionals and educators.

My thanks are due to all my family members who took all the pains to see that I work on the book with full concentration. My thanks are also due to the Publisher, Mr. Sumit Sethi who brought out the book within a very short time.

Although every care has been taken to check mistakes and misprints, yet it is difficult to claim perfection. Any errors, omissions and valuable suggestions for the book brought to my notice will be thankfully acknowledged and incorporated in the next edition.

Dr. Amjad Ali

E-Mail: amjad_alig@yahoo.co.in

Contents

1
CONCEPT OF INFORMATION TECHNOLOGY

Information technology is a recent and comprehensive term, which describes the whole range of processes for generation, storage, transmission, retrieval and processing of information. The history of IT may be traced to early civilizations when the art of recording the information developed. It followed mechanical and later electronic path as in today's society. For centuries together information was recorded on stones, metal plates, cloth, paper and alike materials. The telephone, radio, television, satellite transmission, transistors, computers and lately Internet represent distinct qualitative changes in the field of information technology with the fact that we now have to accept the composite term information technology to include a whole range of new developments.

CONCEPT OF INFORMATION TECHNOLOGY

Information is a collection of data that communicates some meaning. Let us first attempt to define data before proceeding on to information.

Data

Data can be defined in many ways. Information science defines data as unprocessed information. Data is converted into information, and information is converted into knowledge. For the purposes of Enterprise, data is a small unit of information, i.e. a learner's name or an exam mark. It can also be defined as facts represented in a readable language (such as numbers, characters, images, or other methods of recording) on a durable medium. Data on its own carries no meaning. Empirical data are facts originating in or based on observations or experiences. A database is a store of data concerning a particular domain. Data in a database may be less structured or have weaker semantics (built-in meaning) than knowledge in a knowledge base

Information

The word 'information' was used for the first time in 1958 in place of document. It was a wide term in comparison with document. The term became very popular soon. As a result the name of the American Documentation Institute was changed to American Society for Information in 1966. Accordingly the Journal of American Documentation was also named as Journal of the American Society for Information Science. Britain also followed the suit and changed the name of ASLIB to Institute of Information Science. The Russian Government also made similar changes to accommodate the new concept.

Simply defined, information is a message received and understood. Information is something that can be recorded, communicated and computed with. Information is fungible, which implies that its meaning can be identified regardless of the particulars of the physical realization. Thus, information in one realization (such as ink on a sheet of paper) can be easily transferred to another (for example, spoken words). Types of information include deterministic, probabilistic and quantum information. Each type is characterized by information units, which are abstract systems whose states represent the simplest information of this type. These define the "natural" representation of the information. Information units can be put together to form larger systems and can be processed with basic operations acting on a small number of units at a time.

Technology

Technology is defined as " a science and techniques of methods of doing or getting things done, related to an art, science or a particular profession." Technology has also been defined as the science of "industrial arts" and it is also defined as the application of science to the needs of an individual and society. Technology is a scientific way of developing new techniques, and a systematic way of evolving and applying these techniques. Technology is thus a method of designing techniques.

Information Technology

The term information technology is manipulated in many ways. Macmillan Dictionary of Information Technology defines IT as "acquisition, processing, storage and dissemination of vocal, verbal, pictorial, textual and numerical information by microelectronic-based combination of computer and telecommunications".

UNESCO defines Information Technology as "scientific and technological and engineering disciplines and the management techniques used in information handling and processing information, their application: computers and their interaction with man and machine and associated social, economic and cultural matters". It is not concerned only with new pieces of equipment but much broader spectrum of information activities such as print, reprography, the telephone network, broadcasting computers and Internet.

Information technology includes all matters concerned with the furtherance of computer science and technology and with the design, development, installation, and implementation of information systems and applications. An information technology architecture is an integrated framework for acquiring and evolving IT to achieve strategic goals. It has both logical and technical components. Logical components include mission, functional and information requirements, system configurations, and information flows. Technical components include IT standards and rules that will be used to implement the logical architecture.

Information technology is the technique of collection, storage, and dissemination of information. Information technology is more in use in America, England and India in comparison with other countries of the worlds. Janiffer Roule has put information technology into the following categories:

- Methods and tools for recording of knowledge
- Methods of keeping records
- Methods of Indexing Documents and Information
- Methods of Communicating Knowledge

NEED FOR INFORMATION

We live in an age where information is a valuable resource. Information is needed to plan and execute about all type of human activities at local, regional, national and international level. The vast emphasis on production and distribution of information has led to develop ways and means for effective management of the information resources and the work has been transformed into a whole industry called the knowledge industry. Heavy budgets of the governmental and well as private agencies for information related activities remind of the importance of information. Proper use of information is possible only when the information is collected and stored in a professional way so that the same can be retrieved with ease as and when required.

All social organizations need information to solve their problems. The information needs of the social groups are varied since the social activities are of diverse nature. It also needs to retrieve information with accuracy and speed. Information is the basis for taking decisions, particularly in business and trade. Information is needed to know the market trends, demand and supply. Information is not only needed to produce an item but also to sell it. Advertizing plays an important role for publicity of a product or service. Information has great value in education and training. In higher education institutions, the availability of different type of information is needed for this purpose. The use of information is increasing day by day in research, specially after the invention of communication technologies. To fulfill the social, economic and political needs, information fills the gaps in the society. In the advanced society, information has become a power.

Information technology has affected the functioning of libraries and offices to a great extent. Online Public Access Catalogue and Electronic Office have been established which provide grater facility in information production and processing. Internet, Electronic Library and Virtual libraries are a few examples of the application of information technology in our daily lives.

Application of Information Technology

Information technology is being applied in almost all areas of human activities. The following are the main field of application:

- Sciences
- Commerce
- Medicine and health care
- Education and entertainment
- Training and development
- Libraries
- Multi-lingual works
- Sports
- Tourism
- Agriculture
- Research and development

Information Technology is applied in libraries for the following functions:

Computer technology

- Database creation and management
- Library management

Telecommunication technology

- Library network
- Information network

Reprographic technology

- Photography
- Microfilm
- Optical/Digital technology
- Audio/video

Library technology

- Classification
- Cataloguing
- Current awareness service
- Selective dissemination of information

Application of IT in Traditional Libraries

- Acquisition
- Cataloguing and classification
- Circulation
- Reference service
- Safety and security

Information technology may be used in special libraries for the following functions:

- Library automation
- Automated in-house functions
- Library administration, classification, cataloguing, indexing, accessioning, database creation etc.
- Reprography, photography, micrography, audio and video, publishing, optical disk etc
- Networking and resource sharing
- Technical writing, editing, publication. DTP etc.

- Access to databases, latest technical training and human resource development
- Collection building on electronic media
- Internet
- Intranet

IT HISTORY AT A GLANCE

The development of Information Technology and its adoption in the society can be characterized under four basic periods of the history as given below:

Premechanical Period

Mechanical Period

Electromechanical Period, and

Electronic Period

The Premechanical Age: 3000 B.C. - 1450 A.D.

At first humans communicated only through speaking and picture drawings. By 3000 B.C., the Sumerians in Mesopotamia (what is today southern Iraq) devised cuniform. Around 2000 B.C., Phoenicians created symbols. The Greeks later adopted the Phoenician alphabet and added vowels; the Romans gave the letters Latin names to create the alphabet we use today. There came paper and Pens—input technologies. Sumerians' input technology was a stylus that could scratch marks in wet clay. About 2600 B.C., the Egyptians write on the papyrus plant. Around 100 A.D., the Chinese made paper from rags, on which modern-day papermaking is based.

Books and Libraries came into existence as Permanent Storage Devices. Religious leaders in Mesopotamia kept the earliest "books". The Egyptians kept scrolls. Around 600 B.C., the Greeks began to fold sheets of papyrus vertically into leaves and bind them together. The First Numbering Systems was introduced from 1-9 as vertical lines, the number 10 as a U or circle, the number 100 as a coiled rope, and the number 1,000 as a lotus blossom. The first numbering systems similar to those in use today were invented between 100 and 200 A.D. in India. Around 875 A.D., the concept of zero was developed. The first calculator: The Abacus was developed which was one of the very first information processors.

Mechanical Age: 1450 - 1840

This was the period of the First Information Explosion. Johann Gutenberg (Mainz, Germany) Invented the movable metal-type printing process in 1450. The development of book indexes and the widespread use of page numbers took place. The first general purpose "computers appeared during this period. Actually people who held the job title computer: one who works with numbers. The Pascaline and Leibniz's Machine was developed in 1600s. The Pascaline. Invented by Blaise Pascal (1623-62).

One of the first mechanical computing machines was invented around 1642. Charles Babbage (1792-1871), eccentric English mathematician The Difference Enginens' Working model was created in 1822. Punch card idea was picked up by Babbage from Joseph Marie Jacquard's 1834) (1752-loom was Introduced in 1801)

Electromechanical Age: 1840 - 1940.

The discovery of ways to harness electricity was the key advance made during this period. Knowledge and information could now be converted into electrical impulses. It was the beginnings of telecommunication. The voltaic battery, telegraph, Morse Code were invented in the first half of the century.

Alexander Graham Bell invented telephone in 1876, followed by the discovery that electrical waves travel through space and can produce an effect far from the point at which they originated. These two events led to the invention of the radio by Guglielmo Marconi in 1894. Electromechanical Computing gained ground and the first census was conducted in 1880 by the new machine.

Electronic Age: 1940 - Present.

In early 1940s Electronic vacuum tubes were invented. The First High-Speed, General-Purpose Computer Using Vacuum Tubes. Electronic Numerical Integrator and Computer (ENIAC) were developed using vacuum tubes (not mechanical devices) to do its calculations in 1940. Hence, first electronic computer came into being. The First Stored-Program for Computer(s) was developed in early 1940s, Mauchly and Eckert began to design the EDVAC - the Electronic Discreet Variable Computer. John von Neumann's influential report came in June 1945 and the British scientists used this report and outpaced the Americans. Manchester Mark I went into operation in June 1948—becoming the first stored-program computer. Maurice Wilkes, a British scientist at Cambridge University, completed the EDSAC (Electronic Delay Storage Automatic Calculator) in 1949—two years before EDVAC was finished. Thus, EDSAC became the first stored-program computer in general use (i.e., not a prototype. Late 1940s, Eckert and Mauchly began the development of a computer called UNIVAC (Universal Automatic Computer). Remington Rand delivered first UNIVAC to Census Bureau in 1951. But, a machine called LEO (Lyons Electronic Office) went into action a few months before UNIVAC and became the world's first commercial computer.

INFORMATION TECHNOLOGY TODAY

Information has become a vital resource in the present time. Information technology is affecting almost every walk of human lives. It needs to device ways for better management of information. There are two basic tools in management of information systems : computer and the communication system. Apart from it there are six types of technologies that also come under the Information Technology:

- Electronic Technology
- Computer Technology
- Communication Technology

- Telecommunication Technology
- Artificial Intelligence Technology
- Human and Machine Interface Technology

COMPONENTS OF INFORMATION TECHNOLOGY

Information Technology developed through out the ages. But there was always a change in the materials and techniques used for recording, storage, processing and communication of information. Depending upon these characteristics of technology at present, Information Technology is put under the following three categories.

- Computer Technology
- Communication Technology
- Telecommunication

COMPUTER TECHNOLOGY

Computer is an electronic tool which works with high speed, accuracy and memory It stores, processes and retrieves information in a very efficient way. At the same time, computer performs a variety of functions. It has become so much effective that the print media which dominated for centuries is seeing a declined trend in its use. Computer technology is further divided into three categories as under:

- Processing Technology
- Storage Technology
- Operating System and Software

Technical Evolution of Computer

The word computer has been derived from the Latin word 'computere', which means to calculate. The term computer may therefore be applied to any calculating device. Now, the term refers to an electronic machine which is used to process numbers, text, graphics or a combination of them. It may also be stated that computer uses electronic devices such as transistors, resistors and diodes

The computer we see today is a recent innovation. It has undergone many stages of development during the last one century. There are some landmarks which led to the development of computers in its present form Charles Babbage first deviced the idea of a general purpose computer. He realized the possibility to design a machine which could carry out an infinite number of possible sequences of operations. The concept of stored programmes provided the basis for all modern computers.

The next landmark in the evolution of computer was the effort of Herman Hollerith who first developed electromechanical calculating machines in 1890. The early decades of the twentieth century witnesses advances in punch card techniques. In 1944 the automatic calculator was designed by Howard Aiken at Harvard University. It was an electronic computer which utilized electromagnetic relays and mechanical counters.

By, 1950, the period was marked by intense research activity to develop stores program, self-sufficient calculating machines and most of these were laboratory prototypes. The later period saw many developments related to computer hardware and software which made the computer an efficient tool for processing of information at a greater speed with vast memory

CHARACTERISTICS OF COMPUTER

Computers of all sizes have common characteristics — speed, reliability, storage capacity, and productivity. Computers are the foundation of business, travel, and leisure life today. Computers provide the processing speed required by all facets of society. The quick service we expect at the bank, at the grocery store, on the stock exchange, and on the Internet are dependent on the speed of computers.

Computers are extremely reliable as well. Most errors are caused by humans, not computers. Computers are capable of storing enormous amounts of data that must be located and retrieved very quickly. The capability to store and retrieve volumes of data is at the core of the Information Age.

A computer is an intelligent amplifier that performs operations in a more faster, accurate and efficient way. Thus it frees humans to use their time in matters involving creativity and judgement. The characteristics possessed by computer can be listed as follows·

Speed

A computer can add and subtract numbers, compare letter to determine alphabetic sequence, move and copy numbers and letter. As such there is nothing profound in these operations. What is significant is the speed with which computers carry out these operations. This speed varies from a few micro second (millionth of a second) to nanoseconds (billionth of a second). For instance a small computer can evaluate investment decisions by performing hundreds of thousands of machine operations in a second

Accuracy

Computers are very accurate. They can perform hundreds of thousand of operations with great accuracy as their circuits have no mechanical parts to wear and malfunction. They can run errorless for days at a time.

Reliability

Computer output is genrally very reliable, subject to the condition that the input data entering to the computer is correct and the program give us computer errors and wrong results only if data is not correct. Hence, the phrase GARBAGE IN GARBAGE OUT (GIGO).

Central Processing

A processing unit in a computer interprets instructions in a program and carries them out. An instruction in general, consists of a part, which specifies the operation to be performed and other parts, which specify the address of operand. In a processor, a string of bits is used to code operations and another string of n operations in binary so that 2x = n. For example to code 16 operations we need 4 bits, since 24=16.

An instruction consisting of an operation code and operand address or addresses designed for a specific computer is know as a machine language instruction of that computer. Machine language instructions for input/output, data movement, arithmetic, logic and controlling sequence of operations are available in all computers. A computer's processor has storage registers to store operands and results. It also has a register to store the instruction being executed called "Instruction Register" and a register which stores the address of the next instruction to be executed called " Program Counter Register".

A sequence of machine language instructions to solve a problem is know as a machine language program. A computer executes a machine language program in two phases. In the first phase, it reads and stores the program in its memory. After storing the program, it initiates program execution. In this phase, instructions are retrieved from memory one after another and are decoded and executed.

Storage

Storage refers to holding information somewhere. RAM, Random Access Memory, is short-term memory. It is volatile memory because the memory is automatically "erased" when the power is turned off or interrupted. The RAM memory is located inside the computer case on the motherboard. A motherboard is not the keyboard. The keyboard is what you type with. A motherboard holds RAM memory, electronic circuits and other computer parts including the central processing unit. ROM, Read-Only-Memory, is not volatile meaning the memory is still there when power is interrupted or turned off. When the computer is turned back on again, ROM memory is still in storage on the internal hard disk.

Operating System (OS) and Software

A big complicated computer program that lets multiple simultaneously executing big complicated computer programs coexist peacefully on one physical computer. The operating system is also responsible for hiding the details of the computer hardware from the application programmers, e.g., letting a programmer say "I want to write ABC into a file named XYZ" without the programmer having to know how many disk drives the computer has or what company manufactured those drives. Examples of operating systems are Unix and Windows NT. Examples of things that try to be operating systems but mostly fail to fulfill the "coexist peacefully" condition are Windows and the Macintosh OS.

The most important program that runs on a computer: the operatign system ("OS") performs basic tasks such as recognizing input from the keyboard, sending output to the display screen, keeping track of files and directories on the disk, and controlling peripheral devices such as disk drives and printers. PCs operating systems include DOS and Windows XP; Macintosh operating systems include OS 9.2 and OS X.

Software

A set of programs associated with the operation of a computer is called software. The electronic circuits used in building the computer that executes the software is known as the hardware of the computer. For example, a TV bought from a shop is hardware; the various entertainment programs transmitted from the TV station are software. An important point to note is, hardware is a one-time expense and is necessary whereas software is a continuing expense and is vital. Computer software may be classified into two broad categories:

Application Software

It is the set of programs necessary to carry out operations for a specified application such as :

* To solve a set of equations
* To process examination results
* To prepare a Pay-Bill for an organization
* To prepare Electricity-Bill for each month.

System Software

These are general programs written for the system, which provide the environment to facilitate writing of Application software. Some of the system programs are given below:

Compiler: It is a translator system program used to translate a High-level language program into a Machine language program.

Assembler: It is another translator program used to translate an Assembly language program into a Machine language program.

Interpreter: It is also a translator system program used to translate a High level language program into a Machine language program, but it translates and executes line by line.

Loader: It is a system program used to store the machine language program into the memory of the computer.

COMMUNICATION TECHNOLOGY

The word communication has been derives from the Latin word 'communico' which means to communicate. The word is used for exchange of information. Communication needs language as well the channel for communication between two or more than two points. The early man communicated messages by primitive means such as by smoke, drum beating, lighting etc, but as the technology advanced, the means to communicate were also improved. In the 16th century, the postal service developed. In India, horse riders were employed for communication of messages till 1930. Later on telegraph, telephone, wireless, and then the communication technology of today mainly Internet made the system of communication much easier and faster.

Communication Systems

Communication system can be divided under the following categories:

Radio Communication

Radio emerged as one of the most potent media of communication since it made possible the transmission and reception of signals by means of electronic wave and without the use of connecting wires. Within a century of its invention radio has grown enormously going out of Marconi's workshop to a permanent fixture in almost all the homes the world over.

Eventually, the industry came to recognize radio as a way of stimulating sales. By 1930, a magazine, Billboard was reporting that "sheet music and record dealers now consider !radio a boon to their business, rather than a detriment." The magazine's initial radio coverage, a one-eighth-page section called Radio Entertainers first appeared in 1928.

Many forms of presentations emerged and met extinction within a short life span of radio spreading over the last fifty years. By 1975, the once-popular nostalgia format was fading, drama radio had been dead for more than a decade, and the disco format was being studied based on the records played in the growing number of discotheques throughout. Since its development in 1895, the radio has long since been revolutionizing the world. It has become so common that it is very improbable that one could ever pass a day without coming into contact with radio in some shape or fashion. In the beginning, radios were the only form of entertainment other than family outings and live shows such as those seen on Broadway. However, it seems like radio has outlived its passion for the programs and evening news and now concentrates almost completely on music.

Television

Television is used to telecast picture and sound simultaneously. It is an ideal medium of communication for the general use. Television signals are received across the geographical boundaries of the countries. Live telecast makes this medium more popular and interesting.

Coaxial Cable

Coaxial cable consists of a single strand of copper running down the axis of the cable. This strand is separated from the outer shielding by an insulator made of foam or other dielectrics. A conductive shield covers the cable. Usually an outer insulating cover is applied to the overall cable—this has nothing to do with the carrying capacity of the cable. Because of the construction of the cable, obviously coaxial in nature, very high frequencies can be carried without leaking out. In fact, dozens of TV channels, each 6 MHz wide, can be carried on a single cable.

Microwave Transmission

Microwaves uses space as transmission medium. As the microwave beams travel in a straight line, it is advantageous to place microwave towers on hills or mountains to minimize interference from land mass. Usually towers are placed between 25 to 30 miles from each other in order to maintain visibility. Microwave transmission may carry 600 to 1800 voice channels. Advantages of microwave transmission include lower cost than coaxial cable where right-of-way must be maintained and higher cost is involved when the cable is laid over long distances. But the signals are subject to fading caused by absorption and scattering from moisture and precipitation in the air. The rain can also cause severe transmission problems.

Optical Fibers

Fiber optics communicates data in digital form and is a very reliable channel for communication of huge quantity of data. A single glass fiber is thinner than the size of a human hair and it can transmit all the characters in dozens of books of the same size across the country in a single second. Such a quantity of information will normally take about 21 hours to send over a copper telephone line. Fiber Optic technology is a cutting edge method of transmitting information over great distances (150 km without using a repeater) using pulses of light.

Fiber optic technology sends data without electricity through a conductor. Instead of electrical signals, modulated light is used to quickly transmit data over great distances through an insulated glass Fiber-type material.

Fiber optics is currently the best long distance communications method because it provides much faster data transfer speeds when compared to traditional interconnection media such as copper wire. The signal cannot be disrupted by outside sources like electricity, rain, humidity, or other things that tend to damage conventional copper wire signals. Fiber Optic Cables are ideal for volatile environments because there is no fear of damage should they break like there is with traditional copper wiring.

Optical Fiber is lightweight compared to copper cabling because it is a thin glass strand and has huge bandwidth because information travels along the fiber at the speed of light. Thousands of fibers can be fit in the same amount of space as required for one cable. The developments in fiber optics suggest that the future cost of broadband transmission capability will be within the reach of small organizations and individuals.

In recent years, it has become apparent that fiber-optics are steadily replacing copper wire as an appropriate means of communication signal transmission. They span the long distances between local phone systems as well as providing the backbone for many network systems. Other system users include cable television services, university campuses, office buildings, industrial plants, and electric utility companies. This is an overview of fiber-optic technology, telecommunication applications, fiber-optic advantages and disadvantages, and fiber-optic economics.

Fiber Optics Technology

At one end of the system is a transmitter. This is the place of origin for information coming on to fiber-optic lines. The transmitter accepts coded electronic pulse information coming from copper wire. It then processes and translates that information into equivalently coded light pulses. A light-emitting diode (LED) or an injection-laser diode (ILD) can be used for generating the light pulses. Using a lens, the light pulses are funneled into the fiber-optic medium where they transmit themselves down the line.

Light pulses move easily down the fiber-optic line because of a principle known as total internal reflection. "This principle of total internal reflection states that when the angle of incidence exceeds a critical value, light cannot get out of the glass; instead, the light bounces back in. When this principle is applied to the construction of the fiber-optic strand, it is possible to transmit information down fiber lines in the form of light pulses.

There are generally five elements that make up the construction of a fiber-optic strand, or cable: the optic core, optic cladding, a buffer material, a strength material and the outer jacket (Fig. 1). The optic core is the light carrying element at the center of the optical fiber. It is commonly made from a combination of silica and germania. Surrounding the core is the optic cladding made of pure silica . It is this combination that makes the principle of total internal reflection possible. The difference in materials used in the making of the core and the cladding creates an extremely reflective surface at the point in which they interface. Light pulses entering the fiber core reflect off the core/cladding interface and thus remain within the core as they move down the line.

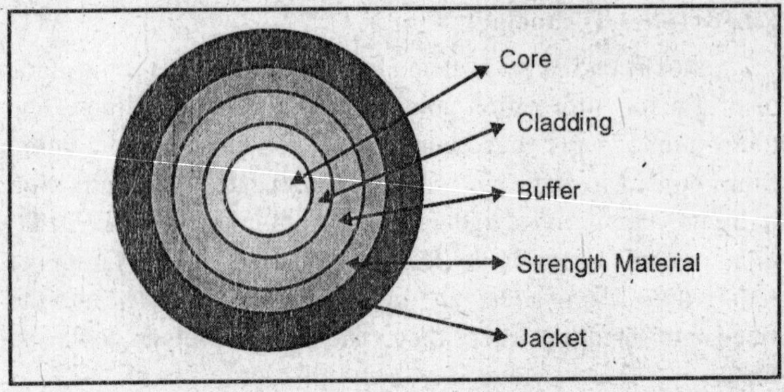

Fig. 1. Cut away of a fiber-optic cable.

Surrounding the cladding is a buffer material used to help shield the core and cladding from damage. A strength material surrounds the buffer, preventing stretch problems when the fiber cable is being pulled. The outer jacket is added to protect against abrasion, solvents, and other contaminants.

Once the light pulses reach their destination they are channeled into the optical receiver. "The basic purpose of an optical receiver is to detect the received light incident on it and to convert it to an electrical signal containing the information impressed on the light at the transmitting end. The electronic information is then ready for input into electronic based communication devices, such as a computer, telephone, or TV.

Application of Fiber Optics

The use of fiber-optics was generally not available until 1970 when Corning Glass Works was able to produce a fiber with a loss of 20 dB/km. It was recognized that optical fiber would be feasible for telecommunication transmission only if glass could be developed so pure that attenuation would be 20dB/km or less1% of the light would remain after traveling 1 km. Today's optical fiber attenuation ranges from 0.5dB/km to 1000dB/km depending on the optical fiber used. Attenuation limits are based on intended application.

The applications of optical fiber communications have increased at a rapid rate, since the first commercial installation of a fiber-optic system in 1977. Telephone companies began early on, replacing their old copper wire systems with optical fiber lines. Today's telephone companies use optical fiber throughout their system as the backbone architecture and as the long-distance connection between city phone systems.

Cable television companies have also began integrating fiber-optics into their cable systems. The trunk lines that connect central offices have generally been replaced with optical fiber. Some providers have begun experimenting with fiber to the curb using a fiber/coaxial hybrid. Such a hybrid allows for the integration of fiber and coaxial at a neighborhood location. This location, called a node, would provide the optical receiver that converts the light impulses back to electronic signals. The signals could then be fed to individual homes via coaxial cable.

Local Area Networks (LAN) is a collective group of computers, or computer systems, connected to each other allowing for shared program software or data bases. Colleges, universities, office buildings, and industrial plants, just to name a few, all make use of optical fiber within their LAN systems.

Power companies are an emerging group that have begun to utilize fiber-optics in their communication systems. Most power utilities already have fiber-optic communication systems in use for monitoring their power grid systems.

Advantages and Disadvantages of Fiber Optics

There are several advantages that have been established with the development and implementation of fiber-optic cable systems. Compared to copper, optical fiber is relatively small in size and light in weight. This characteristic has made it desirable as intra-floor conduits and wiring duct space has become increasing plugged with expanded copper cable installation .

Optical fiber is also desirable because of it's electromagnetic immunity. Since fiber-optics use light to transmit a signal, it is not subject to electromagnetic interference, radio frequency interference, or voltage surges. This may be an important consideration when laying cables near electronic hardware such as computers or industrial equipment. As well, since it does not use electrical impulses, it does not produce electric sparks which can be an obvious fire hazard.

Advances in optical fiber technology have led to decreases in signal loss, or attenuation. As an electric pulse or a light pulse travels down it's respective cable line, it will eventually lose signal energy due to imperfections in the transmission medium. To keep the signal going, it must be boosted every so often along the medium line. A signal regenerator is used to boost the electronic pulse in a copper cable. An optical repeater is used to boost the light pulse in a fiber-optic cable. The advantage of optical fiber is that it performs better with respect to attenuation. Fiber-optic cable needs fewer boosting devices, along the same length of line, than copper cable.

A characteristic feature of optical fiber that has yet to be fully realized is it's potentially wide bandwidth. Bandwidth refers to the amount of information that a fiber can carry. The greater the bandwidth, the greater the carrying capacity of the optical fiber. It is said that currently, the fastest fibre circuits used in trunk connections between cities and countries carry information at up to 2.5 gigabits per second, enough to carry 40,000 telephone conversations or 250 television channels. Experts predict larger bandwidths than this as light frequency separation becomes available. Private communication systems are already using much higher bandwidths.

A disadvantage of the fiber-optic system is it's incompatibility with the electronic hardware systems that make up today's world. This inability to interconnect easily requires that current communication hardware systems be somewhat retrofitted to the fiber-optic networks. Much of the speed that is gained through optical fiber transmission can be inhibited at the conversion points of a fiber-optic chain. When a portion of the chain experiences heavy use, information becomes jammed in a bottleneck at the points where conversion to, or from, electronic signals is taking place. Bottlenecks like this should become less frequent as microprocessors become more efficient and fiber-optics reach closer to a direct electronic hardware interface.

Fiber Optic economics

One of the initial economic factors to consider when converting to fiber-optics is the cost of replacing wire systems with fiber. Increased demand for optical fiber has brought the prices down within competitive range of copper. Cable sales are expected to increase. However, since transmitters, converters, optical repeaters, and a variety of connecting hardware will be needed, the initial cost of changing over to fiber can be expensive. Increased demand, advances in the technology, and competition has brought the prices down somewhat.

Short term and long term gains should be considered when updating a communications system. In the short term it is often less expensive to continue using copper cabling for covering expanded communication needs. By simply adding more wire to an existing system, expanded needs can be covered. This avoids the expense of adding the transmitters and receivers needed for integrating optical fiber. Long term needs, however, may require more expansion in the future.

In the long term it may be more cost effective to invest in conversion to fiber optics. This cost effectiveness is due to the relative ease of upgrading fiber optics to higher speeds and performance. It has already been seen in the industry as communication providers are wiring customers with optical fiber bandwidth that exceed consumer bandwidth needs. This is in anticipation of future bandwidth needs. It is generally accepted that customers will need increased bandwidth as the information highway grows. Replacing copper with fiber today would avoid continued investment in a soon to be outdated copper system. Recent changes in the laws regulating the telecommunications industry have helped to promote and spur the use of fiber optics. The passage of the Telecommunications Act of 1996 has helped this effort by allowing television and telephone companies to enter each others markets. Fiber optics will play a pivotal role in this race since the bandwidth needed for providing an all-in-one service with television, telephone, interactive multimedia, and internet access is not available in much of the wiring of America.

Satellite Transmission

Satellite transmission has turned the entire world into a global village. Satellites relay or transmit information such as TV, phone, weather, military intelligence, and data. Communications satellites provide a worldwide link. In 1960, Echo 1 was launched becoming the first communications satellite. The primitive Echo 1 was an inflatable metallic sphere with instruments that bounced radio signals back to earth. Two years later, Telstar 1 became the first active communications satellite. These satellites orbit the earth at a relatively low altitude. This made them difficult to track and not very suitable for communication. Active satellites receive, amplify, and retransmit signals to different locations. Telstar 1 was responsible for the relay of the first live television broadcast across the Atlantic Ocean.

Weather forecasting has undergone a revolution because of the availability of pictures from geostationary meteorological satellites—pictures we see every day on television. All of these are important aspects of the space age, but satellite communications has probably had more effect than any of the rest on the average person. Satellite communications is also the only truly commercial space technology. By the time EARLY BIRD was launched, communications earth stations already existed in the United Kingdom, France, Germany, Italy, Brazil, and Japan. Further negotiations in 1963 and 1964 resulted in a new international organization, which would ultimately assume ownership of the satellites and responsibility for management of the global system. On August 20, 1964, agreements were signed which created the International Telecommunications Satellite Organization. By the end of 1965, EARLY BIRD had provided 150 telephone "half- circuits" and 80 hours of television service.

In 1965, when EARLY BIRD was launched, the satellite provided almost 10 times the capacity of the submarine telephone cables for almost 1/10th the price. Satellites are still competitive with cable for point-to-point communications, but the future advantage may lie with fiber-optic cable. Satellites still maintain two advantages over cable: they are more reliable and they can be used point-to-multi-point (broadcasting). Cellular telephone systems have risen as challenges to all other types of telephony. It is possible to place a cellular system in a developing country at a very reasonable price. Long-distance calls require some other technology, but this can be either satellites or fiber-optic cable. Cellular telephony has brought us a new technological system, the personal communications system (PCS). In the fully developed PCS, the individual would carry his telephone with him. This telephone could be used for voice or data and would be usable anywhere. Several companies have committed themselves to providing a version of this system using satellites in low earth orbits (LEO).

The inherent "broadcast" nature of satellite communications has made direct-broadcast a recurrent theme—yet one never brought to fruition. Each year from 10-20 communications satellites are launched making the process of communication of information more easy and effective day by day.

The confluence of satellite and multimedia resulted in making the communication technology available at an unimaginably lower cost to the betterment of the common man although it originated in labs for scientific researchers. Now, Internet services are primarily based on these technologies.

TELECOMMUNICATION

Telecommunications refers to long-distance communication (the Greek tele means "far off"). At present, such communication is carried out with the aid of electronic equipment such as the Radio, Telegraph, Telephone, and Television. In earlier times, however, smoke signals, drums, light beacons, and various forms of semaphore were used for the same purpose. The information that is transmitted can be in the form of voice, symbols, pictures, or data, or a combination of these. The physical equipment for a telecommunications system includes a transmitter, one or more receivers, and a channel or means of communication such as the air, water, wire, cable, communications satellite, or some combination of these.

It also refers to preparation, transmission, communication, or related processing of information (text, images, sounds, or other data) by electrical, electromagnetic, or similar means, the transfer of information between computers over telephone lines. Just plug in a modem, fire up some communications software, and you can make contact with the office computer or the Internet or the communication of information over a distance by means of radio waves, optical signals or along a transmission line.

Telecommunication can also be defines as transmission of information between remote locations by electronic means. The information may be in the form of voice,, video or data generated by a computer. There are many similar term which denote to the same process like data communication, communication technology, computer communication, compunications, telecomputing but all of them are used in context of the electronic transmission of information.

Modern telecommunication began with understanding of electrical transmissions over wire and the development of electrical telegraphy. From there we have progressed to the present utilization of the electromagnetic spectrum in wired, wireless, and recently with fibre optics & computers. More and more information is digitally coded. During the last 150 years high speed long distance technology has appeared for general use.

Telecommunication has replaced & will continue to acquire many of the functions that were traditionally required transportation of messages & people. It is now the glue that holds nations together, but can also be one of the forces that destroys them. The 'Global Village' is the product.

Modern communication networks have become essential for all countries. Modern com technology will not use traditional wired networks in underdeveloped areas. Satellite & cellular and other wireless com reduces the need for physical point to point connections. Optical fibre links have greatly expanded the capacity of a cable so that fewer trunk connections are required. Switching & other terminal technology may be progressing at a somewhat slower pace than transmission. Switching & terminal technology is essential for utilization.

DATA TRANSMISSION

Analog Communication

In analog communication, there is a continuous up and down pattern. For example one wave constitutes one cycle, which is measured in the units called Hertz (cycle per second). The term cycle and Hertz may nay used interchangeably. Thus it is customary to describe channel as transmitting a certain number of cycles per second.

Digital Transmission

In digital transmission, wave patterns are translated into discrete bits and are separated by intervals. Bit are the smallest units of information in data processing. They may be compared to light bulb, which is either on or off. When the bulb is on information is being transmitted; when it is off there is a blank or interval. The telephone network originally intended to carry only the human voice, operates mostly in the analog mode, although all digital transmission is available as well. Digital transmission has the advantage of being entirely compatible with computer and terminal originated messages.

Frequency and Bandwidth

The information may be available in the form of sound, picture or digital data. It must be converted to electric signals for the purpose of transmission. Such signal must be modulated in some way to fit them into the carrying medium. The amount of information that can be sent over a given channel in a given time is dependant on the bandwidth. The bandwidth available increases with increasing carrier frequency.

Frequency is the rate at which wave or cycle alternates between high and low or on and off. One cycle per second is called Hertz (HZ). The concept of bandwidth can be explained with the help of the traffic network. If there is a two way street consisting of signal lanes, one in each direction only one line of vehicle can travel in each direction. On super highway, however there may be three or four lanes in each direction and cars can travel on them in parallel each at its own rate of speed. In the same way the width of the electronic path determines how many cycles or bits can travel along this given path at a given time; the more the bandwidth available the more bits may be transmitted.

COMMUNICATION CHANNELS

Communication channel consists of two points which allow communication links. A telephone is the simple example of communication channel. Other channels include coaxial cables. Fiber optics, satellite, a beam, microwave and others. Transmission may take place in a number of different modes as simplex, half duplex and full duplex. Libraries generally use the later two modes of transmission.

Synchronous Communication

Synchronous transmission of data is a method in which blocks of characters are transmitted in timed sequences. Rather than using start and stop bits around each character, each block of characters is marked with synchronization characters. The receiver device accepts data until it detects a special ending character of a predetermined number of character at which time the device knows the message has come to an end. Synchronous transmission commonly uses the faster (greater than 1200 bps) voice band and broadband channels and is usually used when data transfer requirement exceeds several thousand bits per second. It is much faster than asynchronous communications.

Synchronous communication is the communication taking place at the same time. Synchronous, or real-time, communication has yet to emerge as a popular technology in online education, but the likely merging of Web and audio/video delivery formats over time may, if successful and affordable, effectively virtualize education on a global scale.

Asynmchronous Comunication

In asynchronous transmission of data one character is transmitted at a time. The transfer of data is controlled by start bts and stop bits. Each character is surrounded by bits that signal the beginning and end of the character. These characters allow the receiving terminal to synchronise itself with the receipt of data on a charater by character basis. Asynchronour transmission is often used to low speed transmission of data in conjunction with narrow band and few slower speed (less than 12000 bps) voice band channels where the transmitting device operates manually or intermittently. It is least expensive of the two methods.

Most PC serial devices such as mice, keyboards and modems are asynchronous. Asynchronous communication requires nothing more than a transmitter, a receiver and a wire. It is thus the simplest of serial communication protocols, and the least expensive to implement. As the name implies, asynchronous communication is performed between two (or more) devices which operate on independent clocks. Therefore, even if the two clocks agree for a time, there is no guarantee that they will continue to agree over extended periods, and thus there is no guarantee that when point A begins transmitting, point B will begin receiving, or that Point B will continue to sample at the rate Point A transmits. See the figure below for an illustration of what happens when transmission clocks differ significantly.

In asynchronous communication, data is preceded with a start bit which indicates to the receiver that a word (a chunk of data broken up into individual bits) is about to begin. To avoid confusion with other bits, the start bit is twice the size of any other bit in the transmission. The end of a word is followed by a stop bit, which tells the receiver that the word has come to an end, that it should begin looking for the next start bit, and that any bits it receives before getting the start bit should be ignored. To insure data integrity, a parity bit is often added between the last bit of data and the stop bit. The parity bit makes sure that the data received is composed of the same number of bits in the same order in which they were sent. See the diagram in Figure 11 for a portrayal of how asynchronous communication works.

Modem — (Modulator, Demodulator) A device that connects a computer to a phone line. A modem allows a computer to talk to other computers through the phone system. Basically, modems do for computers what a telephone does for humans. Modems are devices which function like translators, changing the digital signals coming out of the terminal to analog so that it can travel along a voice-grade terminal.

The need to communicate between distant computers led to the use of the existing phone network for data transmission. Most phone lines were designed to transmit analog information - voices, while the computers and their devices work in digital form - pulses. So, in order to use an analog medium, a converter between the two systems is needed. This converter is the MODEM which performs MODulation and DEModulation of transmitted data. It accepts serial binary pulses from a device, modulates some property (amplitude, frequency, or phase) of an analog signal in order to send the signal in an analog medium, and performs the opposite process, enabling the analog information to arrive as digital pulses at the computer or device on the other side of connection.

Modems, in the beginning, were used mainly to communicate between DATA TERMINALS and a HOST COMPUTER. Later, the use of modems was extended to communicate between END COMPUTERS. This required more speed and the data rates increased from 300 bps in early days to 28.8 Kbps. Today, transmission involves data compression techniques which increase the rates, error detection and error correction for more reliability. In order to enable modems of various types and different manufacture to communicate, interface standards were developed by some standard organizations

Today's modems are used for different functions. They act as textual and voice mail systems, facsimiles, and are connected or integrated into cellular phones and in notebook computers enabling sending data from anywhere. The future might lead to new applications. Further dramatic speed increases will require digital phone technology such as ISDN and fiber optic lines. New applications might be implemented such as simultaneous voice and data. Videophones are an example of this.

SWITCHING MECHANISM

Switching mechanisms are devices to send messages in many directions without the delay in transmission. Provision is made for an alternate path in case the routine channel is engaged. Switching is carried out by computer in most cases. Computers also serve to collect messages for transmission over higher capacity lines. The lines used in the telephone network are wires, coaxial cables, microwave and satellite links. The different techniques of switching mechanism are described below:

Circuit Switching

In circuit switching system a communication path is actually established before the message is accepted for transmission. For voice communication system circuit switching is the norm where by a path through connected circuit is established. This method is suitable to telephone traffic for not very efficient or economic for data which is transmitted at different bit rates in a varying amounts.

Message Switching

According to this method the system accepts all messages, store them in a computer or transmits them as and when channel a become available.

Packet Switching

The method used to move data around on the Internet. In packet switching, all the data coming out of a machine is broken up into chunks, each chunk has the address of where it came from and where it is going. This enables chunks of data from many different sources to co-mingle on the same lines, and be sorted and directed along different routes by special machines along the way. This way many people can use the same lines at the same time. You might think of several caravans of trucks all using the same road system to carry materials.

FAX

Fax is the transmission of photographs, drawings, maps, and written or printed words by electric signals. Light waves reflected from an image are converted into electric signals, transmitted by wire or radio to a distant receiver, and reconstituted on paper or film into a copy of the original. Facsimile is used by news services to send news and photos to newspapers and television stations, by banks, airlines, and railroads to transmit the content of documents, and by many other businesses as an aid in data handling and record keeping. Facsimile systems involve optical scanning, signal encoding, modulation, signal transmission, demodulation, decoding, and copy making.

Scanning

Scanning is done in a manner similar to that used in television. An original, a photo for example, is illuminated and systematically examined in small adjacent areas called pixels (picture elements). Light reflected from each pixel is converted into electric current by an electronic device, a photocell, photodiode, or charge-coupled device (CCD).

A single such device may be used to cover one pixel after another in a row, row after row from top to bottom until the entire image has been translated into electric impulses. This is rectilinear scanning. Scanning may also be done a row at a time by a battery of devices; this is array scanning. In multispot scanning, a vertical array of photodevices moves across the image, examining the pixels column by column. As the array passes down the copy, it produces a set of current pulses from each photodevice. The separate currents, however produced, are then transmitted successively over a single circuit to the distant receiver.

To secure fine detail in the reproduced image it is necessary to use very small pixels. In one standard, Group 3 of the International Telegraph and Telephone Consultative Committee (CCITT), each pixel is a rectangle 0.12 by 0.13 mm (1 inch=25.4 mm). On this standard, subject copy measuring 8 by 11 inches (20 x 28 cm) is divided into 3.6 million pixels.

This compares with about 200,000 pixels for televised images. The pixels used in high-resolution facsimile systems have dimensions one-fifth those of the CCITT standard mentioned above, whereas in low-definition systems the dimensions may be twice as great.

The image may be illuminated as in rectilinear scanning, or a relatively large area of the image may be illuminated, the photodevice viewing the image through a lens aperture that restricts its field to a single pixel at a time.

In a commonly used facsimile scanning system (invented

by Frederick Bakewell in 1848 and based on Alexander Bain's work of 1842) the subject copy is wrapped around a drum. A finely focused spot of light falls on the copy and the light reflected from that pixel is picked up by the photodevice. The drum is rotated so that the light spot traces a line across the copy, examining each pixel in turn.

As the drum rotates, the light source is moved slowly on a carriage parallel to the drum axis, tracing out a spiral of adjacent lines until the entire area of the copy has been scanned. At least once in each rotation of the drum a signal transmitted to the recorder keeps the scanner and the recorder in step.

In drum scanning, the copy may also be illuminated broadly and examined by a photodevice fitted with a lens aperture.

Copy cannot always be conveniently wrapped around a drum. In such cases, flat copy may be scanned by a spot of light directed across its surface by a moving mirror. Mirror scanning may also be used when the copy is wrapped on a drum, or while it is being pulled from a roller. Laser light produces a very fine beam that travels across the copy, row by row, as the copy moves vertically.

In one arrangement the mirror is rocked back and forth, moving the beam across the copy. In another, a rotating polygonal mirror is used. This mirror typically has 18 flat mirror surfaces on its periphery, each capable of scanning a row of pixels.

Very fast scanning can be achieved by rapid rotation of the mirror and corresponding vertical motion of the copy. The beam is reflected from each pixel into a photodevice that converts successive light values into corresponding currents. Electronic scanning of flat copy may also be done by arrays of photodiodes or charge-coupled devices.

For scanning rates higher than about 6 rows per second laser beams with polygonal mirrors and arrays of photodevices are favored.

We owe development of fax to a Scottish inventor,

Alexander Bain, who was granted a patent for his creation back in 1843. Bain's original concept is still the basis for modern facsimile machines.

Fax Machine

Alexander Bain invented a machine capable of receiving signals from a telegraph wire and translating them into images on paper.

Facsimile (Fax)

Invented in 1842 by Alexander Bain, a Scottish clockmaker, who used clock mechanisms to transfer an image from one sheet of electrically conductive paper to another.

Early Telegraph Facsimile

Bain's fax transmitter was designed to scan a two-dimensional surface (Bain proposed metal type as the surface) by means of a stylus mounted on a pendulum.

Analog Telephone Facsimile - Digital Facsimile

Between 1920 and 1923 the American Telephone & Telegraph Company (AT&T) worked on telephone facsimile technology, and in 1924 the telephotography machine was used to send pictures from political conventions in Cleveland, Ohio, and Chicago to New York City for publication in newspapers.

Background

Demon Internet have introduced a service that allows faxes to be delivered to an email addressee. With the service, a fax number is allocated to the user who can publish it just like any other telephone number. Fax messages arrive in an email format and are forwarded over the Internet. The user can pick them up as email from anywhere around the world.

How does it work?

Customers of the service are allocated a unique fax number on registration and select an email address for the delivery of incoming fax messages. The service allows customers to receive faxes on their desktop, via email, that have been sent manually via an ordinary fax machine.

Benefits of using fax to email

1. Faxes are received straight to the desktop and can conveniently be read as email
2. Captured in electronic format and can be forwarded easily
3. Faxes can be received and stored 24 hours a day, 7 days a week
4. The personal fax number ensures privacy and confidentiality of sensitive faxes
5. Can be printed straight to the printer, which retains its original quality
6. No special equipment is required by the user
7. Received faxes are accompanied by a status page giving transmission information.

Features

1. Unique fax number

A unique number is allocated to the customer on registration. Once a fax is sent to this number, it is delivered as an email to the recipient.

2. Inbox email account

This allows users to specify an email address as the destination for faxed documents to be delivered to. This allows the user to mix fax and email deliveries on a one to one basis. These can then be downloaded, forwarded, stored and printed as emails.

NETWORKING

Computers have acquired the capability to communicate. The advancement in technology have ushered an era of not only the computing power but also of access to information services at least in those countries which have been extensive and reliable computer networks. The transmission over telephone not only of voice but most recently of text and illustrations through telefascimile laid the foundation for this age in which communication is taken for granted in developed countries.

The Oxford English Dictionary defines that a 'network is an interconnected chain or system of immaterial things'. It is also defined as two or more libraries and/or other organizations engaged in a common pattern of information exchange through communication for some functional purposes. Libraries may be in different jurisdictions but agree to one another on the same basis s each service its own constituents.

UNISIST II working document defines information networks a set of interrelated information systems associated with communication facilities which are operating through more or less formal agreements and institutional arrangements in order to jointly implement information handling operation with the view to pooling their resoureces and to offer netter service to their users.

TYPES OF NETWORKS

The following type of networks are in operation

Communication Networks

Such networks are made up of transmission lines, concentrators, switching mechanisms and non data processing components. New and specialized common carriers and value-added networks with data processing equipment is also linked to communication network Depending upon the area of jurisdiction, communication networks fall into the following three categories:

* Local Area Networks (LANs),
* Wide Area Networks (WANs), and
* Metropolitan Area Networks).

Local Area Networks

Local Area Networks extend the usefulness of one

computer by connecting it to others. Often a computer on a network is connected to other networks as well, and has essentially unlimited access to resources and services around the world. At the local level, the network may be any of several popular types. Local area networks have very low error rates and propagation delay that is negligible for most purposes. Transmission in most local area networks is by broadcast — every station on the network receives every transmission. Thus, there are no routing decisions to make. Every packet (message unit) follows the same path, so reordering does not occur. These characteristics make LANs suitable for applications that depend on timely results, for example interactive processing involving files or other resources located on several different systems or time-critical response to a monitoring device. The broadcast mode of operation is suitable for applications requiring message exchange among a number of stations, like checking individual calendars to schedule a meeting or searching for a processor able to share in a demanding computational task.

A combination of technology and the performance expectations of LANs limits the distances they can cover. A small LAN might connect a few computers in an office, or in a home; a large LAN could extend over an office park or university campus, connecting computers and other devices in a number of buildings. Common speeds are 10Mbps (mega bits per second) or 16 Mbps.

Very simple network systems that allow limited sharing between two or more personal computers (for example, at home) are sold at most computer stores. The simplest of these use the computers' serial ports, standard telephone wire, and software that allows printer sharing, file transfer, and sending messages between computers.

This system has the three essential components of any network: a communication medium (telephone wire), an interface between the computer and the medium (the serial port), and software to send and receive on the interface. Each computer can send a message to, access a file, or use a printer on any of the other connected computers.

Most local area networks are more complex than this. Many local area networks have servers — designated stations that provide access to disk storage or printers or other resources shared by users at other stations. Regular use of the servers increases traffic on the network and suggests that individual LANs be kept small, limited to a small cluster of computers that can efficiently share a common set of resources. Communication and sharing among clusters requires that the small LANs be connected. A popular way to interconnect local area networks is to attach each to a high speed backbone network. The distributed queue dual bus (DQDB) is another high speed fiber-based network for times when high data rates are required. Because of their potential for city-wide installation, high speed fiber-based networks are sometimes called Metropolitan Area Networks.

All local area networks have the same components: communications medium, an interface between the computer and the medium, and software to drive the interface to send and receive transmissions. The software coexists in the computer with other hardware drivers, such as those for printers and modems; and with other software such as compilers and databases, text editors and spreadsheets. All the network services are simply extensions to the large collection of services already offered by modern operating systems. Local area networks are sometimes described by the topology used to connect the machines. For the most part, the topology is transparent to the user and to the application developer. Sometimes, there are implications that affect the development effort.

The use of repeaters allows a network to spread over a larger distance than it could otherwise span, and also allows more flexibility in getting the cable where it is needed. Multiple port repeaters also make it easy to expand a network. A new segment can be run where the additional stations are needed, then joined to the network by connecting to a port in the repeater.

Routers are connecting boxes that participate in network protocols to the network layer. Routers can decide the path a packet should take to reach its destination, can participate in distributed congestion control schemes, and can fragment large packets and reassemble them when necessary to get through intermediate networks. Routers rely on information in the data packet to determine what action to take, so routers are considered protocol sensitive, i.e. a separate router is needed for each protocol used on the connection.

Networks can be connected at higher layers as well. The higher the protocol layer implemented in the gateway, the deeper the gateway looks into the data that it transfers. An example of a Layer 7 gateway is a mail gateway, which connects two incompatible mail systems and allows them to exchange messages. This arrangement is convenient when a network includes stations on several floors of a building. A wiring closet on each floor provides a convenient place to look for problems, without requiring the extensive wiring that a single hub needs.

Wide Area Networks

Unlike local area networks, wide area networks consist of specific point-to-point links. Messages pass from one network station to another through a communications subnet. The communications subnet consists of nodes whose function is to pass the message from its origin to its intended destination quickly and accurately.

Wide area networks are characterized by significant propagation delay in message transmission and by high incidence of lost or damaged transmissions. Message units, called packets, are passed from one intermediate node to another until they arrive at the destination. Effective routing techniques are important to network performance. Packets from a single message may travel by different routes and arrive at the destination out of order. Typical transmission speeds range from 56 Kbps to 1.54 Mbps.

Since a wide area network is composed of point-to-point

connections, connectivity is an important design consideration. Routing is easy: each station only has to know which direction to go to reach the destination. The obvious weakness is vulnerability: in case a single node (other than the ends of the chain) fail to function correctly, communication is lost across the faulty node.

Again, routing is easy: every node connects directly to every other node. Vulnerability to failure is minimized, since no node is dependent on any other. The problem here is cost. From graph theory, we know that a complete graph with n vertices has edges, where is the combination of n things taken two at a time. Fully connecting five nodes might be extravagant; fully connecting a hundred nodes (links) is probably unreasonable. Networks of many thousand nodes clearly require another approach.

No single node loss would cut off any operating node from the others. On the other hand, loss of two nodes could interrupt communication among the remaining nodes, depending on which two nodes failed. Routing is no longer obvious in this network. Since there is a direct link from node A to node B, it is likely that is the best route for communications between those nodes.

Often the station connected to the subnet is a gateway to a local area network. Thus, the user with access to the resources of a local network can reach out to a larger network for still more resources. Local area networks (or Metropolitan Area Networks) connected to other networks combine to form very complex patterns with characteristics similar to point-to-point wide area networks. Similar problems concerning routing decisions, dealing with failures, temporary conditions, etc. arise. A further complication concerns the differences among the types of local area networks: the required format for transmissions, maximum lengths, conventions for acknowledging successful delivery of a packet, etc. The stations that join two or more local area networks and address these issues are called routers.

Transparent access to very remote files and printers is not impossible, but is rare. Although the most common application of a wide area network is explicit communication (electronic mail and file transfer) another popular use is to login to a remote computer that offers a particular service. Thus, for instance, the NSFnet gives access to supercomputers to researchers working at sites far removed from such a resource. Travelers also use wide area networks to login to their own computers while away from the home or office.

Metropolitan Area Networks

The term Metropolitan Area Networks is often applied to the new high-speed network technologies to distinguish them from wide area and local area networks. These technologies have pushed the carrying capacity of the communication links into the gigabits range. They can be used over larger areas than LANs, and are often used to connect LANs together to form a greatly extended LAN environment.

Another important potential for these networks is the ability to carry information in forms that require many more bits than conventional text or simple graphics. An ordinary computer monitor screen displaying 25 lines of 80 characters contains only 2000 characters. At 8 bits per character, only 16,000 bits are needed to fill the screen. At 10Mbps, the standard speed of LANs, only 1.6msec would be needed to fill the screen. However, when that same screen displays high resolution, bit-mapped images at 1024 by 768 bits, 786,432 bits are required to fill the screen. At 10Mbps the screen is refreshed every 78.6 seconds. If the display includes color (256 color images are common), the time required to deliver the information for a full-screen display (at 10Mbps) grows to 20.13 seconds — hardly suitable for smooth motion video. Clearly, the standard LAN speeds are not adequate. High speed networks, approaching gigabits per second, are needed to provide the ability to deliver the full potential of multi-media displays to the user from a source on a different machine and to connect LANs together and deliver timely access to resources.

Open System Interconnection (OSI)

Communication between two different system is a difficult process since there are many different protocols for LANs and WANs.The International Standards Organization (ISO) has attempted to solve this problem by the introduction of Open Control Interconnection (OSI). OSI defines a set of procedures and standards grouped into seven layers for the exchange of information between terminals and computers. Some countries have also developed their own standards in order to meet their individual requirements

Integrated Services Digital Network (ISDN)

ISDN's name refers to the combining of voice and data services over the same wires (so computers can connect directly to the telephone network without first converting their signals to an analog audio signal, as modems do). This integration brings with it a host of new capabilities combining voice, data, fax, and sophisticated switching. ISDN uses the existing local telephone wiring, it's equally available to home and business customers. Most important for Internet users, however, is that ISDN provides a huge improvement in access speed.

A given pair of wires connecting two parties for communication can carry electrical signals in one of two forms: analog or digital. An analog signal changes gradually through an infinite number of values, while a digital signal changes instantly between just two values. The human voice and a musical instrument are examples of analog signals — both produce complex variations in frequency and amplitude. A light switch typifies a digital signal — it can be either on or off.

An analog signal's infinite number of variations makes it impossible to reproduce exactly. An analog signal will go only so far in copper wire; to go further the signal must be regenerated electronically with a device called a repeater. The repeater converts the weak input signal to a stronger output signal, unavoidably distorting it in the process. Each regeneration degrades the signal a bit more (in the same way that photocopies of photocopies get worse at each iteration). In a large telephone network, the "copy of a copy" problem becomes very expensive to solve, requiring sophisticated equipment and costly cabling.

Digital signals, on the other hand, are easy to regenerate precisely. Because there are only two possible states for the signal, even a heavily degraded signal can be regenerated into an exact copy of the original. What's more, the cost (and complexity) of equipment to regenerate digital signals is trivial compared with that for analog. Not surprisingly, telephone companies recognized this cost advantage a long time ago and have since converted all long distance transmission to digital signaling. When a subscriber makes a long-distance call, the central office (CO) converts the analog signal to digital using a technique called sampling in which the state of the analog signal is captured about 8,000 times per second. Each state is converted to an 8-bit binary number, and the resulting string of binary numbers becomes a digital data stream at 64 Kbps. This digital stream is routed along the long-distance network, being regenerated as needed. Each regeneration produces an exact copy of the original digital data stream, so no information is lost. When the destination CO receives the digital data stream, it reverses the sampling process and transmits the resulting analog signal to the receiving subscriber. Many local telephone companies are converting to digital switching, even for local calls.

A modem can't get 64 Kbps out of an analog line because the CO's signal sampling, at 8,000 times per second, limits the bandwidth of the analog signal to about 3 kHz, which in turn invokes Shannon's Law setting the practical speed limit for such a channel to about 30 Kbps. To get higher analog speeds requires higher fidelity in the audio signal, dictating faster sampling in the CO's analog-to-digital conversion, which would result in a digital data stream faster than 64 Kbps. Telco's aren't about to change out all their voice digitizers for faster versions or upgrade all their digital circuits to carry channels faster than 64 Kbps. So the probability of the phone system ever supporting faster analog signaling rates is zero.

ISDN cuts out the middleman by eliminating the need for voice digitizers in the CO. ISDN carries through the 64 Kbps digital signal from the CO right to the subscriber, and the subscriber can use it for voice or data as required. Advances in electronics make it practical to do voice digitizing right in the subscriber's phone, and direct digital attachment of computers eliminates the need for modems.

TELECOMMUNICATION STANDARDS AND PROTOCOLS

Standards

Communication between two devices might work only when the interface is defined and agreed. For modems, the standards define techniques used for modulation, for error correction, for data compression, and other attributes. There are some standard organizations for the development of interface standards. The ITU - International Telecommunications Union an agency of the United Nations (Geneva, Switzerland), ISO - International Standards Organization, and CCITT - International Telegraph and Telephone Consultative Committee a group of ITU.

The modem standards were developed during the years and published as V series of recommendations. In the United States the primary standards body is the ANSI - American National Standards Institute. Its committees, concerned with information processing and data communication, are designated X3 and X3S3, respectively. The organizations deal with De Jure standards.

Protocols

Protocols are rules governing the initiation and maintenance of data flows. They are implemented in different ways for different types of equipment and networks. The two major components relating to WAN are the protocol and the media. The media are the actual pathways that the protocol travels in. The network protocol defines the format in which data are sent through the media.

2
Introduction to Computers

The word computer has been derived from a Latin word 'Computare' which means to count. Computer means differently to different people depending upon its use. For a common man, computer is a calculating machine but for an educated and business professional, it is an effective tool of data storage and manipulation in different ways. Computer is regarded as extension of human mind. It is popular because of the characteristics of speed, accuracy and memory.

A computer is an electronic device that operates under the control of a set of instructions that is stored in its memory unit. A computer accepts data from an input device and processes it into useful information, which it displays on its output device. Actually, a computer is a collection of hardware and software components that help you accomplish many different tasks. Hardware consists of the computer itself, and any equipment connected to it. Software is the set of instructions that the computer follows in performing a task.

HISTORY OF COMPUTER

Early man counted by finger to manage business. Then he used the other materials like stones, trees, stars etc to remember numbers. Abacus was invented in Egypt about 13,000 years back and it is still in use in some of the countries.

The first computer of the world ENIAC was developed in the year 1945. Funds were made available by the U. S. Department of Defence and it was used for military purposes.

ENIAC cost millions of dollars to build, took up a lot of space and was initially used for number-crunching tasks. The worlds' first main frame computer used vacuum tubes for its millions of switches.

The first computer in India was acquired by the Indian Statistical Institute, Calcutta in 1955. Additional computers in the country were purchased from IBM. By 1972, there were 172 computers and three-fourth of them were made by IBM. Microcomputer was developed as a result of miniaturization of the computer in the early 1970s using semiconductors. Microcomputer was later converted into personal computer.

The credit for production of the super computer in India goes to the National Aerospace Laboratory, Bangalore. In this field C-DAC also has earned fame by making 'Param 8000'. India has made considerable progress in the technology of supercomputer which in the long run will boost the Information sector of the country.

The advent of PC witnessed a boom in India during the decade of 1980s. Many large institutions including the Air Lines, Railways, banks, hospitals introduced computer for managing their inhouse functions. It proved to be very effective and also user-friendly with the passage of time. Then came the turn of medium and small entrepreneurs since its cost became affordable for them also. By the turn of the 1990s, millions of Indian began to use computers in their workplaces and homes for varied purposes including the Internet applications. Sale of PCs crossed the mark of one million by 1999. In 2000, the installed base of computers in the country was about five millions, translating into about five computers for every 1,000 people.

Many factors influenced the decision of buying computers by a middle class family but the main reason was the ever falling cost during the last few years. The availability of the assembled systems with warranty to run them on annual contracts eliminated the fear of machines from the less computer literate. Moreover the systems of varied configurations were also available in the market. The owners of cyber café who provided Internet search facilities became the main centers of such business. Still the rate of adoption of computers in India remained about 1% by the end of 2000.

In 1642 a Frenchman Blaise Pascal intoroduced the first mechanical calculating ,machine. It could do both addition and subtraction. About three decade later, a German scholar improved Pascal's machine to make it perform addition, multiplication, subtraction and division. This machine proved very useful in lengthy and scientific calculations.

In 1883, Charles Babbage, a professor of mathematics in Cambridge University with the assistance with Lady Augusta Ada Lovelace, started developing a machine called analytical engine which could store information, calculate number and solve algebric expressions based on instructions given by the programmes. Later on, a French weaver named Joseph Marry Jacquard invented punch cards to control his mechanical looms to develop the designs of his yarns. Punch cards used punched holes in a card to control the process. In 1887, a statistician based on the above concept developed a machine called the Census machine for the Census Bureau, which used punch card for inputting data. It was capable of reading numbers, characters and also special symbols. The 1890 census was completed in less than three years because of this machine.

In 1944, there came the MARK 1, a digital computer in which the internal operations were carried out automatically with the help of relays and mechanical parts. Even arithmetic counter were mechanical.

Chronology of Computer Development

3000 BC: Dust abacus is invented, probably in Babylonia.

1800 BC: Babylonian mathematician develops algorithms to resolve numerical problems.

500 BC: Bead and wire abacus originates in Egypt.

1617: Scottish inventor John Napier uses bones to demonstrate division by subtraction and multiplication by addition.

1622: William Oughtred develops the slide rule in England.

1642: Blaise Pascal builds the first numerical calculating machine in Paris.

1833: Charles Babbage designs the Analytical Machine that follows instructions from punched-cards. It is the first general purpose computer.

1886: William Burroughs develops the first commercially successful mechanical adding machine.

1938: Hewlett-Packard Co. is founded to make electronic equipment.

1940: At Bell Labs, George Stibitz demonstrates the Complex Number Calculator, which may be the first digital computer.

1941: Konrad Zuse builds the Z3 computer in Germany, the first calculating machine with automatic control of its operations.

1944: Mark I (IBM ASCC) is completed, based on the work of Professor Howard H. Aiken at Harvard and IBM. It is a relay-based computer.

1946: ENIAC (Electronic Numerical Integrator and Computer), with 18,000 vacuum tubes, is dedicated at the University of Pennsylvania. It was 8 by 100 feet and weighed 80 tons. It could do 5,000 additions and 360 multiplications per second.

1946: Term bit for binary digit is used for first time by John Tukey.

1948: Transistor is invented by William Bradford Shockley with John Bardeen and Walter H. Brattain.

1951: IEEE Computer Society is formed.

1951: UNIVAC I is installed at the Bureau of Census using a magnetic tape unit as a buffer memory.

1952: IBM introduces the 701, its first electronic stored-program computer.

1953: First magnetic tape device, the IBM 726, is introduced with 100 character-per-inch density and 75 inches-per-second speed.

1954: FORTRAN is created by John Backus at IBM. Harlan Herrick runs the first successful FORTRAN program.

1958: ALGOL, first called IAL (International Algebraic Language), is presented in Zurich.

1958: First virtual memory machine, Atlas, is installed in England by Feranti. It was developed at the University of Manchester by R.M. Kilburn.

1958: First electronic computers are built in Japan by NEC: the NEC-1101 and -1102.

1959: COBOL is defined by the Conference on Data System Languages (Codasyl), based on Grace Hoppers Flow-Matic.

1960: Benjamin Curley develops the first minicomputer, the PDP-1, at Digital Equipment Corporation.

1960: COBOL runs on UNIVAC II and RCA 501.

1960: Removable disks first appear.

1962: First general-purpose simulation languages are proposed: (1) SIMSCRIPT by the Rand Corporation, and (2) GPSS by IBM.

1964: BASIC (Beginners All-purpose Symbolic Instruction Language) is created by Tom Kurtz and John Kemeny of Dartmouth. First time-sharing

1969: IBM unbundles hardware and software; introduces a minicomputer line, System/3.

1971: Floppy disks are introduced to load the IBM 370 microcode.

1971: John Blankenbaker builds the first personal computer, the Kenbak I.

1975: Microsoft is founded after Bill Gates and Paul Allen adapt and sell BASIC to MITS for the Altair PC.

1976: Superminicomputers are introduced by Perkin-Elmer and Gould SEL.

1977: Apple Computer is founded and introduces the Apple II personal computer.

1979: The Source and CompuServe Information Services go on-line.

1979: Wordstar, one of the best-selling word processing programs for PCs, is released by Micropro (now called Wordstar International).

1980: Microsoft licenses UNIX operating system from Bell Laboratories and introduces its XENIX adaptation.

1981: IBM enters the personal computer market, creating a de facto standard.

1983: Cray 2 computer introduced with one billion FLOPs (floating point operations per second) performance rating.

1991: Intel introduces the 486SX, a lower priced 486 chip.

1993: - Microsoft unveils Windows NT.

1993: Pentium-based systems start shipping.

1994: Macintoshes using the PowerPC start shipping.

USES OF COMPUTERS

Computers are being used in our daily lives for varied purposes. Airlines, railways, banks and educational institutions are far ahead in using computers in comparison with the other organizations. Due to lowering cost, computer is being used in households as well. Their main uses are as folloes:

Record Keeping: Record means a collection of different fields. A number of records make a file. Records of different types are maintained in households and organizations. The information once fed in a computer can be stored, manipulated and duplicated as and when needed. A computer helps in avoiding duplication of efforts. It economizes the expenses on record keeping comparing with the manual system, which is more time taking, expensive and needs more space for the records to keep.

Banking : Computer is used in banks to maintain bank accounts transactions. Money withdrawl and deposits are directly entered into the customer bank account already maintained on the computer and the amount in the account is updated immediately.

Railway Reservation : Computer is highly useful for Railways in reservation. With the interlinking of computers on national and international level and also among the various agencies, it is possible to keep record of the available seats and ticket reservations from anywhere to anywhere instantly..

Health Services : Some of the most common applications of computer in health services are as the following:

Computer Aided Tomography: It shows the picture of organs inside the body on a computer screen. Any abnormality like swelling in the liver, the enlargement of the heart etc. can be detected through computer easily.

Computerized Electrocardiography (ECG) : The condition of heart is depicted on screen by using computer.

Electrocardiograms: These are the machines that bounce ultrasound off the beating heart to produce an on-screen 3-D computer image to predict the heart defects.

Computerized Stethoscope: Doctors use computerized stethoscope that listen to the heart beats of a patient and then digitize the sound. This digitized data is stored on the disk for further reference and sent to the computer for analysis. The doctors can examine the display on the monitor to find out the changes in the rhythm which they might not have picked up, by using an ordinary stethoscope.

Computer Simulation: Computer simulation means providing a real life situation through computers. It is used to train pilots for flying aeroplanes within different situations as created on the screen of the computer. Simulation is achieved through super computer in different conditions:

- Super computers are used to stimulate the performance of nuclear weapons, replacing the live test of weapons.
- Super computers are also used to predict weather conditions which involve massive mathematical calculations.
- To enhance the vehicle safety and comforts, the VPP 300E super computer is used by one car manufacturer to stimulate and optimize the behaviour of the vehicle bodywork in crash situation. It is also able to perform calculations to enhance the body comfort situation like reducing vibration.
- Computer Animation: In computer animation, computer graphics are created and made to move with the help of computer animation. The famous movies like Titanic, Godzilla, Jumanji etc have used computer animation to create special effects. Even Hindi movies are making use of computer effect.

Internet: Internet is a global network which consists of many networks through out the world. It provides facilities like e-mail, and video conferencing.

E-Mail: It is the means to transmit messages including text, audio, video from one place to the other electronically using Internet. Computer is the basic requirement for the e-mail facility.

Video Conferencing: Video conferencing is an electronic way of conferencing whereby people at different places, even in different countries can hold conference and see each other, interact, share views, and exchange data with one another through computers without actually gathering at one place. Video conferencing saves a lot of traveling time and expenditure.

Aviation and Space Technology: Computer plays an important rol in training of pilots to fly aeroplanes, guiding missiles and launching satellites in space.

Auto Pilots: The auto pilots have components like sensors and control systems which assist the pilots during flight. In aircrafts, in case a pilot becomes inconscious or non-functional due to some reason, the computer on board can take over and the pre-programmed flight schedule becomes operative to bring the aircraft safely to the ground.

Satellite Control: Computers are being used to monitor and control satellites sent to the outer space. Computers fitted inside the satellites, monitor and ensure its proper functioning.

Guiding Missiles: Computers are being used to calculate trajectories to guide missiles so that they can hit the target accurately.

GENERATIONS OF COMPUTER

First Generation Computer: These are the computers produced between the period 1951 to 1959. They used vacuum tubes, which made them very bulky and a lot of heat was generated by them when in operation. ENIAC was the first electronic computer which used about 18,000 vacuum tubes, weight about 30 tons and occupied the space of a house. The operating instructions were fed externally through switches and it could do about 300 multiplication in a second. EDSAC became the first computer with the stored programme concept. Here there was no need to give instructions externally with the changes of wire or switches. Instead the instructions were stored inside the machine. In 1951 UNIVAC 1 (Universal Automatic Computer) became operational. A few years later, IBM introduced IBM 650 machine which was cheaper than the other alternatives available at that time.

Second Generation Computers: In 1959, second generation computers appeared. They used transistors instead of vacuum tubes which made them smaller in size, more efficient in computing, less heat generating and comparatively inexpensive in cost. Second generation computers were having the following characteristics:

- Tape and Disk Secondary Storage
- Magnetic Core Internal Memory
- Modular Hardware Elements
- High Level Language
- New Computer Application

Third Generation Computers: The advancement in technology led to the development of semi conductor chip. Hunderds of transistors and electronic components were placed on small chip of silicon called Ics (Integrated Circuits). Each IC had a large number of instructions which were built into the chip to perform various operations. Due to these features, computer became more efficient, smaller in size and with enhanced computing power. Computation speed increased to nanoseconds. With this type of computer the concept of sharing became possible with the development of mini computer which also belong to this generation. . The other characteristics of the third generation computers are as follows:

- More Advanced Application Software
- Rise of Mini Computers
- Word Processing

Fourth Generation Computers: Efforts were continued for improvement in computers specially towared packing of maximum number of circuits on a single chip. This led to the development of microprocessor on a single chip which contained all the required circuits to do arithmetical, logical and control functions. Fourth generation computers used VLSI (Very Large Scale Integration) technology. With this development the size of the computer was reduced substantially and enhancement of speed was tremendous. The main characteristics of the fourth generation computer are:

- Micro, Mini
- Semiconductor Internal Memory
- Improvement in Software
- High Level Language

Fifth Generation Computers : Fifth generation computers are going to use the concept of artificial intelligence (AI). Using AI, a computer can think and take decision like a human being after consulting the huge knowledge database.

CLASSIFICATION OF COMPUTERS

Computers can be classified into the following two categories:

- Classification according to the logic used
- Classification according to the size

Analog Computers

These computers recognize data as a continous measurement of a physical property. There input is usually in the form of reading on dials or graphs, voltage, pressure. Speed and temperature are some of the properties that can be measured in this way. The examples are:

(i) Service station gasoline pipecontains an anlog processor that connects fuel flow measurements into quantity and price values.

(ii) Automobile speedometer etc

Digital Computers

These are high speed programmable, electronic devices that perform mathematical calculations, compare values and store the results. They recognize data by counting discerte signals representing either a high (on) or low (off) voltage state of electricity. Numbers, alphabets and special symbols can all be rduced to representation by 1's and 0's. Examples of such computers are

(i) Personal computers

(ii) Score board that directly counts discrete value such as the time left to play and the score of each team.

Digital Computers are further grouped into two categories:

General Purpose Digital Computers

The digital computers which can theoretically be used for any type of application are called general purpose digital computers. For instance, the computers that are used for payrol, graphs analysys, accounts, banking system etc.

Special Purpose Digital Computers

These are those digital computers which are made and used for specific job. For instance, the computers installed in automobiles to control fuels, ignition instruments and breaking system.

Classification according to size:

Microcomputer : Microcomputer refers to small computers which can be used by individuals at home or in business. The two sub categories of microcomputers are as follows:

Home Computers : In these computers, a CPU and the key board form a single unit and a TV can be connected to it as the monitor. For storing the data and the programmes, audiocassett players can be used. These are genrally used for home entertainment and educational purposes. A few popular home computers were Commodore-64, BBC Micro etc.

Personal Computer : A personal computer has all the functional elements found in a large system like the CPU, the Input/Output devices connected to the CPU and storage devices to store the data. These are the computers which are used in the day to day functioning.

Mini Computers : The Minicomputer was bigger than the microcomputer and is supposed to be more powerful.

Minicomputers are generally designed to simultaneously handle the needs of many users. They can support a larger number of users at a time with the concept of time sharing. Mini computers can be divided into the following three categories:

Mini Mini Computer

Midi Mini Computer

Maxi Mini Computer

Lap Top Computers: Lap Top Computer is a brand of microcomputer, which can be accommodated in a small bag and can be transported easily. It is operated with battery as well as electricity. Apart of this, computer works like LCD monitor. Lap top is generally used in training programmes, industrial establishments and exhibitions where it is not possible to bring the other forms of computers.

Mainframe Computers : These are large and powerful computers, which are used for complex and lengthy computation, used in scientific and engineering applications. These computers can support large number of input and output devices. Mainframe computers can provide all the processing power needed by an organization from a central site.

Super Computers: The most powerful computers are the super computers. Many processing units are integrated together to perform billion of scientific and arithmetic operations every second. Super computers play a vital role in the area of defence, molecular structure analysis, medicines, industry and space explorations. CRAY 1, XMP, CRAY-2 are some models of super computers.

COMPUTER HARDWARE

The computer is a collection of devices that function as a unit. The most basic collection includes a Computer CPU, a Monitor, a Keyboard, and a Mouse. The Computer CPU is normally a rectangular box that sits on your desktop (called a "Desktop Case") or next to your knee under the desk (called a "Tower Case"). The computer's CPU is actually a small electronic device inside the case but the term is often used to refer to the whole collection of electronics inside the box.

Processor Unit

All computation takes place in the Central Processing Unit (CPU). The CPU is attached to the Main Memory and this combination is the basis of the modern general purpose computer. The CPU has two main tasks:

* To control the fetching and interpretation of instructions from memory and the movement of data between memory and the CPU.
* To carry out (execute) the instructions.

The main components of the CPU and their role are:

* The Control Unit controls the fetching of instructions from main memory, the interpretation and the execution of these instructions and the passing of data to and from the Arithmetic/Logical Unit for computation.
* The Arithmetic/Logical Unit (ALU) carries out arithmetic operations on integer (whole number) and floating point (with a decimal point) operands. It also performs simple logical operations on Logical (True or False) operands and can make comparisons between numeric operands.
* The registers are small units of memory that the Control Unit and the ALU use for the storage of intermediate results and control information. The number and size of the registers depends upon the particular computer. Typically there will be sixteen or thirty two General Purpose Registers. It is important to note that since the registers are internal to the CPU they can be accessed at high speed by the CPU.
* Special Purpose Registers Vital to the operation of the CPU are the Program Counter (PC) and the Instruction Register (IR). The Program Counter holds the address in memory of the next instruction in the program and the Instruction Register holds the instruction currently being executed.

To run or execute a program it is first stored in consecutive locations in memory. The program must be written in the internal machine language of the computer. Each model of CPU has its own machine language.

Once the program is loaded into memory the following sequence is carried out.

Input/OutputDevices

All interaction with a computer must take place using some form of device that can convert computer-readable information to or from human-readable information. Common devices include:

* **Keyboard** The keyboard is used for the input of textual
* **The mousese** The mouse is used to select a position on the computer screen and hence allows selection from menus etc. Similar devices include tracker balls, light pens and touch sensitive screens.
* **Monitor** The monitor is the most common output device. This is usually a Cathode Ray Tube device which can display text and graphics. However it is gradually being superseded by various types of flat-screen devices.
* **Printers** If hard-copy output is required then some form of printer is used, commonly a laser printer or an inkjet printer.

All input/output devices, including hard disk drives, are slow in access time and speed of information transfer compared with the CPU. For example even a fast typist is probably only keying characters at about 6 characters per second. In contrast the CPU can transfer characters to or from main memory at many million characters per second.

All input/output devices will have some form of controller. The CPU communicates with input/output devices via this controller. An important aspect of input/output controllers is data buffering. Data buffering allows for the gross mismatch in transfer rates between CPU and main memory and the transfer rates of most peripheral devices. The data buffer is a block of memory which is used to act as an intermediate staging post for data as it flows to and from peripheral devices to main memory. For example when sending text to a printer the characters will be transferred at a fast rate to the buffer area associated with the printer controller which will then send them on to the printer at the printer's transfer rate. Similarly in the opposite direction an input controller will fill the buffer with input data before alerting the CPU that data is available. The CPU will then transfer the data from the buffer to main memory at high speed. This means that the CPU is not held up waiting for slow input but can carry on with some other task until the input data is available.

The Keyboard

Tip Sheet

Alphabet	**Alt**	**Backspace**	**Calculator**
Capitals	CapsLock	Ctrl	Cursor
Delete	End	Enter	Escape
Function	Home	Insert	Lights
New line	Number	Numeric	NumLock
Overwrite	Page Up	Page Down	Print Screen
Shift	Space	Tab	

Note: a Toggle key is one that switches on and off, or from one function to another, every time you press it.

The computer keyboard is divided into the following sections, plus additional keys.

* **Alphabet / number keyboard** - normal keyboard keys containing ordinary alphabet characters in the same sequence as the typewriter.
* **Function keys** - the F keys or the function keys are programmable and mainly used by advanced users.
* **Numeric keyboard** - a block of numerical keys grouped

together in the same way as most calculators. Most of these keys have two functions. When the NumLock light is shining, the keys act like a calculator keyboard. When the NumLock light is not shining, it acts like a cursor key pad. Change between these functions by pressing the NumLock key once.

* **Cursor keys** - the arrow keys indicating the direction of movement of the cursor on the screen.
* **Esc (Escape)** - this key is used in different ways by different programmes. It is mainly used to escape to the previous screen of a programme, or to undo what you have just done.
* **Tab** - this key enables the cursor to jump a couple of spaces to the right on the screen, see Tab settings. To jump the equivalent spaces to the left, use the Shift-Tab keys together.
* **Caps Lock** - (a toggle key) when this key is pressed, everything is typed in capital letters. A light usually indicates that this key is active. Press the CapsLock key again to de-activate this function.
* **Shift** - as with the typewriter, some keys on the keyboard have more than one character. To type the 'top' character the Shift key must be pressed down first, and then the required key is pressed together with the Shift key.
* **Ctrl (Control)** - this key is used in combination with other keys in specific programmes.
* **Alt (Alternative)** - this key is used together with other keys, often with numerical keys to get a particular ASCII character .
* **Space bar** - moves the cursor one space to the right every time you press the bar.
* **Backspace** - used to delete a character to the left of the cursor.

* **Insert** - (a toggle key) the keyboard is normally in "insert" mode i.e. you are able to insert words in the middle of a sentence or letters in the middle of a word. If you toggle (press) the Insert button it will change to Overwrite (also known as Typeover) mode i.e. whatever you type, will overwrite or type over existing text on the screen.
* **Home** - moves the cursor to the beginning of a line or the top left hand corner of the screen (varies with different programmes).
* **Page Up** - displays the previous page of a document.
* Enter - used to move the cursor to the beginning of a new, blank line or to start a new paragraph.
* **Lights** - the lights indicate which of the toggle keys are on.
* **Print Screen** - this key is used with graphics programmes to capture a screen image
* **Num Lock** - (a toggle key) this key activates the keys of the numeric keypad. A light usually indicates that this key is activated.
* **Delete** - used to delete a character to the right of the cursor.
* **End** - moves the cursor to the end of a line or the bottom right hand corner of the screen
* **Page Down** - displays the next page of a document (varies with different programmes).

The Mouse

Named for the resemblance of the wire coming out of it and a mouse's tail, the mouse was introduced to computing in the early 1980's when Macintosh created its graphical user interface (GUI). The mouse is another input device used to point at objects on the computer monitor and select them. Using the mouse and keyboard in combination allows the computer user substantial latitude in how to accomplish a wide variety of tasks.

The Floppy Diskette Drive

Once the most advanced of storage devices, floppy diskettes are normally used a temporary storage containers or transportation media for data. A standard floppy diskette can hold 1.44 MB of computer data. This amounts to a rather large number of pages if translated to the paper standard for textual information. Computer diskettes are not as reliable or fast as the internal storage drives on the computer. They are also the primary vector of virus infection in the computer world.

The CD-ROM Drive

This modern miracle gained prominence in the late 1980's and has become the primary distribution medium for software to consumers. The Compact Disk-Read Only Memory (CD-ROM) disk itself is a collection of concentric circles containing millions of pits and plateaus which correspond to on/off bits of data. The disk is read with an optical laser similar to the one used to scan your groceries at the supermarket. Most disks of this kind are "Read Only" meaning that the computer can retrieve information from the disk, but cannot place information on it. New developments have improved this technology to allow writing and rewriting data to the disk. A different kind of hardware mechanism is needed to employ this innovation.

Computer Printers

Printers is an output device. It is used to obtain hardcopies of the documents which are entered or stores in a computer system. Printers are of different types:

Impact Printers

Non-Impact Printers

Plotters

Impact Printers : In impact printer there is some impact between print head and paper to form the character. Impact printers can further be categorized into Character Printers and Line Printers

Character Printers

These are slow type printers. The main character printers are as follows

Dotmatrix Printer: It produces the output with lines consisting of dots

Daisy Wheel Printer: These are character printers which print one character per impact.

Line Printers

These are fast type printers and are of the following types:

Chain Printers : Here, the characters are embossed on chain

Drum Printer : Here, characters are embossed on a drum which prints one line at a time in each revolution.

Non-Impact Printers

In Non-Impact printers, there is no such impact as in the case of Impact Printers. The are of the following types:

Lase Printers : These printers print the desired output with the help of a laser beam, which operates under the computer control.. The print quality is exellent and the graphics can also be printer without any distortion.

Inkjet Printers: In Inkjet Printers one or more nozzles in the print head emit a stream of ink drops, which are guided to the paper by defection plates to form the character with tiny ink dots.

Thermal Printers : Here, characters are formed by the heat of pins in the print head. Thermal printers use heat sensitive papers. Since the price of heat sensitive paper is high, its use is less popular.

COMPUTER PERIPHERALS

Computer peripherals are any electronic devices that can be hooked up to a computer other than the standard input-output devices (monitor, keyboard,mouse). Peripheral devices include speakers, microphones, printers, scanners, digital cameras, plotters and modems. Peripherals often require special software packages called "drivers". These drivers are usually included with the peripheral at purchase time.

COMPUTER MEMORY

One of the most misunderstood computer concepts is memory. Often confused with hard disk space, memory is the computer's active working "space." Metaphorically, memory is the computer's desk, while a hard drive is a computer's file cabinet. Your computer's main processor can act on data in memory far more quickly than it can on data stored on a hard drive. That's why a computer primarily uses hard-drive space for longer-term storage.

Most memory chips need constant power to maintain their stored patterns of 1s and 0s. If the power is lost, then all the memory switches revert back to the "off" state, erasing the data from memory. Turning off the power is like going home for the evening: if you don't move your work from your desk to the file cabinet before you leave, the janitorial crew certainly will, trashing everything you forgot to file.

It's also good to be aware that your system probably contains quite a few different types of memory. Some are used for long-term storage of your computer's configuration, some for video operations, and some for basic system operation. It is this last type that we usually associate with "memory".

System Memory

System memory is called RAM or Random Access Memory. It is nothing more than a collection of integrated circuits (ICs) that store data as patterns of 1s and 0s (which are ons and offs) in the chip. Unfortunately, some memory chips are far less efficient than others. (The Keen Grasp of the Obvious Award goes to the readers who figure out which are cheapest.) The industry deals with this disparity by building systems with different, umm, layers of memory. Most systems have three such layers: base RAM, L2 cache, and L1 cache.

When we talk about how much RAM is in our system — 16 megabytes (MB), 32 MB, etc. — we're usually talking about the base layer of memory. All of our system's data get stored here. When people talk about adding memory or adding RAM to their computers, they're almost always talking about adding to this base layer. These RAM chips usually sit in sockets on the motherboard and are easy to install or replace.

There are a couple different types of chips the computer might use as base RAM:

· DRAM

Dynamic Random Access Memory (DRAM) uses tiny built-in capacitors to store the 1s and 0s that make up your data. If a charge exists in one of these tiny capacitors, it is read as a 1. No charge in the capacitor is read as a 0.

Capacitors, however, don't hold charges forever — and tiny capacitors hold their charges for a very short time — so a constant refresh signal is needed to keep the information in memory. When your computer's power is turned off, the refresh signal disappears and everything that had been stored in memory is lost.

Two major types of DRAM are Fast-Page Mode (FPM) and Extended Data Out (EDO) DRAM. While most older computers use FPM, EDO is found on many Pentiums.

Physically speaking, most DRAM in computers sold from 1990 through 1997 comes packaged in Single Inline Memory Modules (SIMMs). These are little rectangular circuit boards about 4 inches long and .75 inches wide. 386s and most 486s use 30-pin SIMMs; new 486s and most Pentiums use 72-pin SIMMs. (We'll get to really new Pentiums and Pentium IIs in a minute.)

It's easy to spot SIMMs: they sit on the motherboard in nice parallel rows. 72-pin SIMMs often rest at a 45-degree angle in relation to the motherboard. For a variety of reasons, SIMMs are typically installed in pairs.

DRAM SIMMs are measured in terms of capacity (e.g., 8MB, 16MB) and speed. A typical speed rating would be 60 or 70 nanoseconds (ns), with the lower number indicating a faster access time.

· SDRAM

Synchronous Dynamic Random Access Memory (SDRAM) is four times faster than standard EDO or FPM DRAM, with a clock rate of 6-10 ns. It typically comes packaged on Dual Inline Memory Modules (DIMMs), which can be installed singly, rather than only in pairs. Most new systems, those built around a Pentium II or AMD K6-2 processor, utilize DIMMs rather than SIMMs.

There is an increasing variety of SDRAM on the market, the newest and fastest of which is called PC100 SDRAM, which is of benefit only to the newest 100MHz-bus motherboards.

Cache-ing It In

Base RAM is the cheapest type of system memory and also the slowest. Unaided, base RAM will slow down our system because it just isn't fast enough to keep up with our Pentium or Pentium II.

To speed things along, two layers of faster Static Random Access Memory (SRAM) are added to keep track of recently used data. All the data in the cache layers are copies of data in the base RAM layer. When the processor needs a certain piece of data, it first polls the cache to see if it's there. If so, that datum can be retrieved and processed much more quickly than if the processor had to go to the base RAM layer to find it.

The L2 cache, the slower of the two cache layers, sits on the motherboard. A typical system will have 256 kilobytes (K) or 512K of L2 cache, though the newer Pentium II motherboards have up to 2 MB. Some systems will allow you to upgrade your L2 cache, but many won't. The fastest memory, the L1 cache, actually resides in the processor itself. How much L1 cache you have depends on your processor. The original Pentium contains two 8 KB-on-chip caches, one for program instructions and the other for data. Most Pentium II chips will have a 512K cache. The new Celeron CPUs have either a 0K or 128K L1 cache. Needless to say, you can't upgrade the L1 cache without upgrading your CPU.

Video RAM

Besides the RAM it uses for basic processing operations, your computer also needs a couple other types of memory. The video card, for example, has its own memory. Video memory is used to store image data for processing by the video adapter. The more memory an adapter has, the higher quality of image can be displayed.

The video image is composed of a set number of dots, or pixels. Your image may be 640 pixels wide by 480 high, 800 wide by 600 high, 1024 by 768, or higher. (Most monitors and video cards allow a range of settings, so you're probably not locked into your current setting.) The total number of pixels you see is calculated by multiplying width by height, e.g., an 800 by 600 image has 480,000 pixels.

Each pixel occupies a certain amount of video memory. If we wanted just two colors — say, black and white — each pixel would take up just one bit of memory because one bit (which is either 0 or 1) would be all that's necessary for defining two colors. For 480,000 pixels, that would require 480,000 bits of memory. Since there are eight bits to a byte, you'd need 60,000 (480,000/8) bytes, or 60K, of memory to support that resolution.

By contrast, a 65,536-color screen requires 16 bits of memory per pixel ($65{,}536 = 2^{16}$) and would therefore need 960,000 bytes, or about a megabyte, of memory to run at a resolution of 800 x 600. The 3D textures found in popular games require even more memory.

Video cards are built with many different types of memory. Some use regular DRAM, which is relatively slow, and some use faster types of memory that have been optimized for use in video subsystems. Sometimes you can add memory to your existing video card, but it's not all that likely a possibility.

BIOS and ROM

Finally, your system needs to "remember" some information after the system is turned off. Otherwise, every time you booted the system you'd have to spend a few minutes reminding it that you've got a 1.44MB floppy as the A: drive, that you use an internal modem so you don't want the second on-board serial port activated, that you'd like the Num Lock key activated at start-up, etc.

These instructions, and many more, are handled by the BIOS, Basic Input/Output System (pronounced "bye-os"). The BIOS lets your hardware and software communicate with each other. IBM computers contain a copyrighted BIOS that only IBM computers can use. Other companies such as Phoenix, Award, and American Megatrends have developed BIOSs for other manufacturers' computers that emulate or mimic the IBM instruction set without using the same code (which is how the phrase "IBM-compatible" was developed). Every time you turn on your computer, the BIOS company's copyright message and BIOS version number are displayed at boot up. BIOS information is stored in yet another kind of memory: Read Only Memory (ROM).

The original ROM chips contained transistors that are created in the on or off position. Once created, the transistors in a ROM could not be changed, so the information was considered "Read Only."

The disadvantage to ROM is that the information cannot be changed once the ROM has been programmed. Since it proved to be very inconvenient to remove an IC chip from the computer every time the software was upgraded, a method was needed to permit erasing and reprogramming the chip in place. The answer was the Electrically Erasable Programmable Read Only Memory chip (EEPROM). The chip can be erased by sending a special sequence of electric signals to the chip while it remains on the circuit board. These signals erase all or part of the chip.

EEPROM chips retain their information when the computer is off by using a small battery. Although the battery's charge is designed to last for several years, it will eventually lose its charge and the EEPROMs lose the ability to store your BIOS settings. You can tell when this is happening to you: the computer begins to lose its ability to keep BIOS settings when the power is off.

COMPUTER LANGUAGES

Machine language

The computers can execute a program written using binary digits only. This type of programs is called machine language programs. Since these programs use only '0's and '1's it will be very difficult for developing programs for complex problem solving. Also it will be very difficult for a person to understand a machine language program written by another person. At present, computer users do not write programs using machine language. Also these programs written for execution in one computer cannot be used on another type of computer. i.e., the programs were machine dependent.

Assembly Language

In assembly language mnemonic codes are used to develop program for problem solving.

Assembly language is designed mainly to replace each machine code with and understandable mnemonic code. To execute an assembly language program it should first be translated into an equivalent machine language program. Writing and understanding programs in assembly language is easier than that of machine language. The programs written in assembly language are also machine dependent.

High Level Languages

High level language are developed to allow application

programs, which are machine independent. High level language permits the user to use understandable codes using the language structure. In order to execute a high-level language program, it should be translated into a machine language either using a compiler or interpreter. The high level languages commonly used are FORTRAN (FORmula TRANslation), BASIC (Beginner's All-purpose Symbolic Instruction Code), COBOL (COmmon Business Oriented Language). Recently developed programming language such as Visual Foxpro, Visual Basic (VB), Visual C++ (VC++) are more popular among the software developers.

COMPUTER SOFTWARE

A computer is just a machine, which consists of various components. To make these components work, a computer needs instruction. It is provided by the software. Software means the instructions and the data which are executed and processed by computer. The software is the information that the computer uses to get the job done. Software needs to be accessed before it can be used. There are many terms used for process of accessing software such as running, executing, starting up, opening, and others. Computer programs allow users to complete tasks. Examples of software programs or applications would be the Operating System (DOS, Windows 9x/Millenium/XP, O/S2, UNIX, MacOS 9.x/10.x and various others), Wordprocessor (typing letters), Spreadsheet (financial info), Database (inventory control and address book), Graphics program, Internet Browser, Email and many others.

There are millions of different pieces of software available for almost every conceivable need. Software is available commercially through stores and mail order and also available on the Internet. As well as commercially, software is also available through an Open Source license which allows anyone to use the Open Source software free of charge.

The largest software companies offer packages of software or suites that include many of the programs that the average person or business needs. Software packages or suites contain programs that work together and share information, making it easier to combine that information in versatile ways. For example when writing a letter you can get the mailing address from a database, include a letterhead from a paint program and included a financial chart from a spreadsheet and combine this collection of information in the body of the letter. Computer software can be broadly grouped undr the following two categories;

- System Software
- Application software

System Software

Programs that control and direct the operation of computer hardware are system software. For example system software control the saving of data and its retrieval from secondary storage devicee. The system software includes the following:

Operating System

All computers need some sort of Operating System (OS). The majority of modern home computers use some form of Microsoft's operating systems. The original Microsoft operating system was called DOS (Disk Operating System) though most computers use Windows. Windows comes in various versions beginning with version 3.x then 95, 98, ME and currently XP. A few computers use IBM's O/S2. Apple's Mac use their own operating system beginning with OS 1 though most modern Macs use version 8.x or 9.x. Apple's latest version is OS 10.1.x. In the past large companies and institutions would have an operating system design exclusively for them but as the commercial operating systems become more sophisticated the benefits of this practice is becoming less apparent. Some computer professionals, Internet Service Providers (ISP) and mainframe computer users use an operating system such as UNIX (or a variant such as Linux), Windows NT or 2000 (Win2k) or one of the other network or server based operating systems.

There are many smaller operating systems out there. The problem is that software is currently being developed only for the main operating systems and only the newest versions of these OS. Many older computers with unique operating systems have lots of software already developed for them but there is very little new software being developed for the older computers. The older proprietary operating systems are less likely to offer technical support than the more modern operating systems.

The operating system controls the input and output or directs the flow of information to and from the CPU. Much of this is done automatically by the system but it is possible to modify and control your system if you need to.

When you turn your computer on it first needs to load the operating system sometimes referred to a booting up. Basically the computer starts from scratch every time you turn the power on.

It checks all its components and will usually display a message if there is a problem. Loading the system is usually automatic.

There are many types of operating systems. Some are made to work on a variety different types of hardware, and some are designed for only one specific type of machine. Mainframe and mini computers generally have their own propriety operating systems. In the early of personal computing systems were single users, APPLE, AMIGA, Commodore and IBM are all computer hardware manufacturers with machines that run single operating systems.

The second type of operating systems described as multitasking, is still capable of having one user but more than one task, operating at a time. The main task that requires the users attention remains on the computer monitor, while the other task is working away in the background. The background process could be a complex statistical analysis program that takes a long time to complete, and the users could spend the waiting time for some other work. A multitasking successor to DOS is called operating system 2.

Microsoft has developed its windows environment, and operating system with multitasking and other advance capabilities. Multitasking operating system must divide the CPU resources between the different tasks. In addition, multitasking itself is a more sophisticated operating system than the single user type, and can take more CPU resources just to run.

The third type of operating system is multi user by definition, multi-user systems are also multi-processing, since each user who is working on the machine accounts for a separate process. Depending on the power of CPU and the size of the computer, the number of users that can be working at one time might go into hundred. The most common examples of multi-user systems are in the large mainframe environment.

For a long time, UNIX is as multi-user operating system become very popular. It was originally developed by AT&T Bell Labs and was designed to be used by engineers and scientists. The most attractive feature of UNIX is that it is open system and multiplateform. A new competitor to UNIX on personal computers, workstations and networks is the Windows NT operating system from Microsoft Corporation.

The three basic types of software are commercial, shareware and open source software.

Commercial software

Commercial software comes prepackaged and is available from software stores and through the Internet.

Shareware Software

Shareware is the software developed by individual and small companies that cannot afford to market their software world wide or by a company that wants to release a demonstration version of their commercial product. You will have an evaluation period in which you can decide whether to purchase the product or not. Shareware software often is disabled in some way and has a notice attached to explain the legal requirements for using the product.

Open Source Software

Open Source Software is created by generous programmers and released into the public domain for public use. There is usually a copyright notice that must remain with the software product. Open Source software is not public domain in that the company or individual that develops the software retains ownership of the program but the software can be used freely. Many popular Open Source applications are being developed and upgraded regularly by individuals and companies that believe in the Open Source concept.

Application Software

Application software may be defined as software that interface between the user and system software to allow the user to perform specific task.

Application packages come in varying level of sophistication and complexity. They need to be user friendly. User-friendly that something that is easy to learn and use.

Application software is developed from two main sources.

- The user themselves. User written application packages
- Another person. Pre writtem application packages

User Written Application Packages

Use written application packages are those that are designed and coded by the users of the package for their own use. For example, payroll program, an inventory control program for specific organization etc.

Pre Written Application Packages

Pre writeten application packages are those packages that have been written by another person or groups and made available to computer users

Five pre written application packages have emerged as the most popular and widely used

(i) Word Processor

(ii) Data Manager

(iii) Electronic spreadsheet

(iv) Graphics

(v) Electronic Communication

(i) Word Processor

It has been the most commonly used software package during the 1980s. and early 1990s. It allows interactive processing of documents, enabling easy redrafting and merging of chunks of existing documents, without the need of existing retyping. Most of the popular programs have features just like spell checkers, outlining, choice of point, line drawing as well as page layout setting to produce any type of document as desired.

(ii) Data Manager

It stores , organizes, manipulates, retrieves, displays and prints data. Data managers are important to corporations and federal and state governments as they can keep track of the vast amounts of data that these organization have to gether and store. It has the following two categories:

- Database Management system
- Relational Database Management System

(iii) Database Management System (DBMS)

These are software packages for maintaining different kinds of database. Database is a collection of related files stored together in a logical manner like address of persons employees records etc. For example dBASE IV, FoxBASE, FoxPro, Clipper etc.

Relational Databse Management System

These are advanced databse management systems which

make the design and development of a database application an easy task. The relational database structure does not rely on a parent-child relationship. Instead, the relational structure groups all the data into tables from which the actual data relationship can be built. A table consists of rows and columns each rwo specifies a record, each column represents individual data items, and the entire table represents a file. Table can be interlinked to pull various data elements together, e. g. Oracle, Ingres, Sybase, Unify, Informix etc.

(iv)Electronic Spreadsheet

It is the software that displays, manipulates and prints rows and columns of data. It is similar to the papper spreadsheet in that both have columns and rows in which data and tables are entered. The difference is that the data in an electronic spreadsheet can be easily edited by the user, and all other dependent figures in the spreadsheet are then recalculated automatically. E. g. LOTUS 1-2-3 and SuperCalc are two popular spreadsheets.

(v)Graphics Packages

These packages display data in the form of graphics images. Even after using a spreadsheet to manipilate an organized data it can sometimes be difficult to see relationships or interpret that information. Graphics packages can extract and display data graphically in pie, barcharts or line. Business managers use graphics packages to present ststistics and other data, their relationship to clients. E. g. Harvard Graphics, Graphic utility of Lotus 1-2-3 etc.

(vi)Communication Package

It allows the user to send and receive data over communication lines. The data/text can be transferred between two points, or it may involve communication through out a network of computers and workstations. Text extended at one office may can be send electronically to other sides. Users at these sides can retrieve and examine the text at their convenience. E. g. PC-TALK, NICMAIL, Xpad, Radix, XTALK, etc.

COMMONLY USED PACKAGES

The commonly used software packages are:

Desk Top Publishing

This software contains many of the features of Word Processing and go further in the capability of laying out the format of a document. It is just like the replacement of typesetting. Sophisticated packages like Ventura Publisher and Page Maker allow in-house department to produce page layouts to include graphic images that were digitized with scanners and print the output by laser printers or high quality devices that produce camera ready output. A new development in DTP is the ability to exchange on various personal computers.

Data Base Software

A Bata Base Software allows the collection of, searching for and manipulation of information about unique entities. One of the early arrivals of the PC database management software market was a product from Ashton-Tate called d'Base. Still used today, d'Base provided sophisticated third generation programming language.

WINDOWS

Windows software was introduced by Microsoft. Its main feature is that it carries out instruction to the computer through mouse. Ever since Windows has appeared in many editions. The following are the main versions:

Windows 2.0, introduced in 1987, provided significant usability improvements to Windows. With the addition of icons and overlapping windows, Windows became a viable environment for development of major applications (such as Excel, Word for Windows, Corel Draw!, Ami, PageMaker and Micrografx Designer), and the sales were spurred by the runtime

("Single Application Environment") versions supplied by the independent software vendors.

In late 1987 Microsoft released Windows/386. While it was functionally equivalent to its sibling, Windows/286, in running Windows applications, it provided the capability to run multiple DOS applications simultaneously in the extended memory.

Windows for Workgroups 3.1, 1992, was the first integrated Windows and networking package offered by Microsoft. It provided peer-to-peer file and printer sharing capabilities highly integrated into the Windows environment. The simple-to-use-and-install networking allows the user to specify which files on the user's machine should be made accessible to others. The files can then be accessed from other machines running either Windows or DOS.Windows for Workgroups also includes two additional applications: Microsoft Mail, a network mail package, and Schedule+, a workgroup scheduler. In 1993 Microsoft ships Windows for Workgroups 3.11.

Windows 95

Windows 95 was released in 1995. A 32-bit system providing full pre-emptive multitasking, advanced file systems, threading, networking and more. Includes MS-DOS 7.0, but takes over from DOS completely after starting. Also includes a completely revised user interface.

Windows 98

It is a very popular software. Windows 98 was released in 1998. Integrated Web Browsing gives your desktop a browser-like interface. You will 'browse' everything, including stuff on your local computer. Active Desktop allows you to setup your desktop to be your personal web page, complete with links and any web content. You can also place active desktop items, such as a stock ticker, that will update automatically. Internet Explorer 4.0 New browser that supports HTML 4.0 and has an enhanced user interface. ACPI supports OnNow specs for better power management of PCs. FAT32 with Conversion utility Enhanced & Efficient support for larger hard drives. Includes a utility to convert your FAT16 to a FAT32 partition. Multiple Display Support can expand your desktop onto up to 8 connected monitors. New Hardware support will support the latest technology such as DVD, Firewire, USB, and AGP. Win32 Driver model Uses same driver model as Windows NT 5.0 Disk Defragmentor Wizard Enhanced hard drive defragmentor to speed up access to files and applications.

Windows NT 4.0

It similar in appearance and style to Windows 95. Windows 3.11 and NT 4.0 share few of the same characteristics. So, if you have been using Windows 95 on your personal computer, the transition to NT 4.0 should be relatively easy. If you are only familiar with the Windows 3.11 environment, you may need to spend some extra time adapting to the new look of the NT 4.0 main screen. Windows NT Run Faster Than Windows 3.11?

Windows 3.11 is a 16-bit operating system and Windows NT is a 32-bit operating system. One big difference between the two systems is that Windows NT processes information twice as fast as the older Windows 3.11 system. This gives Windows NT the power to process higher-end applications, such as Word 7.0 and Access 7.0.

Merits of NT

* NT works quickly (when using programs running under NT)
* NT is less likely to crash
* All resources are accessible from the desktop
* Desktop windows can be resized and moved, and resource icons can be added and removed
* File names can have as many as 255 characters, and the file name can have spaces in it

Some Drawbacks of NT

* Every computer hardware may not be capable of running NT
* NT cannot run all programs (Some DOS, Windows 3.x and Windows 95 programs may not run at all)

Windows 2000

Windows 2000 provides an impressive platform of Internet, intranet, extranet, and management applications that integrate tightly with Active Directory. You can set up virtual private networks - secure, encrypted connections across the Internet - with your choice of protocol. You can encrypt data on the network or on-disk. You can give users consistent access to the same files and objects from any network-connected PC. You can use the Windows Installer to distribute software to users over the LAN. The hardware requirements for Windows 2000 are:

* 86 Pentium or Pentium Pro System
* 32MB Ram or More
* 10GB Hard disk Memory
* CD ROM Drive
* PCI-VGA or AGP Dispel Card Monitor
* Mouse
* Modem Card

Characteristics of Windows 2000

* Task Manager
* File System
* Open With For opening the File
* My Document
* Explorer
* Network
* Internet or Multimedia
* TV like use

* Universal Serial Bus

Windows Me

In 2000 Microsoft released Windows Me, short for Millenium Edition, which is aimed at the home user. The Me operating system boasts some enhanced multimedia features, such as an automated video editor and improved Internet plumbing. But unlike Microsoft's Windows 2000 OS which offers advanced security, reliability, and networking features Windows Me is basically just an upgrade to the DOS-based code on which previous Windows versions have been built.

Windows XP

It is a new kind of Windows for consumers. Under the hood, it contains the 32-bit kernel and driver set from Windows NT and Windows 2000. Naturally it has tons of new features that no previous version of Windows has, but it also doesn't ignore the past—old DOS and Windows programs will still run, and may even run better.

XP comes in two flavors: Home and Professional. XP Home is a $99 upgrade ($199 for the full version) and Professional is a $199 upgrade ($299 for the full version). Recognizing that many homes have more than one PC, Microsoft also plans to offer discounts of $8 to $12 off the price of additional upgrades for home users (the Open Licensing Program is still available for business or home users who need 5 or more copies). That's fortunate because you'll need the additional licenses since the Product Activation feature makes it all but impossible to install a single copy on more than one PC.

Other Software

Virus : Computer virus is a very harmful programmes which after entering into computer corrupts the data files It acts on the Boot Sector of the hard disk which stops the working of the computer. It named virus because of the way of its infection like a biological organism which similarly affects on the living beings. In case of a seviour infection of the virus software even the operating system fails. The computer viruses spreads through floppy disks, tapes and networks.

Translators : A computer understands instructions in the machine language. All instructions imparted to a computer are converted into the machine language first and then the processing work is carried out.. Programmes are written in Assembly Language or High Level Language like BASIC, Pascal, Cobol, Fortran etc which are translated into machine code and the programmes which carry out this work are called translators. Translators are of the following three categories:

- Assembler
- Compiler
- Interpreter

Library Software

Library software are developed keeping in view the needs of the libraries. There are as many types of library software as are the categories of libraries.

3
THE INTERNET

Internet has revolutionized the world of information. It is one of the two technological innovations that have greatly influenced the development of communication strategies and practices in both the general and the business communities of the world. The first innovation was the invention of the printing press by Johann Gutenberg around 1450 in Mainz, Germany. Gutenberg's invention served to democratize the possession and transmission of texts, for it made the production of books much easier and, thereby, much cheaper than did the manuscript method it replaced. A little over four hundred years after Gutenberg began printing books with his press, Alexander Graham Bell invented the first telephone for practical use.

In the twentieth century, the invention and development of radio and television, like the invention of the telephone in the nineteenth century, have further led to the democratization of communication in both the social and business spheres. Like printing, radio and television have generally been confined to unidirectional communication. The users of these communicative channels have almost entirely been receivers rather than transmitters of information.

The invention of computer and the development of Internet have recently begun to alter the historical unidirectionality of mass communication. By creating pages for the World Wide Web, E-mail messages for Mailing List subscribers, and articles for UseNet news groups, most people can now for the first time economically publish their ideas for world consumption. If for no other reason than this one, college students would be well advised to learn how to use these latest technological innovations,

innovations so powerful that they could perhaps be characterized as potentially the most revolutionary since Gutenberg's invention.

Equally important is the growing centrality of the Internet to the myriad functions of the world's business communities. Indeed, most of the major newspapers (and many of the major news magazines) have themselves, being well aware of the revolutionary promise of the Internet, begun to publish special Internet editions. Even more importantly, most of the major businesses organizations of the world have created, or are in the process of creating, websites that supply information about their products.

Students of the process of communication in general and of business communication specifically are also increasingly becoming aware of the revolutionary nature of another Internet application specially, electronic mail. While in 1860 the postal system could deliver a business letter in eight days and today under the best of circumstances a similar letter between the same two cities in two or three days can be delivered almost the same time through a posted E-mail. The implications for businesses daily facing competitive pressures are obvious.

WHAT IS INTERNET?

The Internet is a global network of computer networks. Thousands of networks are linked together, forming a worldwide network. This network makes it possible for millions of people to communicate, to share information about common interests and to work on the same documents in multi-media format. This network is also a new way to do business electronically through the World Wide Web or Web, which is an enormous collection of web sites facility that brought the sudden popularity to the Internet. Many people think of the Internet as the WWW. It is a web of multi-media hypertext documents linked around the world.

The most popular feature of the Internet is the Web sites or electronic documents (files) that are stored on computers (servers) all over the world. The documents are written in a special programming language called HTML (hyper text markup language), which are read using a web browser such as Microsoft's Internet Explorer or Netscape's Navigator. A web site can have formatted text, images, animation, sound, music, movies, and more. With more and more sophisticated and easy-to-use Web browsers, an Internet user can access many documents with a mouse click.

Internet has become user-friendly for computer-illiterate people to use. Originally, the Internet was created for government use, to make military communications more secure. It was started so that technical data could be transferred more easily. Since then, however, the Internet has expanded to much more than that.

The Internet is composed of Local Area Networks (LAN), Metropolitan Area Networks (MAN), and Wide Area Networks (WAN). This is a way of breaking down the huge web of networks into smaller groups to organize them better. The Internet is not really owned or run by a single person or organization; rather, it is a collection of networks all over the world that is comprised of many organizations and companies. One of the main reasons why the Internet has become so popular is because nobody really rules over it and so users have a lot of freedom in what they do. There is one group, however, which tries to organize the Internet to make it more usable. This is the Internet Society, based in Washington, DC. The purpose of this group is to sponsor agencies that "bring order from chaos in such a huge Undertaking" .(http://www.mozcom.com/user/ig/history.html)

The Internet is a packet-orientated network which means that the data someone transfers is divided in packets. This principle is not new, It was already used in the 1960s. The networks are linked by special computers, the so-called Routers. A Router checks where the packet goes and decides in which direction to send it but not every Router is linked with every other Router, they just decide on the direction your data takes. So if the Routers know where the data is going, there must be some address. There is an address, namely the IP - protocol. The data transferred with IP is divided in packets. This is handled by another protocol, the TCP. It was soon discovered that the IP - addresses that are, in fact, just numbers are easy to handle for computers, but not for us humans. So the Domain Name System was introduced in 1984. This was a brief description of how the Internet functions.

Development of Internet

The Internet was born in 1969 during the cold war when the United States Department of Defence created the ARPANET or Advanced Research Projects Agency Network, a network that provided research agencies access to software they could not afford. Since then the Internet has grown and is used for many more purposes. E-mail is one of the most prominent components of the Internet because it is a quick and easy way to communicate with other people. For the next decade, the Internet was used mainly to support e-mail and discussion groups, as well as the transferring of government files.

The first test network built on these principles was installed in National Research Laboratory in Great Britain in 1968. Shortly afterwards, the Pentagon's Advanced Research Projects Agency (ARPA) wanted to installed a more advanced network based on the same principles in the USA. The network consisted of four high speed computers. In 1969, the first node was installed in UCLA.

The 1970s

There were 23 nodes on ARPANET: The first node (1969) was in UCLA, other nodes were in the Stanford Research Institute, the University of Utah and the UCSB.

ARPANET was constructed because computer time was precious and expensive at that time and the ARPANET offered the scientists possibilities to share their computers using long distance computing. This is nearly unbelievable nowadays, for instance a normal PC has 16 Megabytes of RAM today. This is very sharp contrast to the University of Utah's computer. This Honeywell 516 mini computer had 12 Kilobytes of RAM!

1972 was a key year. Ray Tomlinson of BBN invented the first e-mail program. Over the years, an odd fact became clear. Instead of using the ARPANET for long distance computing, the scientists used it for communicating with each other, of course for sharing results of their experiments.

The first international nodes were set up. These were located in England and Norway. The growth of ARPANET was to use any platform to connect to it. This is still the case with today's Internet. In 1976 UUCP (Unix-to-Unix Copy) was released and in 1979 USENET was established using UUCP.

The 1980s

The TCP/IP protocol was established for ARPANET. This protocol became standard (instead of NCP) on 1st January 1983. The name "Internet" was first used. ANET split into ARPANET and the military segment, MILNET. MILNET became integrated with the Defence Data Network created the previous year. The new protocol standard and even more the split-up were important cut-overs for ARPANET. Thanks to TCP/IP and its decentralised structure, ARPANET grew considerably during the early eighties.

In 1986 the National Science Foundation (NSF) wanted to make supercomputers useable for research projects, so they decided to link five super-computing centres. First they wanted to use ARPANET for connecting the computers, but ARPANET's bureaucracy and shortage of staff kept NSF from using this solution. So they built their own network using the IP-protocol of ARPANET. NSF linked the five centres. (56 kps). But apparently they could not link the universities with this network, simply because they didn't have enough money for building cables to every university.

The solution: The schools and universities of one region were linked together and this network was linked to one of the supercomputers. The "traffic" in this network increased steadily and so the computers and the lines were soon to slow to handle the massive amount of data.

In the 1980s, the Internet was still at a experimental stage and, therefore, was not widely available to the public. In the early '80s, the networks began to switch to the TCP/IP protocol. TCP/IP stands for Transmission Control Protocol/Internet Protocol. It is used for transferring data back and forth. The ARPANET then became the main backbone of the Internet, based around the TCP/IP protocol.

1990s

1990 saw the creation of HTML, or Hypertext Markup Language. HTML is the language source code used for current webpages. The purpose of HTML is to make pages more graphical than plain documents. The World Wide Web (WWW) was created, and this was a huge network of webpages all around the world gathered into one web. In the 1990s, the Internet has gone from being in a test-stage to being free for public use. To connect to the Internet, you needed to dial up an Internet provider, or a company who can more easily bring the information on the Web to your computer and make it more user-friendly. Some examples of very well-known, popular providers are America Online and CompuServe. Although it was originally created for the use of the government, the Internet is now used in many homes all over the world, and the number of people beginning to use the Internet for business and personal use is continuously increasing. In fact, the growth of the Internet is more than 20 percent per month. 1990 ARPANET ceased to exist, but its users scarcely noticed that because ARPANET's functions were continued.

The WWW was invented at CERN, an institute for particle physics situated in Switzerland. Originally, WWW was developed only for high energy physics (for world-wide communication). In 1991 Files were available for download on four newsgroups (alt.hypertext, comp.sys.next, comp.text.sgml and comp.mail.multi-media). Tim BL was the driving force behind the development of the WWW. He wrote the first WWW client and the first WWW server and defined standards such as URL, HTML and HTTP while working at CERN. Prior to that, he was a founding director of Image Computer Systems and a principal engineer with Plessey Telecommunications in Poole, England.

In 1991 WAIS and Gopher were released. WAIS — (Wide Area Information Servers) A commercial software package that allows the indexing of huge quantities of information, and then making those indices searchable across networks such as the Internet. A prominent feature of WAIS is that the search results are ranked (scored) accordingto how relevant the hits are, and that subsequent searches can find more stuff like that last batch and thus refine the search process.

WWW was released in 1992 by CERN and the number of hosts broke 1.000.000. A year later, the first browser, Mosaic, was released. The growth rate of Internet was an incredible 341% and it stills grows and grows now. It is a valuable source of information for anyone and on any topic, and also a new, exciting way of communicating with people thousands of kilometres away.

Present and future

Internet is continuously growing internationally. Within the last one decade, its services have spread among all nations of the word. In 1991, it was within the reach of 73 countries only but by 1995 it reached 148 countries. The number of Internet users is also growing tremendously. It almost doubles after every two years. The scope of Internet is also widening as it is being used for publishing of ideas apart from being an effective tool for storage and retrieval of information.

Internet services are developing fast in almost all the nations. The following institutions are responsible for its growth and development:

- Internet Architecture Board

- Internet Registration Service
- Internet Engineering Task force
- Internet Assigned Number Authority
- Internet Engineering Steering Group
- Internet Research Task Force

Internet services are becoming easy and affordable day by day. Its speed and memory have been enhanced greatly. Mass media is also showing interest in the Internet and one can find articles on it nearly in every magazine out there.

USES OF THE INTERNET

There are basically three uses of Internet:

- Communication
- Research
- Publishing

Communication

E-mail

The primary Internet communication tool is electronic mail. E-mail is nothing more than sending and/or receiving messages through computer. It combines the immediacy of the telephone with the word processing power of the computer. E-mail is being increasingly used for business, to keep in touch with friends and relatives, and to work on a project with someone at a place of choice.

E-mail is an extremely low-cost form of communication. Unlike telephone or standard postal services, there are no volume or long distance surcharges for sending e-mail. One can send one e-mail message across the city or 10,000 messages to the other side of the world for the same fee.

If you are hooked up to the Internet through an Internet Service Provider (ISP) or Commercial On-Line Service, e-mail is part of the service. Alternatively, one can get a stand-alone e-mail account that allows to send and receive messages without ever seeing the rest of the Internet. For people who do not have their own account, or who will want to access their e-mail remotely, Web e-mail accounts are also available. These accounts are hosted entirely on a Web site and your mail is protected by a login name and password. Many of these accounts are free. Anytime one can access to the World Wide Web will have access to e-mail. Web e-mail accounts are particularly appealing to people who anticipate moving frequently because their address would stay the same even as they changed ISPs. Some people prefer the relative anonymity of Web e-mail or wish to avoid the unsolicited bulk e-mail, or spam, that may result if users participate in a newsgroup that is subsequently "harvested" for addresses by bulk e-mail companies. With the advent of pre-paid usage cards, Web e-mail accounts may become more popular yet. To a lesser extent, the Internet is also used for communicating in chat rooms, newsgroups, list serves and through telephony.

Internet Telephony

Internet telephony (IPT) is the transport of telephone calls over the Internet. IPT could use traditional telephony devices, multimedia PCs or dedicated terminals to take part in the calls. The calls could entirely or partially be transmitted over the Internet.

Phone, fax and video calls (IP telephony) can now be placed over the Internet (or any IP network) using market available client software or hardware. In most instances, users will only need to make a one-time purchase of client software or hardware to begin placing unlimited long distance calls for the cost of an Internet connection. The quality of the calls will not match that of calls placed over the traditional phone network. However with additional hardware and software purchases, higher quality communications can be achieved.

Briefly, an Internet telephony application compresses and digitizes analog voice signals and sends them as individual packets across an IP network (a digital network) to the recipient

Internet telephony application. The recipient application then decompresses the voice transmissions as a result you have Internet voice communications.

Generally, one needs at least a 75 MHz system, with a sound card, microphone, speakers, a connection to the Internet and the software or hardware application that will enable you to place and receive calls over the Internet. Most of the Internet telephony applications will only allow you to communicate with other users of the same application, so both you and your call's recipient must be using the same Internet telephone application.

Research

For researchers. Internet is the library of the present and future. A growing number of people are using the Internet for research. Business people are assessing new markets, students and writers are looking for information and concerned parents are searching for the latest facts on nutrition. The Internet is the library not only of today, but also of the future.

The quality of information on the Internet ranges from stunningly poor to excellent. Thankfully, there are a large number of quality sites on the Net, and with a little experience, it is fairly easy to differentiate the good from the bad.

Internet Information Sources

Newsgroups

Special interest Usenet newsgroups are excellent places to locate expertise in a given field. Newsgroups act as electronic bulletin boards through which people exchange information, ask technical questions, offer solutions, gather leads and forge new contacts. One can log into a newsgroup, check any or all of the messages that have been posted, add your own message if desired, or simply leave. Anyone on the Net can participate, and it's free. With ten of thousands of newsgroups in existence, it is difficult to imagine a subject matter that is not covered.

List Serves

List serves, or mailing lists, are useful tools for gathering information. They are similar to newsgroups in that individuals post messages to a centralized location, and everyone on the list gets the message. The biggest difference between newsgroups and list serves is that newsgroups require active monitoring, whereas list serves are passively monitored. If you subscribe to a list serve, every message posted to that list by other users will wind up in the e-mail in-box. List serves are good for individuals who do not have the time to actively monitor a range of newsgroups, but who still want to remain current on a specific topic.

Information Services

Other types of information-gathering services are available on the Internet, including commercial information services and research companies. Also, thousands of libraries are connected to the Internet, permitting even casual users to access their catalogues and request loans through inter-library programs.

In addition to those information services, the number of on-line journals, newspapers and trade magazines increases each month. Much of the information in these publications is free, although some are accessible only to paid subscribers.

One of the best ways to locate meaningful information is through any of the public and private sector organizations that have established an Internet presence. Government departments and agencies, private corporations, law firms, retailers, trade associations and educational institutions publish a tremendously rich and diverse collection of information. And as more organizations develop their own Internet sites, the value of the Net as a research tool will only increase.

Publishing

In 1995, the World Wide Web emerged as the most popular part of the Internet. The multi-media Web allows for the display of still images, moving video, audio and text in any combination, and its growth is phenomenal.

A site on the WWW is open 24 hours a day, seven days a week. Sites can be as simple as a one-screen greeting designed by a hobbyist, or as complicated as an interactive catalogue designed for a major corporation. Anyone can design and maintain a site for whatever legal purpose they wish. How many Web sites are there? No one knows – but best estimates put the number of sites added to the World Wide Web every day in the thousands. The information on World Wide Web sites is not restricted to technology issues.

Home Paging

The concept of homepage grew along with the World Web, also known as the Web, WWW or W3. The term has multiple meanings. The sense in which it is used today is not the same as used in the past. Earlier, being represented by many terms, a homepage now refers to the first page of a website or the page which is approached first by a searcher while connected with a website. It is also the page, which is referred to in the website repeatedly as the search within the website generally starts afresh from the homepage.

A homepage establishes the identity of an individual or organization on the net and is like putting up a flag for someone in the cyberspace. It is the Guttenberg's press of our time with extended facility for low cost publishing. Anyone cab publish any kind of information including text, graphics, sound and video or a combination of all on the web through the homepage. It opens the doors of the millions of Internet users all over the world to receive ideas floated by someone. A homepage can be a full service front and for an organization.

A homepage is needed for global recognition of an individual or organization. Universities stand for teaching, research and extension and what distinguishes them from college is the facility for research. Higher the intended level of research in an academic institution, more is the need for a good information system that is effectively provided by homepage across the geographical boundaries of the institutions. The basic requirements for creation of a homepage are computer, Internet connection, Web space, contents creation and file transfer.

SEARCHING ON INTERNET

A Web page may have hypertext links to other documents. That is, a word, group of words, or an image can be an anchor referencing another page somewhere on the Internet. Using this feature, someone can go from one page to another with a click on the mouse button.

Most pages have links to other pages of the same topic or interest. Once you have found a page of your interest, you can easily find references to other pages. The pages are linked together like a spider web, hence the name World Wide Web. While reading the pages of certain interest, you may see a link to a page of another interest and decide to read it also, thus you wander around the Web from home. This activity is called "surfing the net".

Search Engine

One problem with the Internet is the difficulty in finding the needed information. Millions of Web pages are out there, but where and how to find them? Search can be started from the home page of Internet Service Provider (ISP). We have listed some of the popular search engines which have a database of Web pages and let you search for pages containing certain keywords. Good search engines have large frequently updated databases, fast results and a wide range of topics.

People search some of the most popular resources. Most of the pages have anchors to other search engines, so if you can't find the pages you want, you can go to other engines from there. When going to the search engine web site, type in what you are looking for and click 'Find', the 'button' next to the search box.

If you find thousands of results, you may want to narrow your search.

Most Popular Search Engines

- Google
- **Yahoo! (Nasdaq:YHOO)** - provider of comprehensive online products and services to consumers and businesses worldwide.
- **AltaVista** - featuring web and newsgroup search engine as well as paid submission services.
- **Lycos** - online destination site combining elements of navigation, community, and commerce.
- **Excite** - provides search, news, email, personals, portfolio tracking, and other services.
- **HotBot** - search engine that offers custom filters, skins, and access various other engines.
- **AllTheWeb** - search engine which indexes web pages, as well as multimedia, audio, FTP, PDF, and MS Word files from around the world.
- Open Directory Project (DMOZ) (6)
- **Northern Light** - customize search folders for integrated web and article searching.

Alphabetical List of Popular Search Engines

- **000search.com** - provides suggested categories to search the web and a keyword search box with a link exchange program available.
- **11AA.com** - offers links for students of Asia, Africa, and Latin America.
- **123World.com** - directory includes transportation, company, country, publication, and international organization links.
- **1DO3.com** - online directory that aims to anticipate the things you might want to do using the web.

- **212.net** - an eclectic directory of sites.
- **411.com** - offers various searches for a number of concepts.
- **4anything.com, Inc.** - features relevant information on a variety of subjects.
- **A Top Quality Site** - offers links, online games, downloads, news, and resources.
- **ABC Search Engine** - directory, offers news, chat, and email.
- **Abig Make Money & Shopping Online** - features links to finance and investment, money making, e-commerce, health and fitness, and online shopping resources.
- **About.com** - extensive network of sites by subject specialists who write articles, host discussions, publish free email newsletters and provide personally-reviewed links for each topic.
- **Abrexa UK** - family friendly U.K. search engine providing site reviews, age ratings, and spam warnings.
- **Aeiwi** - indexes sites according groupings of keywords.
- **Ajdee Internet Directory** - manually edited, advertisement-free, commercial Internet directory.
- **ajiffy** - provides pay-per-click advertising and an affiliate program.
- **Albert** - search the web using the company's Albert Meaning Interpreter (AMI) technology.
- **Alexa** - offers a web search and browser toolbar that learns from users and provides them with context sensitive information about sites.
- **All Academic** - provides free academic searches of the Internet. Authors can index academic work as well.
- **All.info** - searchable directory of topics focused on web site credibility.
- **Allestra** - offering a variety of links organized into targeted categories.

- **allsearchengines.com** - lists the major search engines and directories.
- **AllTheWeb** - search engine which indexes web pages, as well as multimedia, audio, FTP, PDF, and MS Word files from around the world.
- **AltaVista** - featuring web and newsgroup search engine as well as paid submission services.
- **AOL Search** - search engine and directory.
- **Argus Clearinghouse** - if you're interested in what the Net has to offer, the Clearinghouse can help.
- **Aryawat.com** - online business directory to find companies, products, services, and information with web advertising services available.
- **AtlasNav** - a geographical directory.
- **Ayna** - Arabic search engine and Internet directory .
- **Azoos.com** - searchable database organized by category and keyword offering same-day site submission for webmasters.
- **Baidu** - Chinese language search engine employing character-matching techniques.
- **Bankoi.com** - specializing in technology services for IT professionals.
- **Bay9** - pay-per-click search engine.
- **Best of the Net** - categorized index of sites.
- **Betabuck.com** - includes links to shopping, search engines, travel, entertainment, city guides, and more.
- **Beyond....**The Black Stump
- **BidSmart** - pay per click search engine offering paid positioning for Web site promotion and Internet marketing.
- **Big US Search Engine** - offers pay-per-click search results with donations to fight child abuse with every deposit.
- **Blackworld** - gateway to Africa, the Indian Subcontinent,

Europe, the Far East, the Caribbean and African America.

- **Blue Collar Internet Guide** - includes news and sports as well as a directory of sites.
- **BoardReader** - search message board information on the web.
- **Boxmind** - online library that categorizes a wide variety of subjects and subject areas, offering carefully reviewed and edited links to external sites.
- **BrainFox Media Services** - search engine which combines an existing directory with paid listings through their pay-per-click program.
- **BUBL Information Service** - subject trees arranged alphabetically and by UDC.
- **Business Center** - directory offers information for businesses and business travelers.
- **Buzzle.com** - offers links, message boards, jokes, stories, and free email. Subjects include sports, arts, finance, family, computers, shopping, entertainment, and more.
- **Care2** - environmental portal full of healthy living tips, eco-directory, click-to-donate sites, e-cards, and more. Generates donations for top environmental nonprofits.
- **CategoryWeb** - offers offers wholesale search results with a search engine which combines the DMOZ directory with paid listings.
- **Cheats.com** - directory of business, shopping, and recreation sites.
- **ChoiceX** - directory of user-submitted web sites listed by subject, country, and local area.
- **Clever Project** - publications and ongoing work at IBM Almaden Research Center to develop algorithms and systems for solving the problem of information overload.
- **Clickey** - keyword based search engine of registered domain names.

- **Clickforchoice** - offers a web directory and keyword searches.
- **Clickla** - search engine serving both pay-per-click and spidered search results.
- **CMN.com** - directory offers free submission, shopping, news, and supplemented metasearch.
- **Community-based Navigation** - enhanced version of Mosaic that supports fast Likert scale rating and automatically pools item-ratings in a community server that can recommend and evaluate URLs.
- **CompInfo** - reference site and search engine for computers, software, and business.
- **CosmicClick** - provides pay-per-click and spidered search results.
- **Cosmosurf** - Internet directory offers search, news, sports, shopping, web hosting, email accounts, and more.
- **Cyber Web Search** - directory and search engine offering postcards, games, classified ads, email, and more.
- **Daypop [read review]** - current events search engine indexes the best news sites and weblogs on the Net every day.
- Deltis
- **Digital Librarian** - a librarian's choice of the best of the Web.
- **Easaseek.com** - search for web pages, categories, and newsgroups.
- **eClickz** - pay-per-click search engine with an affiliate program.
- **EncycloZine** - hybrid portal/encyclopedia.
- ePilot
- **Espotting.com** - European search engine where advertisers can bid to be listed higher on search results and have their company logo appear as well.

- **Essential Links** - quick links to popular Web resources.
- **Eurekster** - offers personalized search results by tracking visited sites and remembering favorite sites and interests from you and others for future searches.
- **ExactSeek.com** - featuring free standard and enhanced site listings.
- **Excite** - provides search, news, email, personals, portfolio tracking, and other services.
- **Explore the Internet** - from the Library of Congress.
- **Family Safe Startup-Page** - family-oriented directory. Includes links for homeschooling and homework help.
- **FetchDog** - search for your favorite sites or participate in online discussion forums or just send a postcard to a friend.
- **Finally** - serves pay per click and spidered search results.
- **Fish4It** - from Urban Desires; limits results to just one "damn near perfect" URL. Discover the other fish in cyberspace.
- **Flipper.com** - features the grouping of Deep Web search results.
- **Freegle** - search engine technology for Freenet.
- **Galaxy** - searchable directory of manually edited listings.
- **Geekin!** - a web directory presented in graphical form as an Internet desktop.
- **GeoIndex** - search tool for geo-environmental professionals.
- **GeoURL ICBM Address Server** - location-to-URL reverse directory that allows users to find web sites by their proximity to a given physical location.
- **Get Favorites** - U.S. and U.K. directory of reviewed web sites covering topics including recipes, shopping, careers, weather, news, and more.
- **Gigablast**

- **Gimpsy** - web site directory organized by activity the user desires sites about.
- **Global Windows** - offers links to a variety of subjects including business, entertainment and recreation, health, and more.
- **Globe Alive** - search engine listing live experts and conversationalists standing by to chat with you and answer your questions.
- **goClick.com** - pay-per-click search engine.
- Google (11)
- **Google Directory** - human-edited directory organized by topic into categories.
- **GOpile** - pay-per-click search engine.
- **GroupWeb Directories** - features an Internet guide by industry.
- **Guidebeam** - returns search results grouped into browsable, related topics.
- **Haddock.org** - invite-only archive of URLs. Also includes an aggregation of weblog sites and books/music reviews.
- **Help Resource** - lists useful and informative resources.
- **Hot Sheet** - carries links to news, shopping, entertainment, and more.
- **HotBot** - search engine that offers custom filters, skins, and access various other engines.
- **HoundDog.com** - search engine and directory with keyword bidding and affiliate programs.
- **I Am Bored** - offers a list of sites with user ratings to visit when feeling bored.
- **Ibeau** - search and navigational directory of sites featuring Asian celebrities.
- **ibiblio** - Internet library and digital archive containing links to online collections.

- **iLOR** - offers different ways for the user to interact with search results derived from Google.
- **InfoGrid** - features indexed guide of the web.
- **InfoTiger** Search Engine
- **Insider.com** - directory of useful sites.
- **Internet Information Services** - serving the Internet industry with information, news, history, reference material, and more.
- **Internet Public Library** - Reference Center
- **InvisibleWeb** - directory of databases, archives, and search engines.
- **IQSeek.com** - search engine allowing sites to bid for placement under specific search terms.
- **Irena** - Web Connections Finder - glean from a target page of this Web server all relevant hypertext links and their annotations. Irena is especially useful for locating links to resources referenced in long, complex and densly written HTML documents.
- **itList** - keep your favorite sites and email addresses on the Web.
- **Jayde Online Directory**
- **Jump City** - The online version of the book,"What's on the Web", published by Internet Media and available in bookstores nationwide.
- **Kanoodle.com** - bid-for-location search engine with a focus on music. Also offers email, chat, a Love & Advice section, and more.
- **KartOO** - presents results and related links in a graphical map based format.
- **KaZaZZ** - includes search, news, tools, personalized lifestyle profiles, comedy, movie and book reviews, articles of interest, and thought provoking questions of the day.

- **keyword.com**
- **KoolPages** Search Engine
- **Last Chance List** - a large list of com sites generated by a worm.
- **Lerra.com** - search engine directory that organizes Internet content into targeted categories.
- **Librarians' Index to the Internet** - librarian selected and annotated index to the Internet, updated weekly.
- **Library Card, Thc** - lists links in the areas of entertainment, home and garden, libraries, government, health, schools, and more.
- **Link-Pimp** - human-edited and categorized directory of web sites.
- **LinkMaster**
- **Linkopedia** - seeks to take the work out of surfing by providing "best of" links.
- **Links2Go** - topical directory compiled using proprietary automated technology.
- **Linksgiving.com** - searchable collection of user-submitted favourite links. Visitors may vote for topics to get submissions.
- **List, The** - offers a directory of sites on topics including email, computers, mobile phones, movies, and shopping.
- **LookSmart (Nasdaq:LOOK)** - provider of commercial search listings products and graphical advertising products that help businesses generate cost-effective sales leads.
- **LuXPoint** - Internet directory and search for Luxembourg.
- **Lycos** - online destination site combining elements of navigation, community, and commerce.
- **Metrobot** - map-based search engine and city guide for selected U.S. cities.

- **MonsterSeek** - bid-for-placement search engine with an affiliate program available.
- **MOSHIx2** - Japanese and English search engine. Also has a browsable directory of sites.
- **MSN Internet Search**
- **Multimedia Educational Resource for Learning and Online Teaching (MERLOT)** - resource designed primarily for faculty and students of higher education. Presents links to online learning materials with annotations such as peer reviews and assignments.
- **Mysearch7** - offers a reciprocal link directory with search capabilities.
- **MySearchOwl.com** - general search engine offering bid for placement along with free games, horoscopes, news, and more.
- **NationalDirectory**
- **Nebraska Electronic Library** - searchable directory created and maintained by the Nebraska Library Commission.
- **NetQuantum** - searchable categorized index.
- **Netscape Search** - combines results from the Netcenter, Open Directory, and the Web.
- **Netword** - a word or short phrase that provides free access to an Internet destination. People & companies are creating Networds so you can find their information easily.
- **New Atlantis** - offers sub-directories organized by subject.
- **Northern Light** - customize search folders for integrated web and article searching.
- **Nutch** - effort to implement an open-source web search engine.
- **Official Site Register** - directory of official sites.
- **Oingo** - offering a meaning-based search service.

- **OneKey** - a child-safe search engine.
- **Onesite.info** - classifies sites by subject.
- **OneWorld** - database of web sites in English and Spanish. Topics include education, music, sports, Latin American studies, and more.
- **OpenFind** - search utilizing the PolyRank technique that aims to provide more flexible and optimized rankings.
- **OpenHere**
- **Oyeme!** - Latino portal.
- **Pay Per Click Analyst** - offers reviews of pay per click search engines.
- **Peekaboo** - business directory and a travel guide. Includes city and town info.
- **Peepo** - icon-based directory of web sites that aims to make it easier for people with learning difficulties to enjoy the web.
- **PepeSearch** - features the option to search using a variety of languages and a browsable Internet directory.
- **PepeSearch UK** - offers commercial web listings, news, and shopping.
- **Pocketflier** - pay per click search engine offering performance based Internet advertising for advertisers and affiliate programs in highly targeted categories.
- **Poke!** - search assistant that uses javascript and frames. It is always with you, an alt + tab away.
- **PolyBot.com** - offers a searchable and browsable directory with a clean interface and a featured sites sidebar.
- **QAZ.com** - U.K. directory.
- **Re: QUEST dot Net** - library of Internet resources for student and professionals.
- **Refdesk.com** - comprehensive index of Internet sites.
- **Resource Discovery Network** - dedicated to providing

effective access to high quality Internet resources for the learning, teaching, and research community.

- **ReverseDirectory.net** - collection of links to phone number and people locators, maps, and other resources.
- **RoPile** - offers a pay per click search engine with an affiliate program available.
- **Scannery, The** - for the investor. Focuses on investment-related information on companies around the world.
- **Scoop Cybersleuth's Internet Guide** - links categorized by subject.
- **Scrub The Web** - includes searching, user submissions, and a meta tag analyzer.
- **Search Adobe PDF Online** - search engine for PDF documents that allows you to view the summaries before viewing the actual documents.
- **Search Engine Dictionary** - aims to establish a standard for search engine terminology by creating an authorative glossary of search engine terms.
- **Search Engines Internet** - offers search results from two different search engines.
- **Search Hippo** - offers free keyword listings and an open HTTP XML API.
- **Search King** - engine that relies on web surfing for quality searching results. Searchers vote on sites, assuring relevant Internet results.
- **Search Mega** - providing pay-per-click advertising.
- **SearchGalore.com** - pay-per-click search engine and directory.
- **Searchgate** - UK-based web search and shopping directory.
- **SearchInfo.biz** - search for information including consumer goods, insurance, and more.

- **SearchIt.com** - pay per click engine.
- **SearchtheIndex.com** - offering relevant, ad free, human-edited search results.
- **SearchUP.com** - categorized Internet directory.
- **SelectSurf** - directory of selected web sites.
- **SightQuest.com** - offers a directory of links for shopping, health, business, affiliate programs, and more.
- **Singingfish** - multimedia search engine for audio and video files. Also licenses streaming media and multimedia search services.
- **SiteRanking.com** - provides a categorized directory of searchable listings.
- **Sitexplorer** - in English, German, Italian, and Spanish.
- **Smarter.com** - provides both algorithmic and editorial search results organized by user intent for popular queries.
- **SmartLinks.org** - easy access to categorized search engines, directories, and a select collection of web sites.
- **SolveYourProblem.com** - targeted to assist individuals in locating solutions to a problem, alleviating a hardship, or improving general well being.
- **Sootle** - half human, half-spider based search engine.
- **Spider's Apprentice, The** - a public service site that offers help on searching the Web. We also analyze and rate the major search engines.
- **Spire Project, The** - interlinked collection of search blueprints work with articles, links, forms, and guidance.
- **SplatSearch.com**
- **Square 1** - provides a pay per click search engine and affiliate program.
- **SunSteam** - search and directory.
- **SurfSafely.com** - offers family-friendly search, using a web directory open only to PICS rated sites, enabling

content selection using parental controls.

- **SurfWolf.com** - pay-per-click search engine providing webmasters and advertisers with targeted positioning and search results.
- **Surfy!** - Internet access, search, email, downloads, and more.
- **Teoma** - compares links of sites that are subject relevant.
- **TheIndex** - for locating commercial, professional, technical, and academic information, products, and services.
- **TheLinks** - includes major search engines, plus 800 numbers, zip codes, usp, yellow pages and medical databases.
- **ThisIsOurYear.com** - searchable website directory and webmaster tools.
- **Thunderstone** - an index of sites, not pages.
- **Tile.net** - reference source for Internet discussion and information lists, Usenet newsgroups, FTP sites, computer products vendors, and web design companies.
- **Top50.to** - features top list web directory, affiliate network, member community, website promotion, and more.
- **Top9.com** - sites in each topical category are ranked by popularity.
- **TopiaWebSearch** - directory, search engine, and merchant product database organized by category.
- **Toppest** - news headlines and a directory of web sites for the creative arts, performing arts, visual arts, humanities, and sciences.
- **TotalSeek** - categorized directory of web sites.
- **TrueSearch.com**
- **Turbo10** - allows you to search the "deep web" via a collection of databases and search engines, which you can

customize. Searchers can also cluster results into topics and sort by relevance, speed, and source.

- **TurboFind.com** - offers a directory of popular categories and search engine for the Web.
- **Tygo** - search engine and directory actively spidering the web.
- **United States of America Web Resource**
- **UniXL** - online university and college education directory.
- **Virtual Voodoo** - includes technical advice and reviews.
- **Visca Online** - selected sites on everything from entertainment to business with quick links for common search terms.
- **Voila** - search the web or browse through categories.
- **Web's Best Directory** - volunteer editors categorize the Web into an organized directory.
- **Web-Search.biz** - search engine combining third party results with pay-per-click listings. Also offers a webmaster affiliate program.
- **WebbieWorld** - features an engine that searches partial search phrases and a ranked directory of sites.
- **WebExhibits** - illustrated educational exhibits, with brief summaries, ratings, and reviews.
- **WebLens** - offers sections for classic and specialized searches, search tutorials, knowledge networking, and more.
- **Webocracy Internetwork** - media think tank committed to furthering the views of a liberal, thinking society through a polemical approach to established, traditional, orthodox, or authoritarian attitudes, views, or dogmas.
- **Webpilots, The** - features tours of the Web with an easy-to-use graphical interface.
- **Webtaxi** - provides a single interface for both parallel and

nonparallel methods of searching multiple sites.

- **What Can You Do On The World Wide Web?** - listing of sites answering the title question.
- **What-U-Seek** - uses Chubba to search the Web
- **Whoisman.net** - family friendly search and directory.
- **WiseNut** - employs a context-sensitive ranking algorithm to return search results by degrees of relevance.
- **World Guide Top Sites** - directory of categorized sites with a built-in search engine.
- **World Portal** - includes directory and services.
- **WorldWebDex** - lists and advertises commercial web sites alphabetically according to category.
- **Wotbox** - independent search engine in development with geo-targeting features.
- **WWW Virtual Library** - catalog of the web run by a confederation of volunteers.
- **WZ.com Inc.** - offering a reviewed sites directory including newsletters focused on hobbies, leisure, business, and online recreation.
- **Xoing** - search engine offering free games, email, websites, and more.
- **Xoron Search** - uses a community of paid infomediaries to give you search results.
- **Yahoo! (Nasdaq:YHOO)** - provider of comprehensive online products and services to consumers and businesses worldwide.
- **Yahoo! Directory** - subject-based guide to web sites and web content.
- **Yahoo! Search** - provides an interface for finding information, news, images, products, and local services.
- **YamWeb Navigator** - Taiwan-based directory of web sites.

- **Yep** - surf engine based on quality and popularity.
- **Yourwebspace.com** - free email, chat, games, search, online auctions, news, geeks areas, and more.
- **Zappo.com** - offers consumer and information based web directory.
- **Zeal.com** - user-contributed and maintained web directory with ratings and reviews
- **ZenSearch** - includes a Web search, email, and discussion forums.
- **Zenzibar.com** - index of alternative culture sites. Topics include the arts, business, health, lifestyle, politics, religion and science.

Meta-Search Engines

Meta Search Engines are Parallel Internet query engines which are used to submit questions to several search engines at one time. Many metasearch engines are now including paid placement sites in their results lists.

Metor Search

Pay careful attention to the menu on the left side of the page. By using General Search, you may choose to use search engines, directories, or listings of reviewed sites for your search. You may specify which search sites are used and the amount of time spent on the search. Specific Search offers the option to do metasearches by topic such as health, MP3, sports or science. This site has a privacy policy and offers no cookies.

Search.Com

Search.Com provides general metasearching using search engines and directories. You must use the advanced search option to specify which engines and directories are searched. There is specialized topic metasearching in categories such as news, people, reference, business, computing, and gaming. From C|Net.

ProFusion

You can choose to submit your search to from one to nine search engines, or let Profusion pick the best search engines to fit your terms. Results are combined and duplicates are eliminated. Searches may also be done in topics such as news, business, health, investing, and others.

HotBot

You can choose to search Google, Teoma, Fast or Inktomi. There are a number of different filtering and search options available through Advanced Search.

Kartoo

Kartoo graphically presents relationships between the web sites located for a topic. Kartoo will give you a new perspective on your search results, but it is a good idea to read the Help and FAQ before doing a search.

Vivisimo

Vivisimo uses 8 search engines and directories. Results are combined, and also organized into folders by topic on the left side of the screen. There is no specialized topic searching.

Ask Jeeves

Ask Jeeves a question in plain English and you will receive a reply from either Jeeves' list of human selected sites or from a metasearch of several of the major search engines. There is also Ask Jeeves for Kids. Jeeves is a fun place to visit, but lacks the relevance and precision needed by the serious searcher. Ask Jeeves also includes advertisments in its search results so your search results may include a site that paid to be there.

Highway 61 MetaCrawler

Submit your search to 9 search engines and directories. References are listed on the search results page in order of relevance, and the search engine from which the reference was retrieved is indicated. There are Boolean AND and OR search options. The amount of time spent on the search can be specified, and there are two options for the number of references retrieved. These folks have a sense of humor too which is nice to see in a search site.

Ixquick Metasearch

Sites in the results list are given star ratings according to the their placement in the top 10 of each of the engines and directories searched. It is possible to choose which search engines are used after you have done your initial search. This option is presented in the results list. There are individual searches for the Web, news, MP3, and pictures. This site offers many cookies.

Mama : The Mother of All Search Engines

The basic metasearch uses 6 search engines and directories to search web sites, news, usenet, stock quotes, MP3 files, images, and sounds. The results are combined and duplicates eliminated. If you go to Power Search, you will find that Mama is searching a rather unimpressive group of sites. If you want a wider search range, try another metasearch site.

MetaCrawler

MetaCrawler uses 10 search engines and directories and the results are combined. Use the power search option to specify which engines are used and the amount of time spent on the search.

Datavor

Datavor is not really a metasearch site but it is quite useful. You may enter your search term and get results from Datavor's collection. Then you can run the same search term on a large number of other search engines and compare the results.

Dogpile

Search the web, usenet newsgroups, FTP sites, business news, stock quotes, weather and newswires. The Web Metasearch uses both search engines and subject directories. Results are returned rapidly, but are not combined. This might be the place to go to locate shopping sites but the serious researcher might be wasting time here.

Chubba

Chubba submits searches to Alta Vista, WhatUSeek, Ah-Ha, Infoseek, and Lycos. You may not specify which search engines are to be used. Chubba searches the web, newsgroups, an encyclopedia, a dictionary, auctions, and the weather. Chubba is operated by WhatUSeek.

Debriefing

Debriefing seems to be another manifestation of the Ixquick search site.

WebCrawler

You may not specify which search engines and directories to use, and you do not know which have been used.

Approaches to Searching

The information on the web is growing and being updated every day. There are millions of web pages and there is a lot of great information. However, one of the most noticeable problems with the web today is the difficulty in finding a specific piece of information. Unlike a library, there is no central card catalog for the web and it follows no organizational standard. Instead, search tools are used to locate information on the web. For the most part, they are fast, easy to use and open 24 hours a day. A search tool performs searches of the Internet based upon input by the user. This input might include topics, keywords or phrases, or any other type of search criteria. Some of the difficulty in finding information is going away because the tools for locating information are maturing, becoming more powerful and sophisticated every day. Because of the enormous amount of information out there, search tools are indispensable.

There are numerous tools available for finding information on the web, and each of these operates somewhat differently.

Some of the tools use a comprehensive approach and try to include all of the information on the web. Other tools only cover a narrow subject matter, for example, there is a tool specific for finding conferences sponsored by the Microsoft Corporation. The results of your search will depend on the type of search tool you are using.

Google and Yahoo are very good at finding general information, because they organize web sites into popular categories. If you wanted to find the Walt Disney home page, Yahoo would be a good tool to use. In comparison, AltaVista is much more comprehensive. If you wanted to find the name of the producer for Walt Disney's movie "The Lion King", AltaVista would be a good tool to use. These two tools demonstrate many of the features found in other search tools and you should be able to apply this knowledge to other tools.

One gets confused when learning about search tools because there are so many terms. This includes terms like "search engines", "meta indexes", "web guides", "directories", etc. The value of spending a lot of time on these terms is questionable as they are often vaguely defined and misused one should not be overly concerned about all of the terms, but rather how to perform a search.

Therefore, rather then dwelling on specific terms, let's look at two general approaches to finding information on the web. These approaches can be used to find the same information, however, each one has its advantages and disadvantages. Many search tools now support both approaches. For the duration of this module we will refer to these approaches as "browsing" and "keyword searching", however, as you spend more time on the Internet, you will see many other names for these same approaches and their variations.

Searching by Browsing: Searching by browsing is like surfing the web. One starts out looking at a very wide range of topics and after following six or seven links you have narrowed your attention to a specific web site. If the specific site does not contain the information you are look for a different page. The search tools that support the browsing approach organize the web sites into categories and sub-categories. You start out with the most general categories and work your way through a series of categories until you get to the information you are looking for. Normally this approach implies that you have some background information related to your search and can identify which categories it will belong to. This approach works well for this simple search because the categories are easy to identify and there is a small number of sub-categories.

Subject Directories: Subject Directories are good for this type of searching because they are good at identifying general information. They group web sites together under similar categories, such as Internet Tutorials, English Universities and Paris Museums. The results of the search will be a list of web sites related to the subject you are searching for.

Keyword Searching

In comparison, keyword searching provides a more direct approach. Most search tools employ a search engine which is a web accessible program that searches a database (index) of words and phrases from web documents, attempting to match key words that you supply. They providea search entry box where you can enter a word (or, a few words). The tool will then produce a list of resources that contain that word. Occasionally, all of these resources are relevant to the information you were looking for, however, most often only a portion of the list will be relevant. At this point you will have to sort through the list to find the results that contain the information you are looking for. This approach can be much faster than browsing, however, depending on the keywords you select, and the number of "hits" returned, it can be much slower. In addition to sometimes being faster, this approach does not require as much background information.

The WWW will almost certainly become a major part of

the infrastructure of the increasingly interconnected world economy. In the near future, using the Web to conduct business will become as commonplace as using a bank card is today. The Web will allow customers to search catalogues, place orders, submit requests, send "digital cash", and more. Companies large and small can do business in their own neighbourhood, or with customers in other countries.

Internet Tools and Services

Domain Name

Domain name is a name that identifies one or more IP addresses. For example, the domain name *microsoft.com* represents about a dozen IP addresses. Domain names are used in URLs to identify particular Web pages. For example, in the URL

http://www.pcwebopedia.com/index.html, the domain name is pcwebopedia.com.

Every domain name has a suffix that indicates which top level domain (TLD) it belongs to. There are only a limited number of such domains. For example:

gov - Government agencies

edu - Educational institutions

org - Organizations (nonprofit)

mil - Military

com - commercial business

net - Network organizations

in - India

ca - Canada

th - Thailand

Because the Internet is based on IP addresses, not domain names, every Web server requires a Domain Name System (DNS) server to translate domain names into IP addresses.

Client Server

A software program that is used to contact and obtain data from a *Server* software program on another computer, often across a great distance. Each*Client* program is designed to work with one or more specific kinds of *Server* programs, and each *Server* requires a specific kind of *Client*. A Web *Browser* is a specific kind of *Client*.

Voice Over Internet Protocol (VOIP)

VoIP is a term used for a set of facilities designed to manage the delivery of voice information using Internet Protocol. In general, this means sending voice information in inconspicuous digital form rather than in the traditional circuit-committed protocols of the public switched telephone network (PSTN). A major advantage of VoIP and Internet telephony is that it eliminates ordinary toll charges.

The delivery of voice information in the language of the Internet, i.e., as digital packets instead of the current circuit protocols of the copper-based phone networks. In VOIP systems analog voice messages are digitized and transmitted as a stream of data (not sound) packets that are reassembled and converted back into a voice signal at their destination. The killer idea is that VOIP allows telephony users to bypass long-distance carrier charges by transporting those data packets just like other Internet information. With VOIP, your PC becomes your phone and you can call anywhere in the world for the cost of a local call.

Uniform Resource Locator (URL)

A URL (Universal Resource Locator) is a general-purpose Internet addressing protocol, used in WWW (HTTP) service. It is of the form: protocol://hostname.domain.name/directory or file names/file name.file extension. One could say a URL is what a telephone number is to a telephone or a street address is to a house. Although Web site URLs are sometimes long and hard to read let alone remember, browsers like Netscape have a bookmark feature, which gives you the opportunity to save the location (URL) of Web sites you want to return to.

URL is an identifier used in the World Wide Web to find and access resources on the Internet. An example URL is "http://fiddle.ee.vt.edu/courses/general/tutorial.html" - it specifies the protocol that should be used to access the resource (HTTP), the Internet host containing the resource (fiddle.ee.vt.edu), and the specific resource, a file (/courses/general/tutorial.html).

Active X

Set of platform independent technologies developed by Microsoft that enable software components to interact with one another in a networked environment, like the Internet. In addition to adding functionality within the browser (for example, by enabling Microsoft Word to be opened in a browser) Active X components can be exploited by malicious mobile code. Since most web pages are static documents with little interactivity, Microsoft created a programing language, called ActiveX, to remedy this situation. ActiveX "controls" promise to make the web-surfing experience comparable to that of highly produced CD-ROMS, where you can listen to music, watch animation and video clips, and interact with the program.

A set of technologies created by Microsoft Corp. that enables a type of interactive content on Web sites. With ActiveX, Web sites become animated using multimedia effects, interactive objects, and sophisticated applications that create a user experience comparable to that of a high-quality CD-ROM. The same effects can be experienced with Java, Shockwave and numerous other applets — the difference is that ActiveX is an exclusive Microsoft product. Ad Banner: An advertisement on a Web page that links to an advertisers site or buffer page. Ad banners are the most common unit of advertising on the Web and cost anywhere from free to upwards of $15,000 per month depending on the amount of page requests the Web site receives. The standard size for an ad banner set by the Internet Advertising Bureau (IAB) is 468 pixels wide by 60 pixels high.

Multimedia

Multimedia describes any application that uses multiple media (graphics, text, animations, audio, video). However, multimedia is primarily thought of as any application that uses high-bandwidth media (audio and video) and is most often delivered on CD-ROM. Multimedia does not describe the purpose of the application, such as game, presentation, or CBT. Nor does multimedia describe the delivery media, such as CD-ROM, only the nature of media used in the application. CBT and WBT may also be considered multimedia applications if they incorporate multiple media to meet instructional objectives.

This originally indicated a capability to work with and integrate various types of things including audio, still graphics, and especially video. Now it is more of a marketing term and has little real meaning. Historically the Amiga was the first multimedia machine. Today in addition to AmigaOS, IRIX and Solaris are popular choices for high-end multimedia work.

Programming language

An artificial language that is used to generate or to express computer programs. The language may be a high-level language, an assembly language, or a machine language. (188)

There are a number of programming languages in existence and no one language is suitable for writing all types of programs. The language a programmer uses to create an application will depend on the desired properties of the program. Some programming languages lend themselves to mathematical and analytical functions while others are better suited for creating business or data processing applications. The programming language field is wide and complex, encompassing a large number of disciplines.

Common Gateway Interface (CGI)

A server-side interface for initiating software services. The specification that defines communications between information services (such as an HTTP service) and resources on the server's host computer, such as databases and other programs. For example, when a user submits a form through a Web browser, the HTTP service executes a program (often called a CGI script) and passes the user's input information to that program through CGI. The program then returns information to the service through CGI. Any software can be a CGI program if it handles input and output according to the CGI standard. CGI applications always run out-of-process. See also server.

Java

A simple platform-independent object-oriented programming language used for writing applets that are downloaded from the World Wide Web by a client and run on the client's machine

Developed by Sun Microsystems, Java is a programming language that is specifically designed for writing programs that can be safely downloaded to your computer through the Internet and immediately run without fear of viruses or other harm to your computer or files. Using small Java programs (called "Applets"), Web pages can include functions such as animations, calculators, and other fancy tricks. Java is a simple, robust, object-oriented, platform-independent multi-threaded, dynamic general-purpose programming environment. It is best for creating applets and applications for the Internet, intranets and any other complex, distributed network.

Java Script

This is a language very close to Java that allows for more interaction with the viewer. It is much more forgiving than Java as doesn't require it's own window in which to work.

JavaScript is an interpreted programming or script language from Netscape. It is somewhat similar in capability to Microsoft's Visual Basic, Sun's Tcl, the UNIX-derived Perl, and IBM's REXX. In general, script languages are easier and faster to code in than the more structured and compiled languages such as C and C++ and are ideal for programs of limited capability or that can reuse and tie together existing compiled programs. Example: The date on the bottom of the page (Page Last Updated) & all pages here change each time I save the file. I do not manually type in the date each time I edit a page. Handy because just saving the file changes the date displayed!

Virtual Reality Modeling Language (VRML)

A language for coding three-dimensional HTML applications.

Virtual Server

Also called a Web site. A virtual computer that resides on an HTTP server but appears to the user as a separate HTTP server. Several virtual servers can reside on one computer, each capable of running its own programs and each with individualized access to input and peripheral devices. Each virtual server has its own domain name and IP address and appears to the user as an individual Web site or FTP site. Some Internet service providers use virtual servers for those clients who want to use their own domain names.

Real Time Communication

Communication occurring at the moment messages are generated. Real Time is a characteristic of synchronous communication.

Push

Frequently used to describe data sent over the Internet; the act of sending data to a client computer without the client requesting it. Example: a subscriptions service that delivers customized news to your desktop. Contrast to browsing the World Wide Web which is based on "pull" technology; you must request a web page before it is sent to your computer

A software program that retrieves information from web sites and deposits a copy on the user's computer to view offline. This is in contrast to traditional pull technology, where the user must manually seek and find information on the World Wide Web. See also channel.

The technology that puts pre-selected content directly on your computer screen from the Internet without your need to browse for it. With this technology, introduced by PointCast and Individual, Inc.and added to 4th generation browsers, you can program your desktop, for example, to automatically receive such things as local weather, news headlines, selected stock reports, and sports scores for selected teams or events.

In client/server applications, to send data to a client without the client requesting it. The World Wide Web is based on a pull technology where the client browser must request a Web page before it is sent. Broadcast media, on the other hand, are push technologies because they send information out regardless of whether anyone is tuned in. Increasingly, companies are using the Internet to deliver information push-style. One of the most successful examples of this is PointCast, which delivers customised news to users' desktops. Probably the oldest and most widely used push technology is e-mail. This is a push technology because you receive mail whether you ask for it or not — that is, the sender pushes the message to the receiver.

Gopher:

Invented at the University of Minnesota in 1993 just before the *Web*, gopher was a widely successful method of making menus of material available over the Internet. Gopher was designed to be much easier to use than *FTP*, while still using a text-only interface. Gopher is a *Client* and *Server* style program, which requires that the user have a Gopher *Client* program. Although Gopher spread rapidly across the globe in only a couple of years, it has been largely supplanted by Hypertext, also known as *WWW (World Wide Web)*. There are still thousands of Gopher *Servers* on the Internet and we can expect they will remain for a while.

Veronica

(Very Easy Rodent Oriented Net-wide Index to Computerized Archives) is a constantly updated database of the names of almost every menu item on thousands of gopher servers. The Veronica database can be searched from most major gopher menus.

Veronica was developed at the University of Nevada, Veronica is a constantly updated database of the names of almost every menu item on thousands of gopher servers. The Veronica database can be searched from most major gopher menus. The name is a play on the less capable Archie program. It is the gopher-based search engine that worked with an index of gopher menus around the world. The last VERONICA search engine on the nets is probably gone for good, but before the web's spectacular growth, it was a real workhorse for searchers . It supposedly is an acronym for Very Easy Rodent-Oriented Netwide Index to Computerized Archives, but since the archie FTP search preceded it in time, the name pretty obviously came before the acronym.

File Transfer Protocol (FTP)

File Transfer Protocol, the protocol used on the Internet for exchanging files. It is a very common method of moving files between two Internet sites. FTP is a way to login to another Internet site for the purposes of retrieving and/or sending files. There are many Internet sites that have established publicly accessible repositories of material that can be obtained using FTP, by logging in using the account name "anonymous", thus these sites are called "anonymous ftp servers". FTP was invented and in wide use long before the advent of the World Wide Web and originally was always used from a text-only interface. See also: Login, WWW

Usually FTP is used to copy files from a personal computer to a server, so that they can be accessed by others. There are several common software programs that are used to transfer files (depending on which operating system your computer is running): WS_FTP, Internet Neighborhood, or Fetch. FTP is often used to download files from Internet sites, many of which allow users to log in anonymously and download public repositories of material (programs, images, text, etc.). These sites are called "anonymous ftp sites."

Archie

A tool (software) for finding files stored on anonymous FTP sites. You need to know the exact file name or a substring of it. By 1999 Archie had been almost completely replaced by web-based search engines. back when FTP was the main way people moved files over the Internet archie was quite popular.

FAQ

(Frequently Asked Questions) — FAQs are documents that list and answer the most common questions on a particular subject. There are hundreds of FAQs on subjects as diverse as Pet Grooming and Cryptography. FAQs are usually written by people who have tired of answering the same question over and over.

RFC

In the Internet community, Request For Comments are the working notes of the Internet research and development community. These documents contain protocol and model descriptions, experimental results, and reviews. All Internet standard protocols are written up as RFCs.

The document series, begun in 1969, which describes the Internet suite of protocols and related experiments. Not all (in fact very few) RFCs describe Internet standards, but all Internet standards are written up as RFCs. The RFC series of documents is unusual in that the proposed protocols are forwarded by the Internet research and development community, acting on their own behalf, as opposed to the formally reviewed and standardized protocols that are promoted by organizations such as CCITT and

ANSI. A complete list of RFCs can be found at http://www.internic.net/rfc/.

FYI : An abbreviation for the phrase "for your information." There is also a series of RFCs put out by the Network Information Center called FYIs; they address common questions of new users and many other useful things.

FYI is a protocol that allows users to converse with others in real time. IRC is structured as a network of servers, each of which accepts connections from client programs. It is a program for synchronous (real-time) communication. Users can log on to an IRC server and choose a channel to participate in or create a new channel.

INTERNET IN INDIA

Internet is the newest of the information technologies and has made a very recent entry in India. The exact date of inception of Internet in India is not known. However, it is safe to assume that the beginning was made less than a decade ago. It made a very slow beginning mainly because of the costs were initially prohibitive and the plans and policies for its growth were either inadequate or silent and definitely not very facilitative. The necessary infrastructure was not at a very advanced stage and was certainly not geared to its use on a large scale. The picture in the last five years or so is showing a major shift both policy-wise as well as infrastructure-wise. Internet has started growing at a very fast rate.

India was one of the few countries to enact the Information Technology Act 2000 to enable Digital signatures and e-commerce. Setting up of gateways for Internet, laying of fibers & cables was freely permitted to the ISPs. Tax incentives were showered on the industry, infrastructure status given & mergers and acquisitions facilitated.

Unfortunately the result is not in line with expectations of what has happened elsewhere in the world. The net users still stagnated at 5 million, less than India's 7 million mobile phones and less than 12% of the 42 million telephone connections in India. What went wrong in India which did not go wrong in the other countries?

The estimated number of Internet subscribers varies from 500,000 to a little over 600,000. It is estimated that there are about 30 million Internet users in the country. It is still largely a metro or an urban phenomenon. However, it is spreading into small towns very fast and it has also made inroads in the rural areas. Indians, by and large, have adopted this technology very fast. This holds true both user-wise as well as business-wise. As it will be seen in the later part of the article, even illiterate persons have started to avail of the services of the Internet facilities. A large number of Indians know English well and this facilitates the use of the technology. In addition, several Indian language based websites are created which makes the use of Internet even more user-friendly and popular.

According to the Indian Government's Planning Commission, the number of Internet connections in the country will grow from more than 3 million now to 23 million during its 10th Five-Year Plan, which ends in 2007. A recent study by the Gartner Group has suggested that the country has topped the list of Internet users in the Asia Pacific region for 2001. India has an estimated 3.1 million regular Internet surfers, although the number of registered users would hover at just about 1 million. The study conducted by India's Manufacturers Association of Information Technology (MAIT) has revealed that the number of Internet subscribers has increased to 1.12 million during the 2000 - 2001 period from just 651,000 in the previous year; the home segment registered a whopping compounded annual growth rate (CAGR) of 215 percent. "The number of active Internet subscribers increased to 1.12 million by March 2001, leading to 67 percent penetration among PC-owning business establishments and 54 percent penetration in PC-owning homes," the annual survey found.

IDC India predicts that the number of Internet users will grow eight-fold to 37.5 million by end-2005, representing a CAGR of 53 percent for the period 2000 - 2003; the research firm had estimated that there were 4.47 million unique Internet users in India in 2000. India is expected to be next only to China in the Asia Pacific region in terms of total number of Internet users by end-2005. IDC also forecasts that India's home and small business segments will drive the growth in the Internet user base for the next five years. For the period 2000 - 2005, the Internet user base in the home segment is expected to witness a CAGR of 87 percent, while that of the small business segment is expected to grow by a CAGR of 72 percent. Despite the differences in actual prediction figures, all agencies have agreed on one point India is expected to see the highest growth rate in the region's Internet market in the next five years. Seeking to promote the spread of the Internet, the Planning Commission said telecom operators must get the required bandwidth and the last-mile connection to achieve that aim.

The use of cable network and DSL technologies may be actively promoted to provide higher bandwidth to Internet users, it said. "For dial-up Internet users, telephone call charges are a major element of cost, with the higher local call charges and multi-metering of local calls discouraging its usage. Call charges for Internet use need to be brought down substantially," added the Planning Commision's report.

Creation of a separate Ministry of Information Technologies and sound proactive policy decisions have helped the growth of IT sector in the country. Internet is one of those technologies to benefit from it. Initially only government agencies like VSNL and Department of Telecommunications were permitted to be Internet Service Providers (ISPs). This sector has now been opened up to private entrepreneurs and there are already about 300 Internet service providers in the country. The exact number of Indian web sites is difficult to determine. But it definitely runs into hundreds. India has slowly started entering into the e-commerce area.

Some estimations of the profile of the Indian Internet users are available through studies of NASSCOM, IMRB etc. 80 per cent of the users are males, they belong to the 19-34 year age group. The average time spent is 10 hours per week and nearly 90 per cent of the use is for email purpose. The estimated advertising spent per user comes to Rs.140/- (about 4 dollars) and less than 5 per cent of the users buy anything on the net.

Usability Factors

The use of Internet is dependent on the following factors:

(1) cost of the computer

(2) cost of subscription and telephone; and

(3) efficiency of the telephone lines.

Cost

The cost of the personal computers has been coming down very substantially. It is possible to obtain a good configuration PC for about 700 to 800 dollars. The rate of growth of the PCs has been very fast. In 1999, the estimated number of PCs was 3.2 million and growing fast. The growth can really now be described as exponential. It is important to look at the other necessary link of Internet, the telephone. The estimated number of telephones is 20 million.

In India the telephone user is required to pay even for in-city calls. A call is for a duration of 3 minutes. So in an hour of continuous usage of telephone, it amounts to making 20 calls. Use of the telephone for an hour will cost approximately Rs. 30/ -. But the there is relaxation now on use on Internet during the nights and on Sundays. The pulse rate for telephone for the purpose of Internet is 10 minutes whereas the Internet connectivity is free of charge for such time. Apart from the cost, a major problem really lies with the state of technology of the telephones. It largely uses a very archaic technology especially while covering "the last mile", i.e. from the telephone exchange to the subscribers. The bandwidth of the line is very low and that slows down Internet especially the download of graphics, sound or even the text material. This would mean that it takes much longer for a transaction to be completed or for downloading of a file or for accessing information and so on. All this adds to the cost.

Apart from the expenditure for the phone call, the subscriber has to pay a fixed amount to the ISP periodically. The exact amount is dependent upon the number of hours per year that one subscribes to. These costs have been coming down steadily because of the increased competition. But still it is on the higher side. In a year if one books 500 hours of Internet use, it would cost the subscriber about 135 dollars. Remember that for using 500 hours of subscription, one has to pay equivalent to 10,000 telephone calls and thus total cost of the subscriber is 360 dollars per year. Given the overall spending capacity of the Indians and taking into account several other priorities Internet subscription will remain by and large a preserve of the rich and the upper middle classes.

However, one must hasten to add the fact that the per capita use of the technology in India is always much higher than the actual subscribers. This has happened in several other technologies in the past. When the number of television sets were fewer, it was observed that a large number of persons of the neighborhoods would come and watch program. Several neighbors and friends use a telephone. Even the newspaper is often borrowed and read by more than one family. Similar thing happens about the Internet. Large number of what have come to be known as cyber café kiosks has come up. A cyber café would charge approximately Rs. 15/- per hour of use of the Internet. A large number of users avail of this facility. The Internet is also very much an institutional arrangement in India. That means in an office one account will be used by a much greater number of persons.

Pragmatic Policies

The Indian Internet had started with a great promise. The policy makers did not fail to recognize the potential of the net for a quantum group in the knowledge-based economy. The ISP policy of the Department of Telecommunications (DOT) was very pragmatic with free licensing to ISPs.

The Incumbency Factor

With all the pragmatic policies, the makers failed to follow these through to the implementation stage. They failed to recognize the daunting role which incumbent operators have played worldwide to make telecom reform difficult to accomplish.

High Usage Charges

In India the usage charges of Internet remain one of the highest in the world. Internet dial up is still charged as local calls, netting approximately Rs.26 per hour to the BSNL/ MTNL. Add to it the ISP charge of Rs.10 per hour. A typical household with 3 hours of Internet access per day would need nearly 3500 per month to have access to the net during the day time.

In fact just 20 hours of monthly net access in India costs 16.8% of GDP per capita. This one of the highest in the world and compares to 0.12% in Sweden,0.65% in USA, 0.84% in Hong Kong, countries where net access has really taken off.

Cost v/s Internet Penetration

The DOT (now BSNL) as incumbent operator did not relent to reduce the charges for local access to the net. Elsewhere in the world, dial up net access began to be offered at flat rates (including dial up charges) of $10-15 per month (USA) & $15 per month (UK) and at similar rates elsewhere. DSL access averaged $40-50 per month.

Basic operators worldwide encouraged volume calling by offering reducing rates, and even offering shares of revenues to callers. Some of the basic operators in India also offered reduced local rates for Internet access. However, the incumbent BSNL in

India thwarted every effort to lose even a fraction of its revenue.

Broadband Access

Broadband was a star performer with Worldwide Broadband Subscribers crossing 46 million in 2002,with 25.6 million being on DSL and 20 million on Cable. Asia has been a strong area of Broadband Internet growth, apart from USA and accounted for 42% share of World's DSL market as per figures released by the DSL forum in Aug 2002. In South Korea, DSL is now operating on 26% of all installed phone lines.

70% of Hong Kong users have broadband access at homes. Even in USA, with much sparser urban density, broadband has reached 17% penetration. Broadband, via either DSL or Cable remains one of the fastest growing modes of net access.

The growth in broadband net access exceeded 50% over the last year, despite a severe economic slump. There were many enabling factors. For example, in USA, the Baby Bells were, by regulation (Telecommunication Act of 1996) required to offer Unbundled Network Elements (UNE) i.e. any piece of their network could be hired by the competitive operators.

DSL operators were therefore able to get local copper loops. In 1998 this type of unbundling fever spread across Asia and Europe. Partially unbundled local loops (i.e. DSL/ADSL) have been made available in Asian markets like Japan, Hong Kong Australia & Singapore. Admittedly some of them have not made much headway yet due to high access charges, but the growth where it has happened is startling. For example in South Korea, the number of internet users leapt from 3.4 million in Feb 1999 to 15 million in May 2000- a four fold growth in a period of just 15 months.

In India nothing of the kind happened with all the copper loops being controlled by BSNL. In the absence of any regulation for offering lines to competitors, no such initiatives took off in India. Except for a couple of hardy operators no one could extract the concessions of local loops in return for additional revenue to

BSNL. It is now, only on 23rd Aug 2002 that he BSNL has came out with a scheme of franchising the local loops for DSL type services at unsustainable rates of revenues share with no costs to be borne by them.

However the services will remain that of BSNL. Bharti, a basic operator has now launched its Broadband DSL offering in India signifying the end of the virtual monopoly of the incumbent.

Broadband Cable Access:

Broadband cable Internet has been one of the success stories in the US, primarily due to the high quality HFC and fibre network. Telephony over cable has been one of the drivers of net access over cable, whether switched, packet mode or as pure Internet Telephony. Internet telephony accounts for nearly 11% of the global International traffic today.

In India the regulations for net telephony were drafted heavily biased towards the Incumbent. First of all no Internet telephony operator can provide Internet phone service within India. In fact no connection to the phone network within India is permitted at all. So if a user buys a "Valufon" or "Bol Anmol" Card, he still can't call Bombay to Delhi.

For cable Internet it is a death knell. Reaching over 38 million homes many of which do not have a primary fixed line phone, it could have provided a cheap phone facility. However, this option is unattractive if a cable phone customer cannot call any one in India-not even emergency services.

With Compulsory Conditional Access (CAS) set to become mandatory, under the Ministry of Information and Broadcasting Initiative, a set top box will soon find a place in a majority of homes. An Internet phone, which can come virtually free with it will not however be possible- you can't call anyone in India – do no local shopping.

The Incumbent BSNL & MTNL have ensured that their turf is protected at all costs. You can however call overseas (with VSNL being divested, the incumbency factor had vanished).

Internet Backbones

In the initial Internet years, USA constituted the hub of Internet and all other operators from Europe, Asia & Australia had to connect to USA in a Hub & spoke arrangement, paying both-way charges for all connectivity to US.

It was expected that with the high growth rates being experienced in Europe and Asia, these would develop into Regional Hubs and US centric Internet would cease to exist. This however, could not be accomplished, though regional exchanges did come into existence.

Due to the high leased line charges in India, backbones of Internet practically did not exist. National Long Distance operators (NDLOs) only could have provided backbones in India. The long distance policy brought into play in 2001 was apparently only to satisfy India's obligations under WTO and not to usher in serious competition to the Incumbent BSNL.

To protect the turf of the incumbency provisions such as Rs.5 billion entry fee ($100 million) and compulsory roll out obligations for the entire country were put into place. The result: Only three operators even applied for the NLD license. The charges across the country for E1 range at Rs.2.2 millon per annum not counting the local loop. Even inter-city connectivity of 100 km costs Rs.500,000 ($10500) as per TRAI rates.

When the operators dropped the tariffs for long distance calls in India – they did not bother to reduce the leased line rates either local,or domestic reflecting the operation of a cosy system. The result: No backbones of Internet in India, fragmented networks & high operational cost for ISPs remains the stark realty today.

There were some views that other extraneous factors are inhibiting the growth of the net in India e.g. the number of PCs and lack of infrastructure. However, this is only partially true. India has over 7 million PCs with 1.7 million being added every year. The cost of PC hardware has fallen to a fraction of what it was seven years ago.

It is not these factors but the environment imposed by the incumbent BSNL - high dial up charges, high cost of backbone capacity denial of network elements such as local loops, which have bottled the growth of the net in this country. The result : Internet business became so bad in India that may companies simply wrote off their dial up & DSL businesses. The number of ISPs halved in India in 2002 while the International Bandwidth used by Internet Service Providers (ISPs) fell to 600 Mbps against 900 Mbps in 2001 as per the ISPAI. (ISP Association of India).

Other service providers are really on thin ice, mostly awaiting regulatory or operating concessions to make a good business of a service which has done very well elsewhere. There can still be hope for the Indian Internet. Most projections for the Indian Internet continue to be very optimistic. As per IDC forecast, the number of net users will grow to 37.5 million by 2005.

This will however require more than a cosmetic change in the operating scenario. A global scale Indian Internet can be a reality only if the costs are kept down to affordable levels. Enabling regulation needs to recognize the need of competitive operators using infrastructure of the incumbent through unbundled network elements and follow through with policies which have been enacted over four years ago elsewhere.

The regulations also need to recognize the synergies in businesses such as internet and telecom, content and broadcasting.

INTERNET APPLICATION IN LIBRARIES

Internet use in libraries has brought efficiency in services ranging from acquisition of documents to the retrieval of information as well as creation of new knowledge. It is used in libraries, broadly for the following functions:

Application in Library management

Library management includes all library functions taking place behind the scene as well as with the users of the library. The important functions are discussed below:

Acquisition

Acquisition process involves the following functions:

- Operation of library budget
- Receipt of approval from the various heads of departments
- Selection of books and other educational materials
- Verfication of bibliographical details
- Ordering of library materials
- Payment of bills
- Creation of orders on computer
- Activity for acqusition
- Transfer of details for classification and cataloguing

Internet can also help in the following functions related to the acquisition:

- Tenders for books can be floated on Internet
- Checking of duplication before ordering
- Book orders can be sent through the Web
- The availability of the addresses of booksellers, publishers , distributors and their catalogues help in selection and purchase of the library materials
- Lbrary orders can be sent through e-mail
- Users can know about the possible availability of the desired books in the library through Internet
- The information available on the Web relating to acquisition of books or for comments can be sent to the library through the Internet.

Technical Processing

- Classification of documents according to the standardized schemes of classification
- Cataloguing of documents in accordance with the standard code of cataloguing
- Assignment of subject headings
- Preparation of book cards etc used in circulation
- Feeding of class numbers and cataloguing details in computers
- Display of new arrivals in the library

Serials Control

The Periodicals section is responsible for the following functions;

- Allocation of budget journals
- Approval of the list of journals on annual basis
- Action on recommendations of library committee and the heads of the departments
- Selection of journals suitable for subscription
- Verification of the cost and other details of journals through the list of publishers
- Ordering procedure
- Payment procedure
- Reciept of the subscribed journals
- Availability of the subscribed journals on OPAC
- Sending reminders for the unsupplied issues of journals
- Display of the titles of journals on weekly basis

To fulfill the above demands, the Internet is used in the following way;

- Communication of the approval for journals on the Internet
- Web based ordering exercise

- Selection of journals through the list of publishers and their catalogues available on the Web.
- Access to journals by users through the Web
- Listing of the received journals through Internet access
- Availability of the Union catalogue of journals
- Viewing of full text of journals

Reference and Information Service

Internet is also used to answer the questions of the users in the library. In research establishment it plays a very vital role now a days. The main activities relating to the reference service in the library are;

- Awareness about the available print and electronic sources
- Identification of the proper source of information to answer a query
- Knowledge of the current sources of information
- Identification of reference tools
- Access to electronic databases available on CD ROMs and Internet
- Providing selective dissemination of information

Internet can help in the above activities by the following means;

- Identification of reference sources according to the needs of the users
- Search of subject directories on Internet and answering the queries
- Guiding users to the reference sources to enable them to search the desired information on their own
- Identification of the available sources and listing them for future use
- Identification of the full-text journals available freely on the Web.

Library Management

The following functions are covered under the library administration;

- Making of policies for library service
- Keeping coordination among the various sections of the library
- Strengthening library automation, networking, CD ROM and on line services
- Provision of budget for books, journals and the other educational materials
- Statement of expenditure
- Work details for the library staff
- Distribution of library publications
- Deciding standards for better library services
- Arrangements of training for the library employees

The above exercises can be carried out successfully through the Internet

Electronic mail (E-mail): Librarians use E-mail to communicate with colleagues and customers. They participate in electronic discussion groups, share experiences and ideas with other librarians, and create and monitor discussion groups of interest to their customers.

Telnet: Librarians use Telnet to connect to remote computer resources. They explore other library catalogs, access commercial and noncommercial database services, and share the resources of campus-wide information systems and community Free-Nets.

File Transfer Protocol (FTP): FTP enables librarians to obtain software programs, text, images, and sound files from the net and then offer them to their customers. Librarians and information professionals contribute to the Internet community by making library catalogs and local databases available on the network; creating Gopher sites that offer logical, well organized, menu-driven access to services and resources on the Internet; and establishing World Wide Web servers that provide graphical user interfaces for browsing the resources of the Internet.

Internet's Impact on Libraries

Internet services and resources influence library services. New opportunities and benefits include:

1. Leadership opportunities. Libraries frequently take the lead by introducing the Internet to user communities in industry, academia, and schools, and often provide training and access for customers as budgets allow. Public libraries are beginning to offer similar services to the public at large.

2. Cost savings and time savings. Listservs and other electronic forums facilitate information exchanges among librarians from all over the world. Librarians now keep up with advances, challenges, and issues without having to attend expensive conferences or subscribing to multiple library journals.

3. Question answering services. AskERIC is a network-based education information service offering library media specialists (as well as K-12 teachers, administrators, parents, and students) access to a question answering service. Another service, Stumpers-L, provides a networking resource for reference questions.

4. International interlibrary loans. Libraries now have customers from all over the world. Internet accessible library catalogs assist research endeavors, provide interlibrary loan verifications, and offer a myriad of reference materials that enhance local library collections.

5. Document delivery services. There has been a rapid growth in fee-based document delivery services that use the network to order and/or transfer documents to libraries and often to endusers, bypassing libraries completely.

6. Online transactions. Major bibliographic utilities are experimenting with the use of real time bibliographic transactions over the network, while already supporting batch mode transactions.

7. Government information. Government information can be distributed over the network to libraries allowing unparalleled opportunities for libraries to inform communities and constituents about government issues.

8. Information sharing. Technical standards, such as Z39.50, coordinate the transfer of information between different systems and formats over the network. These standards are essential to libraries as automated library systems share information and streamline processing using the Internet.

9. Other impacts. Using Internet resources may include some increase in workload for librarians, but that is offset by the library's increased visibility and value to the community and the opportunity for the library to become an information provider rather than a dispensary.

Current Issues

1. Academic libraries. Academic libraries are on the leading edge of Internet developments because of the information resources they provide for research. Distance education degrees and library catalogs available on the Internet provide a global customer base for academic libraries. Academic libraries often distribute academic authors' unpublished documents via the Internet allowing subject experts to be direct sources of information for the user. The roles and responsibilities of librarians, the library, campus computing services, campus administration, publishers, and vendors need redefinition in a networked environment.

2. Public libraries. The public library community has been slow to connect to the Internet. Public libraries serving large communities, however, are more likely to have an Internet connection than those serving smaller communities. The cost of connectivity is the main barrier to a public library presence on the Internet. Public librarians consider federal government assistance essential for connection and equipment costs. Staff support, expertise, and training are other issues that need resolution to ensure Internet access for public libraries and their customers. Some suggestions for training include "post-MLS certification and sabbaticals for public librarians to be reeducated" (McClure, 1993).

3. Special libraries. National Science Foundation policy on what constituted acceptable use of the network kept corporate libraries wary of connectivity in the late 1980s and early 1990s. With the arrival of network connectivity specifically for commercial customers and the enticement of lower cost connections to commercial database retrieval services, corporate libraries are becoming an active presence on the network.

4. School libraries. School library media specialists are working hard to bring the Internet into their schools. Resources they introduce include online catalogs, CD-ROM periodical indexes, full-text encyclopedias and reference resources, interactive multimedia, and other network technologies. Funding for equipment, infrastructure upgrades, and connectivity is often difficult to obtain, however, and educational goals must be coordinated. Working to coordinate existing school programs with Goals 2000 and National Research and Education Network (NREN) objectives is one challenge faced by media specialists and teachers.

Librarians and media specialists need to have a stake in the development of policies and roles as their communities adopt Internet technologies. They need to consider the following as they develop visions for implementing technology:

1. Librarians need to take an active role during formulation of national policy and legislation to ensure that libraries receive adequate funding to be major players in the National Information Infrastructure (NII).
2. Internet connectivity does not guarantee equitable access

to the Internet. Librarians as a profession need to become network literate and in turn need to provide programs and facilities so their customers will become network literate.

3. The services and resources of the Internet need to be created and organized by librarians. A catalog of network services and resources is essential for efficient use of the Internet.
4. Library administrators need to include staff training and practice time in any budget for Internet connectivity.
5. Librarians need to take an active role in new legislation being proposed concerning intellectual property and copyright in an electronic environment.
6. Librarians need to have significant influence on the evolution of Internet services and need to be prepared to share their ideas with administrators and project planners.

Internet Reference Sources

Internet is a very effective tool to provide reference service. About all popular and specialized databases are available to Internet to satisfy the queries of the library users. While it takes more time to answer a query manually, Internet searches the pinpointed information and presents it before the users within a very short time. Some popular reference sources available on Internet are given below:

Citing Electronic and Printed Sources

Dictionaries

Encyclopaedias

Directories

Maps and the World

Citing Electronic and Printed Sources

A collection of references on how to cite both electronic and printed resources. Includes APA & MLA citation styles, Harvard Systems of Referencing, How to organize Reference Resources and many others.

You can also use the guide on How to wirte a Bibliography that is available both, electronic and printed copies, at the Library. For further information ask at the Library Issue Desk.

Citing Electronic Sources

APA Style

A complete guide on how to cite information from the Internet and other electronic resources from APA.

Citing Electronic Sources

Examples for citing resources from materials such as: films; legal; maps; recorded sound; photographs and drawings; special presentations; and texts.

Citing Online Resources

Gives information on citing the most common types of online material.

Cyber Bee Advice

Includes examples for citing electronic information according to the APA and MLA styles, as well as additional links for consultancy.

Dictionaries

Acronyms and abbreviations dictionaries

The World Wide Web Acronym and Abbreviation Server

A list of acronyms and abbreviations. You can search to find out what an acronym means, search for a word to see what acronyms are used, or you can submit a new acronym in the database.

Journal Abbreviations Sources

Journal Abbreviation Sources is a registry of Web resources that list or provide access to the full title of journal abbreviations.

Biographical dictionaries

This dictionary covers more than 28,000 notable men and women who have shaped our world from ancient times to the present day. The dictionary can be searched by birth years, death years, positions held, professions, literary and artistic works, achievements, and other keywords.

Who is and who was

Search over 25,000 of the greatest lives, past and present.

The Nobel Prize Internet Archive

This site maintains information on all winners in all categories. Click on any Nobel category (literature, physics, chemistry, peace, economics, or physiology & medicine) to see an annotated, hyperlinked list of all Nobel laureates in that category.

English Language & Foreign dictionaries

Dictionary.com

The dictionary includes definitions, related words, grammar and usage, finding books or related Web sites, etc.

Dictionaries Index

Lists of 230 on-line dictionaries of all types and for most languages.

Merriam-Webster Online

Online dictionary and thesaurus.

Oxford English Dictionary

The Oxford English Dictionary is the accepted authority on the evolution of the English language over the last millennium. It is an unsurpassed guide to the meaning, history, and pronunciation of over half a million words, both present and past. It traces the usage of words through 2.5 million quotations from a wide range of international English language sources, from classic literature and specialist periodicals to film scripts and cookery books.

Roget's Thesaurus

On-line version from the ARTFL Project at the University of Chicago. 1911 version - supplemented 1991.

Webster's English Dictionary

ARTFL Project: Webster's Revised Unabridged Dictionary, 1913 Edition.

Language resources on the Internet

Internet Resources for Language Teachers and Learners

This is a collection of annotated links to websites of use to both teachers and learners of languages. The collection is broken up into six broad categories, each of which contains various sub-categories. The 'top level' categories are : general (eg linguistics, translation), Language Specific (eg national newspapers), Multilingual (eg literature in multiple languages), Search Engines (Internet sites in a specific country or geographical area), Internet (sites related to the use of the Internet as a medium for language teaching and learning), Commercial (companies selling language products and services)

Subject dictionaries

Grove Dictionary of Art

The most comprehensive online reference resource for all aspects of the visual arts worldwide, from prehistory to the present day. With the exception of film, all the visual arts are examined: from Greek architecture to Nazca ceramics, Giotto to David Hockney, Chinese snuff bottles to Louis XV wallpaper, 14th century painting treatises to feminist art history. All of the 41,000 articles of the Dictionary have been published and are fully searchable. Free trial is available.

Free Online Dictionary of Computing

FOLDOC is a searchable dictionary of acronyms, jargon, programming languages, tools, architecture, operating systems, networking, theory, conventions, standards, mathematics, telecoms, electronics, institutions, companies, projects, products, history, in fact anything to do with computing.

Harcourt Academic Press Dictionary of Science and Technology

The largest scientific dictionary ever compiled in the English language to the Web. Fields covered: Engineering Sciences, Life Sciences, Medicine, Physical Sciences, Mathematics and Computer Science, Social Sciences, General and Miscellaneous

ODLIS: Library and Information Science

Online Dictionary of Library and Information Science (ODLIS) is designed to be a hypertext reference resource for library and information science professionals, university students and faculty, as well as for users of all types of libraries.

Yahoo's Collection of Dictionaries

Includes commercial, English, language, slang and subject dictionaries.

Encyclopaedias

Britannica.com

The worlds best web sites plus magazines, books and the complete Encyclopaedia Britannica.

Encarta.com

Encarta.com features a reference library (including a dictionary and atlas), a homework help section, pre-college and graduate-school departments, a section especially for parents, a centre filled with online course offerings, and a shop stocked with great deals on educational products.

Encyclpedia.com

Encyclopedia.com is the Internet's premiere free encyclopaedia. Newly updated and expanded with more than

50,000 articles plus links giving you access to millions of articles and pictures in Electric Library, Encyclopedia.com puts tons of information right at your fingertips. It is free, quick and useful.

Infoplease.com

Online encyclopaedia, dictionary, almanac, atlas.

World Fact book 2001

Information for each country of the world including area, boundaries, climate, disputes, population, political system and economy.

Xrefer

Xrefer's free reference site contains encyclopaedias, dictionaries, thesauri & books of quotations from the world's leading publishers. All cross-referenced, all in one place - providing you with a single source for reliable factual information.

Directories

Company directories & reports

Corporate Reports

Online summary pages for Company Reports, Accounts and Financial Information from UK companies.

CAROL World

Carol is a free corporate online service offering one point access to Company Annual Reports Online from major European, Asian and US companies as well as a range of other investor information.

EDGAR Database

Online Annual Reports from US companies.

European Interactive Directories

The interactive European Internet directory for, business, banking, shopping, etc.

Directories of organisations

Union of International Associations

Telephone directories

Find Phone Books

The World's Phone Books on the web, is one of most complete indexes of online phone books, with over 400 links to Yellow Pages, White Pages, Business Directorics, Email Addresses and Fax Listings from over 170 countries all around the world.

University and College directories

American Universities

Alphabetical list of universities and colleges in the United States.

UK Universities and Higher Education Colleges

Alphabetical list of universities and colleges in the United Kingdom.

UK Universities – Admissions

The main link for each site is to general admissions information, or to the site's home page. There are also links to specific information for prospective Undergraduate (U/G), Postgraduate (P/G) and International (INT) students where this exists.

International Universities

General Education Online v2 is a free database of links to higher education facilities worldwide for researchers, students, and others, hosted and sponsored by Simple End User Linux.

World Wide University Index

Search for any university and college throughout the world.

electronic_reference.htmelectronic_reference.htm

Maps and the World

Expedia

Street maps of the United Kingdom, United States, Canada,

France and Germany and topographic maps of places around the

globe.

Mapblast

Street maps, driving directions, yellow pages from many

European and other countries.

MapQuest

Maps, driving directions, road trip planner, yellow pages from

worldwide.

National Geographic Maps and Geography

Maps and geographical information, photography, adventure & expedition, from all over the world.

Library Home Page

A Library homepage contains the most needed information searched by students, faculty and others for a various reasons ranging from admissions to the result of examination. A homepage can be compared with the main menu of a user-friendly software which encourages interaction and promotes its use by presenting the contents in a logical order.

A homepage establishes the identity of an individual or organization on the net and is like putting up a flag for someone in the cyberspace. It is the Guttenberg's press of our time with extended facility for low cost publishing. Anyone cab publish any kind of information including text, graphics, sound and video or a combination of all on the web through the homepage. It opens the doors of the millions of Internet users all over the world to receive ideas floated by someone. A homepage can be a full service front and for an organization. Here we restrict to discuss a home page about the universities only.

Requirement of a Library Home Page

The basic requirements for creation of a homepage are:

- computer,
- Internet connection,
- Web space
- contents creation and
- file transfer.

Computer is the basic requirement for converting data into electronic to facilitate upload and download of information with speed and accuracy. Most of the computer systems available in the market fulfill the requirements, however a PC 486 of Pentium series suits to the needs. Now a days, computers have become a necessity for the universities and about all of them are already having it which can be used for a variety of tasks including the homepage creation and hosting.

The pre-requisite to Internet connectivity apart from computer is a telephone line and modern in order to transfer signals from and to the other computer systems. An Internet connection, which is the license to transfer information is generally of three types i.e. Dialup, Leased line and VSAT.

Availability of web space is the most significant requirement. Many Internet Service Providers (ISPs) offer web space for hosting homepages free of cost up to certain amount of memory. They generally do it for the sake of advertisements, which bring revenue. The advertisements are generally in the corners of the homepage an do not hinder the process of information exchange. The larger sites are hosted on prescribed rates.

A thorough survey of the nature of clientele and the needs of the library is necessary before undertaking the work of content development. This can be achieved by contact with the users of the site followed up with the usability testing to make sure that work goes in the right direction. The following guidelines may be followed in developing the contents:

1. Keeping in mind the type of content or information intended to be put on the web
2. Keeping in mind the goals for presentation of content
3. Organization of contents into main pages
4. Coming up with a general structure of pages and topics by storyboarding the homepage
5. Foreseeing readers reaction while searching the homepage
6. Avoiding having too many layers of information as users want to get information quickly and having too many steps will annoy them

The homepage may begin with general details about the institution, which can be followed by information on collection, services and staff. The collection may include books, journals and the other media while services may reflect the list of additions Current Awareness Service etc. A homepage should also offer links to the similar sites.

In order to make a homepage easy to search, a logical order of content be followed and the extensive use of graphics and colours be avoided since they hinder the speed of retrieval. The easiest way is to refer to the related websites before undertaking the work of creation. About all major universities of the world maintain homepages.

Once the contents of a homepage are finalized and put into a logical sequence on paper, they are be keyed in and made available on a computer system. The task of content verification and designing is undertaken to ensure that it looks on the desired pattern while retrieving. The results can be checked on Netscape as well as Internet Explorer or on some other browsers. In case of the expected results, the next step is to transfer the contents to the web servers of an ISP. This is achieved by File Transfer Protocol (FTP).

In order to ascertain if the contents have been successfully transferred, one has to check it by typing the URL address in the local browser. The attempt is considered successful if it is retrieved on the desired pattern. While submitting a homepage, it is also necessary to assign the category of URL, descriptors and keywords. The search engines put page under various categories depending upon their descriptions. In case of universities, the popular terms higher education, universities etc. may be assigned for search engines.

In India, about all premier institutions have developed their websites. The representation of libraries is also growing day by day on Internet.

4
MULTIMEDIA INTRANET AND E-COMMERCE

MULTIMEDIA

Multimedia is a method of instruction that uses the computer to present information with text, graphics, audio and/ or video. It is also referred to as computer-based training (CBT) or Web-based training (WBT). It can take the form of training, presentations, software simulation, job simulation, testing, reference or online help. Since multimedia instruction is often delivered over the Internet, it can look just like a set of Web pages, but it also can be delivered on CD-ROM, on diskette or over a local area network (LAN) or company intranet.

Applications of Multimedia

As a good example of using multimedia instruction, one specialty sporting goods firm provides its sales representives with a CD to use in clinics to educate dealers about their products. When the clinic is over, the dealer gets to keep the CD as a reference tool. Updating the materials is easier on CD (especially if CDs are burned on demand) than on paper, and it reduces paper waste. The same content can be delivered throughout the company regardless of the sales rep's instructional style. And the dealer can pass the same information along to the store sales staff.

Multimedia instruction works well for all kinds of content. Both very complex material and very simple information can be delivered this way. For companies whose products or services are dangerous or sensitive, multimedia instruction can safely allow trainees to "practice" on the computer. When the trainee makes an error, he or she gets immediate feedback and an opportunity to correct the error ("Nope, not down the kitchen sink! Try again!").

Audiences for multimedia training may have a wide range of skills, educational levels and computer experience. It has been used to deliver training to such disparate groups as pilots using sophisticated flight simulators with detailed graphics and tightly controlled user responses and teenagers using touchscreen kiosks to learn the dangers of alcohol and tobacco. (In the touchscreen application, a user doesn't need any computer skills at all, and information can be entirely graphic, with little or no text.)

Advantages

The advantages of multimedia are as under:

* **It's interactive.** Learners are actively engaged. Interactive tools may include multiple-choice questions, fill-in-the-blanks, selecting all right answers or matching by dragging and dropping graphics. Feedback engages the learner even more. For example, an incorrect answer could provide a hint along with a "Sorry, that's incorrect" response.
* **It's tailored to learner needs.** Learners can take the training when they want, as often as they want, and at a pace that's right for them.
* **It's cost-effective.** Companies don't need to pay for trainers, travel or classrooms. It's especially useful in situations where users are spread over a wide area.
* **It's efficient and effective.** Learners typically learn more in a shorter period of time with multimedia instruction.
* **It's easy to revise and update.** Especially with Internet delivery, changes made to one copy are immediately available to all learners. For example, a company that manufactures car utility racks can easily alter installation instructions for consumers as car manufacturers introduce new models every year.

Suitability of Multimedia

* **Cost.** The expense can vary widely. One can find off-the-shelf or off-the-Web training at very reasonable cost, and sometimes even for free. Custom development of computer-based training can be expensive, but may be worth it if employee or customer training is crucial.
* **Number of learners.** A very large audience, such as a large customer base, may reduce costs greatly and possibly allow to deliver instruction more effectively and economically than with paper-based instruction.
* **Location of learners.** If the learners are spread over broad geographical areas, such as with sales reps or traveling technicians, CBT or WBT may be the only way to provide accurate and effective training to everyone.
* **Availability of computers.** Equipment doesn't have to be sophisticated—all you may need is an Internet connection.

More Information

One can probably find training on any topic, either online or on CD-ROM. For generic computer-based training, such as tutorials and other instruction on software packages, look in your local computer store. On the Web, search by subject area or use keywords like online learning, CBT, WBT, online training, courseware, or e-learning. The following Web sites are just a few that provide online courses on a vast range of topics:

* ElementK—www.zdu.com
* DigitalThink—www.digitalthink.com
* Blackboard—www.blackboard.net

If you consider customized, company-specific instruction, look for consultants with experience in both instructional design and multimedia development. You may be tempted to use a Web design company, but keep in mind that the goal of multimedia instruction is different from the goal of a Web site. A Web design firm can develop effective marketing tools and information delivery, but only an instructional design firm follows instructional principles to help people learn. An independent instructional developer does most of the multimedia instructional development. Courseware, Inc., a Kansas City–based performance.

Multimedia Formats

* Presentation Tool
* Public Information Kiosks (Point of Sale)
* CD Encyclopaedias
* Commercial CD 'Titles'
* Games ('edutainment' or otherwise)
* Communication Systems
* Computer Based Training (CBT)
* Computer Based Learning (CBL)
* Interactive Multimedia.

Multimedia Publishing

Publishing has evolved to the point where word processors are ubiquitous and desktop publishing is used by middle school children for history reports. Once complex technology becomes widespread, commonplace, and a part of daily life.

Multimedia publishing is the next frontier. In a few years we will all be including video and audio in multimedia publications, the same way we now include images, photos and text in print publications today. And these new multimedia publications will be "printed" on DVD.

Low Cost DVD will lead the way

The laser printer triggered the desktop publishing revolution. What is required to trigger this next step change for multimedia publishing are the low cost DVD "burners".

Multimedia Publishing Requirements

As with every new technology, new uses emerge that the

designers don't anticipate. This is now happening with DVD. Designed as an entertainment media, the many powerful DVD features are now being exploited for multimedia uses that go far beyond entertainment and movie distribution.

These new uses put new demands on DVD "authoring" applications, including:

* Support for different types of media
* Improved tools for integrating multimedia
* Ability to publish on all the variations of CD and DVD
* Control over movie and menu timing and actions

Publishing Applications for Everyone

Just as there is a range of desktop publishing solutions, a number of applications are being provided to publish on DVD. Sonic's focus is to go beyond traditional "entertainment" applications, and to provide capabilities for true Multimedia Publishing with products like Sonic DVDit! and MyDVD.

INTRANET

An Intranet is a private system that uses computer hardware and software specially developed to provide communication, information management and information publishing services within an organization An organization, which has many computers usually owns and operates a private network that connects all the computers. Such a network is called Intranet. It is independent of any external support but to provide Internet services, an Intranet is connected with Internet Unlike public access networks, Intranet is restricted to provide security. Only authorized computers at the organization can be connected to it The restrictions allow computers inside the organization to exchange information but keep the information confidential and protected from outsiders.

Applications of Intranet

As Intranet is a connecting device for many computers

within an organization it can solve many problems related to input, storage and dissemination of information without much inconvenience. The other services expected from Intranet are the following:

1. World Wide Web publishing
2. File Transfer Protocol
3. Indexing and Searching Services
4. Facility to run scripts

Intranet if employed in a larger set up like the Library of a major organization will bring efficiency in work and help improve the standard of education and research.

Advantages of Intranet

* It will connect all libraries/departments of the University
* It will be a private network
* It will provide connectivity round the clock
* It will permit decentralization of the library work, like accessioning, classification, cataloguing etc.
* It will allow resources sharing within the campus including the stored data and e-journals
* It is cost effective since only one software package can be used for the entire library system.
* It will provide connectivity from and to the libraries to residence of the authorized users
* Recording and dissemination of information/meetings/ lectures from any location
* Data is secured from external risks

Besides the above advantages, the facility may be used for other purposes like vigilance and security of the campus.

The basic requirements for installation of an Intranet are computer hardware, software and a connecting device.

Intranet is based on a client server system where the server is a computer that has the following functions:

* Running the Intranet service software
* Storing some or all of the content that is available to the users

Requirement of Intranet

The requirements of the server computer depend upon the number of connections expected to be provided per hour. For a few hundred connections, a Pentium 4 with 1.6 Gh speed, 64 MB RAM and 40 GB memory is more than sufficient. In case the load increases on the sever, users will find them waiting for retrieval of information. The capacity of a computer system may be enhanced by adding more memory and processors and splitting the contents among them.

Software for the Intranet is available in two categories, the server software and the client software.

Software Sever

Intranet needs a server software that runs a computer and provides services such as World Wide Web publishing and File Transfer besides indexing and searching facilities. Server software is available on the Internet free of cost and the commercial packages such as Microsoft's Internet Information Server and Netscape Navigator are available for a variety of operating systems including UNIX and Windows NT server.

Client Software

The software that runs a client is called a browser, which is used to access and browse Web pages. It may also be acquired free of cost or at a reasonably low cost. The most popular server is Netscape Navigator Some other browsers are also available at the Web addresses in Table 1.

Internet is a gold mine of free software. One can find any type of software to run a full featured Intranet service but the software downloaded from Internet should be used with great care. It is always better to take precautions and invest some money for a well designed, listed and supported software.

Table 1. Web Address of Browsers

S. No.	Name	Web Address
1.	Midas WWW	
2.	Mosaic	ftp://ftp.ncsa.uiuc.edu/mosaic
3.	Netscape	htt://home.netscape.com
4.	Emacs	ftp://mouse.cs.indiana.edu/pub/elips/w3
5.	Lynx	ftp://ftp2.cc.ukans.edu/pub/lynx/
6.	Internet Explorer	

A connecting device provides links between the server and the client. It is mainly based on the following two devices

* Networking Device capable of running on radio frequencies
* RF Links comprising of Mast and Antennas

There are many devices, which can be used to connect a server with browser but their usage depends upon the convenience and the financial resources of an organization to install and support the device The geographical location of the various departments of an organization is to be taken into consideration because sometimes it is hard to manage the connections besides being in the position of installation of the costlier systems.

The most significant feature is that it does not require a major expenditure and utilizes the existing hardware of the library systems. Most of the software are available on Internet free of cost. The expenditure is to be incurred mainly on the connecting device.

It is better to take up the project in a phased manner connecting more significant points at first and then extending the facility to the less used libraries. This will reduce the expenses at one time. Additional facilities like audio and video conferencing and installation of video cameras for security checks etc. may be introduced at a later stage.

Intranet like Internet is a very significant system of

information. It is being used for many purposes but hardly installed for the university libraries which are the largest body of information within an academic and research institution. There is no much cost involved for two or three points of communication. The existing hardware of computer can be utilized with the software available form the Internet free of cost.

Gyandoot: A Rural Intranet in India

On January 1, 2000, Dhar district began the new millennium with installation of low cost, self-sustainable and community owned rural Intranet project. Dhar district is located on the south western corner of the central India and has a population of 1.7 million, with 54% population being tribal (Bhils, Bhilalas, patleiyas) and 60% population living below poverty line. Computers in 20 village centres in five Blocks of the district were wired through an Intranet network (presently there are 31 such wired village centres). Local rural youth act as entrepreneurs for running cybercafes-cum-cyberoffices on commercial lines without salary or stipend. The computers in the network have been established in Gram Panchayats (Village Committee). They have been called Soochanalayas (Information Kiosks). The Soochanalayas provide user-charge-based services to the rural people. This Intranet system has been named Gyandoot (Messenger of Information).

SOOCHAK (Manager/owner of the kiosk)

The person operating the Soochanalaya is a local matriculate operator and is called Soochak. A soochak is not an employee but an entrepreneur. Soochak only needs maintenance and numeric data entry skills. He needs very limited typing skills since most of the Intranet software is menu-driven.

The Soochaks for originally started 20 centres were selected interactively by village committees and the local community. Three member panels were selected by the community who received training at their own cost at the District Council. At the end of the training. the best trainees were selected out of a panel of three as Soochaks. He/she runs the Soochanalaya on commercial lines. He has an initial one year agreement with the village committee. He does not receive any salary. He bears the cost of stationery, maintenance and electric and telephone bills. He pays 10% of income as commission to the Zila Panchayat (District Council) for maintaining the net.

The 11 centres started as private enterprise, the Soochak is the owner of the establishment who pays Rs. 5,000 as a license fee for one year to district council. Each Soochak is expected to earn a net income of at least Rs. 36,000 per annum at conservative projections.

Services and facilities

During the formation of the project proposal a detailed RRA/PRA exercise was taken up involving the villagers and the community. The selection of the services was a result of this interactive exercise and was based upon the advice and the felt needs of the villagers. In these meetings, it was learnt that due to lack of information regarding the current and prevailing mandi (agriculture produce auction centres) rates, the farmers were unable to get the best price for their agricultural produce. Villagers also informed that copies of land records were difficult to obtain. The villager who requires a copy of the land record had to go out in search of the patwari (village functionary who maintains all land records) who may or may not be available on that particular day at his headquarters. For small complaints or for giving applications, people had to go to district headquarter which resulted in waste of time, money and potential livelihood earnings. The services offered on the Gyandoot network are:

Agriculture Produce Auction Centres Rates:

The variety-wise current and prevailing rates of prominent cereal crops of the district like wheat, gram, soybean, etc. at local and other prominent auction centres of the country are available on-line. Other statistics of the auction centres e.g. the volume of incoming agricultural produce, previous rates etc. are also provided on demand. The facility is available at a nominal charge of Rs. 5. Horticulture crops like tomato, potato, peas, green chillies, guava etc. are also produced in substantial quantity in the district. The rates of these commodities are also available.

On-line Registration of Applications:

So far, the villagers had to go to the local revenue court to file applications for obtaining income / caste / domicile certificates or for getting demarcation done or for obtaining landholder's loan passbook (rin pustika) etc. For this, they would again made repeated visits to the court to enquire about the progress of the application as well as to finally collect the prepared document. Now, through Soochanalayas they may send the application at a cost of only Rs. 10 and thereafter, in a maximum period of 10 days, preferably less, an intimation of the readiness of the certificate is sent back to them through e-mail at the concerned Soochanalaya. Thereafter, they may go to the concerned court to collect the certificate.

On-line Public Grievance Redressal:

Wherever there is some problem in the delivery of services, the villagers travel at the cost of time, money and livelihood to Block, tahsil or district headquarters without any certainty that they would even be able to meet the officer concerned. Now through the Soochanalaya, a villager may send his / her complaint with assurance of reply within a maximum period of seven days, preferably lesser, at a charge of Rs. 10. The reply to his complaint after redressal is sent back at the Soochanalaya through e-mail. Complaints available on the intranet include complaints regarding drinking water, scholarship sanction / disbursement, quality of seed / fertiliser, employee establishment matters (like leave or provident fund sanction) queries, functioning of school, public distribution system, beneficiary oriented schemes, functioning of village committee etc.

Rural e-mail facility:

A fee based e-mailing facility, which is provided in the intranet, and it has all the features and facilities of a state-of-the-art web based e-mail.

Village auction site:

This facility is started since July 2000 where auction facilities are available to farmers and villagers for land, agricultural machinery, bullocks or equipment or other durable commodities. It opens a new horizon of e-transactions in the rural areas. The middlemen involved in the rural commodity transaction market are sought to be eliminated through this facility. One can put one's commodity on sale for charges of Rs. 25/- for three months. One can browse the list of salable commodities for Rs. 10/-.

On line matrimonial site:

A fee based on-line matrimonial service for the villagers to choose the right match for a prospective bride/groom. Every entry from a Soochanalaya by a villager gets added on to a centralized database with search facility on various criteria. The user charges for service rendered is Rs. 25/- for three months. The program has been designed to suit the requirements of the villagers.

Information regarding government programmes :

Detailed Information regarding over a hundred government programmes is now available on the Gyandoot Intranet. The villagers have an access to the information regarding all government programmes related to rural development.

Sawaliram se puchiye:

This site provides opportunity to schoolchildren to ask inquisitive questions regarding career counseling or any other field from Sawaliram at no cost. A team of experts at the district headquarter provide the answers within three days. The facility is created to promote inquisitiveness, ability to inquire and scrutinize among the school children.

Ask the expert:

This facility is aimed at farmers and villagers who can inquire about latest techniques, advice for their problems, new technologies etc. from a group of experts pertaining to fields of agriculture, animal husbandry, health, or related to legal opinion. The service is provided at Rs 5/- user charge.

Free E-mail facility on social issues:

Free of cost option are available to the villagers to inform regarding child labour, child marriage, illegal possession of land belonging to Scheduled Tribes etc. Besides they can send e-mails to others connected through the net with the help of this facility in Hindi.

Avedan Patra:

This facility provides on-line application formats required by local administration and departments of the state government. Thus, application forms are available at the doorsteps of the villagers and avoid their running from pillar to post for these application forms.

Transparency in government working:

Updated and latest information regarding public distribution system, list of below poverty line families, beneficiaries of social security pension, beneficiaries of rural development schemes, information regarding government grants given to village committees, etc. are available on the intranet which makes the government functioning transparent.

Gaon ka Akhabar (Village Newspaper):

A local web-based newspaper is available to cater to the rural people. The newspaper delivers micro-news about the happening around the villages where Soochaks act as correspondents.

E-education (shiksha gyandoot):

This site contains reading material to supplement and help the students in understanding and learning their subjects in a better way. It contains things like syllabuses of various subjects taught in class X and XII, question banks developed by a team of experts to help in preparation of exams, chithi to help them keep in touch with other schools connected to the intranet etc.

Employment News:

This site contains employment news for semi skilled employees.

Below Poverty line list:

The site contains the whole list of below the poverty line families and anyone can check his her name in the list.

Strengthening of project:

In order to make Soochanalayas economically viable entities and to improve the functioning of the project following steps are being taken:

Additional facilities at Soochanalayas :

To make Soochanalayas economically viable soochaks are given licenses to vendor government judicial stamps and powers of petition writer are also delegated to them. Due to the delegation of above mentioned powers additional incomes are possible and the Soochanalayas are becoming virtual cyber offices. .

On-line linking of all departments with gyandoot server :

A local Area Network (LAN) linking all the major district offices has been installed. As a result, the district heads of various government departments like health, education, tribal development, revenue, food, agriculture, public health engineering, District Council and District Magistrate etc. are connected directly to gyandoot network. This provides backup support and logistics to gyandoot network.

Wireless in Local Loop:

The Gyandoot Samiti is introducing low cost TDMA based Wireless in Local Loop (WiLL) technology in collaboration with Indian Institute of Technology, Chennai. This technology will facilitate large scale multiplication of Soochanlayas in the hinterland where traditional plain old telephone system has not reached. The technology has power to increase access speed and provide reliable connectivity. The technology will also help the kiosk operator to run two connections at a time, e.g. STD PCO (voice connectivity) and Internet/Intranet (data communication).

E-education initiatives:

The Gyandoot Samiti, with the help from Member of Parliament, has established 34 kiosks at the high schools and higher secondary schools. We are providing them local educational contents through the server. They are also accessing internet for other educational contents. Each school is having Computer Club to promote activities related to IT among rural students.

Expansion of the project:

Some fundamental guidelines were framed for future expansion. They were:

1). Centers to be opened only in the villages where local telephone exchange is having OFC and fair connectivity,

2). New centers to be created through private investment.

3). New services and facilities to be introduced in phased manner.

The new facilities planned over next two years :

1. E-News for the district
2. Distance education
3. Registration of property transaction
4. Feedback system on the development programmes
5. "Bare foot doctor"

Action plan for increasing usage of the network

A comprehensive and integrated multi-media mass campaign concentrating on IEC activities has been launched in the district. The campaign focuses on penetration and propagation of the project in the hinterland of the district. Indian Institute of Management, Indore is collaborating to provide structured inputs for the IEC activities. The steps taken include:

Gyandoot medhavi chhatra (talented students) scholarship:

From the funds available with gyandoot, two scholarships each of Rs. 1,000/- per month for 5 years have been announced. For the scholarship, only those students of the district would be eligible who motivate 10 or more villagers to use gyandoot facilities between the period 1st September to 31st December 2000. The scholarships will be finalised through an on-line test of the eligible students and the result of the test would be declared on 26th January 2001. This scheme uses the services of the students to propagate new technology and its power among the rural masses.

Visit of school children to nearest Soochnalaya :

Students of class IX, X, XI, XII are taken to the nearest Soochanalaya on study tour. These students are given elaborate demonstration on the gyandoot Intranet system and the facilities available at the centre.

Gramsabha in the villages in the project area :

Special gramsabhas (Meeting of all villagers) in each village in the project area have been started which will be completed by January, 2001. These specially convened village meetings will deliberate on gyandoot and its services, which are available there at nominal cost.

Audio-Visual campaign

Posters and pamphlets have been distributed to all the concerned village committees. TV cable network and cinema halls are being used to popularise gyandoot services.

Audiocassettes carrying gyandoot messages are being used in weekly haat bazaars (market places).

Use of ISRO-DECU communication project

A communication project has been established by ISRO (Indian Space Research Organisation) which is already functional in 200 villages of the district. The said project carries message on the gyandoot project.

Gyandoot Computer Clubs

Gyandoot Computer Clubs are being established in major high schools and higher secondary schools of the district.

Incentives

Incentive in the form of cash awards (Rs.5,000/-, Rs.3,000/-, Rs. 2,000/-) along with certificate of excellence were given to three best performing Soochaks and certificate of appreciation were given to the village head of the concerned village committee on 15th August,2000. These incentives are being offered twice a year.

Sir Ratan Tata Trust Healthy Child Competition

Sir Ratan Tata Trust has granted Rs. three lakhs to organise healthy child competition based on Soochnalayas. The scheme has dual objective of promoting good practices of child rearing among rural masses and at the same time let them know about IT and its usages. The competition is organised with Soochanalayas as nodal points. It will motivate villagers to come to the kiosks. This competition was recently organised (between 9th to 19th April 2001) and was a huge success with 29140 children (12113 boys and 16027 girls) participating in it. All the people coming to the soochanalaya for this purpose were explained the utility of the Gyandoot network. It is expected that this will popularise the use of the network for various purposes.

PROJECT PARTNERS

No	Organisation name	Role in the project
1	District Council (Zila panchayat)	Conceptualisation of the project, bringing together the financial resources, management of the server room
2	District Administration	Conceptualisation of the project, co-ordination, Commanding the back-end human system, Liasing with the State Government
3	State Government of Madhya Pradesh	Providing vision to use IT for rural masses
4	District planning Committee	Monitoring and evaluation
5	National Informatics Center	Software Maintenance & all required Technical Support.
6	Gyandoot Society	Enrichment and expansion of the project, IEC, software development, induction of new technology, capacity building

Stockholm challenge award 2000

Gyandoot project of Dhar District has been awarded Stockholm Challenge IT Award 2000 at a glittering function in Town Hall, Stockholm on 6th June 2000. In the words of the organisers, Stockholm City Economic Development Agency in partnership with the European Commission:

The Stockholm Challenge Award is a challenge between pioneering IT projects world wide ... The Stockholm Challenge award focuses on the benefit that information technology can bring people and society. The technology itself is not the issue.

... The single most important criterion is the benefit the project can bring to individuals, society and the environment by using inspirational approaches within the local context."

Gyandoot was declared winner in "Public Service and Democracy" category out of 109 IT projects from all over the world. The gyandoot project is the only Indian project to receive the award in any category in last four years.

The 29 member international Jury has stated its motivation in identifying Gyandoot Project as a winner as follows:

"Project "Gyandoot" is a unique government to citizen Intranet project implemented in a tribal district (Dhar) in Central India, with numerous benefits to the region, including a people-based self-reliant sustainable strategy. "Gyandoot" is recognised as a breakthrough in e-government, demonstrating a paradigm shift which gives marginalised tribal citizens their first ever chance to access knowledge, with minimum investment."

CSI-TCS national IT award

The project is awarded CSI-TCS National IT Award for best IT usage, instituted by the Computer Society of India, for the year 2000. The final contestants for the award were ICICI Bank, Global Trust Bank, SAIL and National Crime Record Bureau, along with the Gyandoot project.

E-COMMERCE

Introduction and Overview

Most people have an understanding of commerce based on their experience as shoppers and buyers, and they bring this experience with them when they start shopping online. In order to meet the user's needs, then, we must understand the typical user's experience of traditional commerce.

World Internet Link makes it easy to do business on the Web. Whether you are just starting out or have complex enterprise-level, Web hosting and e-commerce needs, World Internet Link has the solution for you. We know what it takes to create a powerful and profitable Web site. Our redundant, T3 backbones and powerful dual processor Pentium II servers provide you with the speed you need to reach your target market.

Reliability, flexibility, high performance, and the most competitive prices in the industry will be at your fingertips when you choose the plan that best suits your needs. And you will never find yourself in a bind since World Internet Link Technical Support is available seven days a week, 24 hours a day.

E-commerce is the future and World Internet Link has the tools you need to begin generating your own Internet profits. Create your online storefront quickly and easily with World Internet Link's powerful lineup of electronic commerce services and products. Choose one of the following plans and begin selling your products and services on the Web today, all World Internet Link e-commerce accounts are ready to integrate with an online merchant account and gateway for instant creditcard and electronic check approvals.

E-Store Value

Designed for entrepreneurs and small businesses with 25 - 50 products, E-Store Value provides a quick and easy way to create an online commerce site. This entry-level solution includes Miva Order. A single page flexible browser based tool that will allow you to set your store up quickly and easily.

E-Store Lite: Designed for entrepreneurs and small businesses, E-Store Lite provides a quick and easy way to create an online commerce site. This entry-level solution includes Miva Merchant, a powerful application that allows your Web site to come alive with interactivity and the power of XML and CGI.

E-Store: E-Store is designed to provide both small and large businesses with everything needed to create robust, high-volume storefronts. In addition to the features in E-Store Lite, this plan includes World Internet Link's PlusRoamerII and SiteBuilder products, which provide customers with a dynamic and scalable approach to creating Internet-based commerce functionality with greater accessibility and expedience.

Most problems with commerce sites are due to misunderstandings on the part of the site creators about how users understand the structure and elements of typical commerce transactions. Users have formed schemas to understand commerce, but commerce sites routinely ignore these schemas.

Commerce is a communicative transaction between two parties playing very familiar roles: *buyer* and *seller*. For commerce to occur, somebody must do the selling, and somebody must do the buying, and these two somebodies must share a basic understanding of how the transaction is generally supposed to flow. Ecommerce web sites can't simply make products available to be bought (*surface it, they will buy...*); these sites must hold up their part of role-playing the commerce transaction.

Branding serves as a marker of corporate identity, and so has *some* value to the user, but the hubbub over branding misses some very important concerns that users have.

Ecommerce web sites must pay attention to how they communicate to users. Ecommerce sites play their role of seller by trying to broadcast two messages to potential buyers: "buy from us" and "trust us". The impact of these explicit messages, though, is often corrupted by contradictory or distracting messages implicit in the site's implementation of navigation flow, page layout, visual continuity, and information space.

Ecommerce sites seem to shout the message that they are trustworthy, that users need have no trepidation over purchasing from these sites, but trust derives not from assertions but rather from experience and judgment. People interact, and they make judgments and form expectations of others based on what they experience and what they surmise; it's a lot easier to decide to trust a merchant when you can speak to them face-to-face and shake their hand. Trusting a web site to deal with you fairly and deliver your merchandise, though, well, that's harder to do when you realize that *anyone* can build a commerce site. Ecommerce sites must work hard to build the impression of trustworthiness.

Internet brings to companies to sell their products or services on-line with ease. Companies can now gain from a global marketplace while reducing drastically the setup, maintenance and operational costs, all this due to the fact that eCommerce is an extremely affordable way of doing business compared to conventional business models. You can have a lucrative online store as an independent business venture or use eCommerce to generate additional revenues to your existing "brick and mortar" business.

However setting up an online storefront can be a laborious endeavor. It includes a proper electronic commerce application, merchant account system, credit card processing gateway, and a secure interface for secure transactions.

Finally the success of an eCommerce site doesn't relay primarily in product pricing, selection and availability, just as any other business, consumer awareness via proper marketing plays a key factor in a successful on-line business venture. Once an eCommerce solution is in place and operating, we can assist with continual support by marketing, monitoring, analyzing and developing proper cross industry promotional campaigns.

Functions of E-Commerce

Transmission of electronic messages

E-mail

Fax

Internet Telephony

Electronic publishing

Advertizing

Corporate Digital Library

Information resource sharing

Cooperative work

Import of e-documents

Transfer of e-documents

Electronic data transmission

Categories of E-Commerce

Electronic Commerce can be divided into three major categories

Business to Consumer E-commerce (B2CE E-Com)

Business to Business E-Commerce (B2B E-Com)

Intra-organizational E-Commerce (B2E- E-Com)

Benefits of E-Commerce

Benefits to the customer

Information on cost and expenditure

Quick Starting facility

Facility of selecion

Purchase details

Purchase facility

Benefits for the Organization

Globalization of customers

Availability

Special purchasing

Cost-effective

Less risk

Important Factors Related to E-Commerce

(i) *Safety*- Confidential for users

Confidential for producers

Safety in Payment process

(ii) *Cost*- For Internet access

For safety

For harware and software

(iii) Rules and Regulations

Governemt action and rules

Consumer protection

Controlling Authority

Global standards and methods

Policy Guidelines in India

Any organization which is registered under Companies Act 1956 can apply to DOT Foreign investment shall not exceed 49% in this field. For such facility the country has been divided into three categories, ABC and separate applications are accepted for them. An individual applicant can be given more than one licenses in the field. No license fee is chargeable by December 2003. Bank guarantee of Rs 2 crores for A, 20 lakhs for B and 3 lakhs for C categories is needed Internet Service Providers have been permitted to provide facility for Internet access and establish private gateways depending upon the clearance from DOT Internet Service Providers have been permitted to provide Internet access to establish optical fiber or radio transmission links.

5
Library Automation

Computer is being introduced in libraries like many other organizations. An automated library performs functions efficiently. It saves time and cost of the library services. An automated library is one where a computer system is used to manage one or several of the library's key functions such as acquisitions, serials control, cataloging, circulation and the public access catalog.

HISTORY OF LIBRARY AUTOMATION 1930-1960

Library automation development began in the 1930's when punch card equipment was implemented for use in library circulation and acquisitions. During the 30's and early 40's progress on computer systems was slow which is not surprising, given the Depression and World War II. In 1945, Vannevar Bush envisioned an automated system that would store information, including books, personal records and articles. Memex" system was the first form of automation described as a techanical library that would allow a user to view stored information from several different access points and look at several items simultaneously. His ideas are well known as the basis for hypertext and computers for their operations. They first appeared at MIT, in 1957, with the development of COMIT, managing linguistic computations, natural language and the ability to search for a particular string of information. Librarians then moved beyond a vision or idea for the use of computers, given the technology, they were able to make great advances in the use of computers for library systems. This lead to an explosion of library automation in the 60's and 70's.

1960's Onwards

The advancement of technology lead to increases in the use of computers in libraries. In 1961, a significant invention by both Robert Noyce of Intel and Jack Kirby of Texas Instruments, working independently, was the integrated circuit. All the components of an electronic circuit were placed onto a single "chip" of silicon. This invention of the integrated circuit and newly developed disk and tape storage devices gave computers the speed, storage and ability needed for on-line interactive processing and telecommunications. The new potential for computer use guided one librarian to develop a new indexing technique. HP. Luhn, in 1961, used a computer to produce the "keyword in context" or KWIC index for articles appearing in Chemical Abstracts. Although keyword indexing was not new, it was found to be very suitable for the computer as it was inexpensive and it presented multiple access points. Through the use of Luhn's keyword indexing, it was found that librarians had the ability to put controlled language index terms on the computer.

By the mid-60's, computers were being used for the production of machine readable catalog records by the Library of Congress. Between 1965 and 1968, LOC began the MARC I project, followed quickly by MARC II. MARC was designed as way of "tagging" bibliographic records using 3-digit numbers to identify fields. For example, a tag might indicate "ISBN," while another tag indicates "publication date," and yet another indicates "Library of Congress subject headings" and so on. In 1974, the MARC II format became the basis of a standard incorporated by NISO (National Information Standards Organization). 1980's witnessed computer application in libraries whereas the later decade dominated by networking.

AUTOMATION OVERVIEW

Automation needs proper planning so that all components should work in coordination and achieve the set objective. It has been observed that even after procurement of hardware and software the work does not start for a long time. This is a very harmful tendency in automation since the expected life of a computer system is about five years. By the time computerization is achieved an entirely new system outdates the existing ones. Then, there arises the problem of maintaining such systems. Most of the maintenance agencies refuse to take annual contracts for the older systems. Alternately, it needs consultancy of high professionals to run the system, which is almost out of reach for the libraries. The time of launching computerization should be fixed up in accordance with the expected availability of hardware software and the data entry staff as most of the problems confront at the initial stage.

In the past, computerization meant involvement of professors, scientists, engineers etc. This tendency still prevails. As a result, many persons are required to coordinate the work. This naturally delays the process. The most unfortunate decision is to allow the technocrats to develop software and ignore the expertise of librarians. Where there is an active involvement of librarians, the rate of computerization is taster such as in case of the libraries of Planning Commission, Parliament House, Indian Institute of Public Administration, IITs and IIMs etc. There is hardly any university in the country now, which can claim such achievements in automation.

Our expectations from computerization are very high at the time of beginning. We usually think of adopting many additional services such as (a) facility to search national and international databases, (b) setting up of the electronic library of CD ROM databases, (c) design and development of Open Public Access Catalogue in machine readable form, and (d) setting up of Desk Top Publishing system. These expectations are hardly realised but the whole process of computerization is delayed because of it.

Computerization of new and smaller libraries is easier compared to the older and the larger ones. But most of the university libraries have emerged from the smaller libraries of the past. They have inherited with them the traditional systems of their maintenance. Computerization is based on the modern and standardized systems, which are rare in the older libraries. Their systems have to be standardized and modified in accordance with the necessity of automation. This is possible by conducting stock and system verification.

In the past, the fear of machines for librarians and the high cost of computers restricted their application in libraries. The fear has been eliminated because of the availability of user friendly and menu driven packages specially developed for automation of libraries. The machines of enhanced quality are available now a days on comparatively lower costs. This has been possible with the advancement in electronics and specially in the microchip technology based on Very Large Scale Integration (VLSI).

The larger library systems can be computerized systematically by computerizing all the libraries under the system one after the other.The office of the librarian should be the central nodal agency with the most powerful computer system. The databases developed anywhere in the libraries should be available on this system. The major divisions of the central library should be provided terminals or computers as per their needs. Each of the major satellite libraries can also be equipped with an independent system to cope with the load and also to meet future needs.

The selection of hardware is made keeping in view the quantum of data to be processed and the services expected. A larger library may have needed a super computer had the automation been planned a decade back. In the changed circumstance of today even a mainframe is regarded as more than sufficient for such a library. Pentium, a personal computer with 40 GB memory that is available with an ordinary computer now can accommodate the whole bibliographical details of an average university library. Its memory can be extended further if needed as applicable in most of the systems. Some peripheral devices can also be attached with Pentium to divide the additional load and to permit decentralization of functions.

Software for a major library should be chosen with great care. Basically, there are two options for it. The software can be developed locally and it can also be procured from the market. Experience shows that the locally developed software generally fail after sometimes. This is particularly relevant in case of the university libraries. The main reason being that the software development needs high professional skills and continuous updating even after its application. It is better to opt for the branded packages since they are the only effective substitute now.

The market is full of the readily available packages specially designed for library automation. Some of them have already proved dependable after their application. The provisions for in-house as well as the retrieval functions have been incorporated. Their vendors undertake warranty to train the operating staff and run the system for the desired periods. These software are menu driven and user friendly and need lesser computer skill compared with the CD/ ISIS and many other packages. LIBSYS has been refined over the years. It is operational on DOS, ZENIX and UNIX environment

There is a provision of conversion of data in most of the packages. It means that the data entered into the system using any library software can be made accessible for the other. Unesco has prescribed some basic entry elements for all the software developers in order to standardize formats and permit global resource sharing among the desired institutions. This format is called the Common Communication Format (CCF).

The accession information is the basis for automation. It is extracted from the documents as well as from all other possible sources at the time of procurement. Thus the maximum details gathered are recorded in a standardized format called the accession register, in a computerized system these details are entered once only, stored properly and manipulated in the desired sequences.

The current data can be entered straightaway from the accession records as a routine work. However, additional staff or private agencies can be engaged for entry of the retrospective data. The agencies undertaking data entry have quite varying rates for their work. Sometimes, they quote charges for data collection also.

Computer has proved to be the most powerful tool for management of information. But in the Indian universities its potential has not been realised properly. The university libraries have to face the challenge of computer as the coming generations will depend more on it. Or, this gap in library profession will adversely affect the overall process of education. The purpose of library automation is to free the librarians from the routine clerical work and to allow them to contribute more meaningfully to spread of knowledge and information. In the functioning of libraries, there are many repetitive jobs, which can be easily handled by computer and a lot of human energy thus saved can be put to a better use.

Standardization allows proper sharing of resources among the desiring institutions. For this, processing of all documents of the libraries is required to be undertaken according to the standardization norms. The work is to be taken up both outside the libraries and inside just as the centralized accessioning has become a common feature in most of the university libraries. This saves a lot of expenditure avoiding ordering of duplicate copies, which are not needed and can be shared by other libraries.

NEED FOR LIBRARY AUTOMATION

Information systems are designed to facilitate access to a huge amount of data. The system may be manual or computerized. But the computerized systems are advantageous over the manual ones. They reduce the energy and time taken in the repetitive processes of the libraries and reflect their holdings instantly and from various angles of search which is not possible in the traditional systems due to physical limitations.

A library stands to collect, store, retrieve and communicate information. In the present time, there is emphasis in application of information technology in almost every walk of human lives. Libraries deal with information, therefore, they are being affected by the new technology more in comparision with the other social organizations. The following are the needs of library automation:

- Growth of library collections
- Availability of information in varied formats like print, non-prints, graphics, audiovisuals and electronic media
- Varied needs of libraries and their limitations
- Challenges of information technology before the librarians
- Excess of repeating and duplication of work in in-house functions of libraries
- Information management and retrieval
- Search of national and international databases
- Networking, resource sharing and Internet applications in libraries
- Impact of communication technologies
- Limitations of traditional information systems in libraries
- Depleting budgets and scarcity of library staff
- Expectation of society from libraries

OBJECTIVES OF LIBRARY AUTOMATION

- Speedy disposal of library work
- Time-saving with quality service
- Suitability for library cooperation and collection development
- Simplicity in library management practices to meet the objectives
- Proper use of human resources
- Development of the new library services
- Management of computerized systems

- Preparation of reports
- Suitability for resource sharing and networking
- Budgetary control of libraries
- Development of human resources

BASIC REQUIREMENTS OF LIBRARY AUTOMATION

- Adequate Collection
- Financial Assistance
- Computer Hardware
- Library Software
- Trained Staff
- Users Training
- Maintenance and Development

Adequate Collection

Collection of a library forms the basis for library automation. Larger the collection the more is the need is the need of automation to increase efficiency of the library services.

Financial Assistance

Computerization involves money. The expenditure is required to be made at the time of installation, purchase of library software, training of staff, entry of library data and also for running the facility as a matter of routine

Computer Hardware

The selection of computer hardware for automation involves careful planning. There are many types of computers available in the market. Moreover, the libraries also have various categories. The computer to be purchased for the library should meet the specific needs of the library. The technology is changing fast. Therefore, the latest computers with adequate speed and memory should be acquired from the market.

Library Software

Software activate computers to perform the desired functions. A large variety of library software are available in the market. But the selection of software depends upon the nature of the library. A simple software may be suited for a school library but for a larger library a special type of software is needed. A software should be user friendly.

There are software which offer management of multimedia and multilingual collections and a also allow remote access not only from the libraries but also to the libraries from one's work place. These options are costly and out of reach generally for an average library but the university libraries being larger enough may go for them for better results. In India, such software are still in the stage of infancy.

Training of Staff and Users

Designing of information systems for automation of university libraries is a joint venture of librarians and software engineers. The former present their requirement into a logical order and the latter incorporate suitable provision to make the system work. Both of them analyze the same functions but their approaches are different. Now, the work of system designing has become easier with the availability of ready made software packages for automation of the libraries.

Library staff needs training in handling the computer hardware, software and perform data entry work. Earlier it was a difficult task but with the advent of user friendly software, the work on computer has been made simple. The training is generally provided by the hardware and software supplying agencies. Users also need training in retrieval.

Training of staff in maintenance of the hardware and software and also in extraction of the required data from the documents is an essential part of the work of database creation. The hardware and software suppliers undertake to impart the working knowledge about their products but the extraction of data becomes the responsibility of the libraries. Moreover, there may be some local variations in respect of the presentation of the various segments of the database as per the needs of an individual library that is taken care of by the library itself.

Maintenance and Development

During the use of computer there may be some disorders in computer hardware, software and databases .For this purpose, professionally trained staff with computer background are employed in large libraries. There is a trained to enter into contract for annual maintenance of the systems also.

Database Creation

A database is a set of data that is related to each other. A dictionary or an encyclopaedia being arranged logically and complete in itself may be taken as an example of manual database. The advantages of computerized databases are many over the manual ones on account of the vast memory, speed and accuracy of computer which stores,' processes and delivers information once fed into the desired sequences.

Types of Library Data

The most time taking process in computerization is data entry. It needs the services of professionals trained in extraction of the bibliographical data from the documents and mounting it on a computer. In case of the retrospective data. It is necessary to ensure that only those documents are taken up for the task which are available in the library physically or on record, otherwise not only the precious time of the staff is wasted but also the complications in automation increases which contributes to confusion and inaction. To avoid such a situation, there are certain practices in the libraries and the most effective of them is the rectification of the library collections; both books as well as the shelf record are arranged properly and then compared with each other. Libraries have two broad categories of data:

Current Data

Libraries normally have to decide a cut off date for automation. All new arrivals are processed in the changed environment after this date. Data entry for such books starts right from the acquisition section, which deals with the selection, ordering and purchase of documents. As per the provisions incorporated in the software packages, the information is required to be entered only once and the same is imported by the other concerned sections of he library to perform a variety of Functions as per their specific needs.

Retrospective data

Retrospective data refers to the record of the documents, which have already been purchased and processed in the library before the cut off date. A large amount of data about the existing collections of libraries belongs to this category, which is required to be mounted on the systems as a pre requisite to automation. It can generally be achieved in two ways i.e. by entry through books or through catalogue cards. The former is done on a regular basis for the current arrivals whereas the popular practice followed in case of retrospective conversion is the latter.

Retrospective conversion of data is the main problem for the university libraries. They generally engage outside agencies for the work. But it largely depends upon the availability of funds. The rates for entry through books are comparatively higher and only a few university libraries are able to meet the expenditure to be incurred in such a case. In the normal circumstances, the rates for data entry through books range from Rs. 7 to 40 per record depending upon the specifications. Since books are the original sources of bibliographical data, entry through books should be preferred if affordable.

Information Sources for Database Creation

Documents

The best and the most appropriate source for data entry is

the document. Being complete in itself, a document provides the maximum possible details. In some cases the body of the text is also consulted for bringing out the required information that is not available anywhere else. Every library maintains record of documents in a standardised format to facilitate the inventory control. The two broad categories of such records are Accession Registers and Catalogue Cards

All possible details about a particular document are copied in the accession register at the time of purchase. The format of the register is approved by the Government of India and it is more for administrative exercises rather than for retrieval functions. It does not provide column for subject headings and key words. Moreover, libraries generally do not write class numbers in it although a column has been provided for the same. In view of these limitations, the accessicn register is generally not used as a source for data entry. But it is of great help when the other sources fail to provide details about a particular document.

Bibliographical Records

Every library maintains catalogue cards of different categories like author, title, subject, classified etc. Another category of card maintained behind the scene are shelf cards. They are of utmost value for automation. It is the confidential record of library kept in the high security zone and maintained in a classified order. University libraries generally go for data entry through this record for retrospective conversion.

Online Databases

Various new methods of data entry have emerged with the advancement in the hardware and software. Big libraries in the developed countries purchase pool of bibliographical data and extract records of those documents which are to be added to the library. The catalogue of Library of Congress may be acquired on CD ROMs or online for transfer of the relevant entries to the developing database of the interested libraries. This allows speed and accuracy. Further, the data so entered is available in a standardised format which can be shared on national as well as the international level. The bigger the library the more advantageous and economic is this method of data entry.

Data Security

Data in a computerised form is the end product of a long exercise and it works as a source for all the operations of the libraries. Such data on the disk of the computer system is always exposed to risk of viruses and other hazards. There are many reasons for loss of the entered data and the risk factor is comparatively higher in the environment of big libraries where suitably trained computer professionals are few in number and the systems are to be operated by many persons.

There are many methods of data security The most common of them is its copying from time to time on floppies or CDs. Viruses generally come through floppies and CDs brought from outside or from the Internet connection, therefore the use of such alien items be avoided as far as possible. It should also be made a regular exercise to run anti-virus software on the systems to free disk from the viruses. Entry of unauthorized users can be restricted by incorporating provision of passwords for the hardware as well as software.

FEATURES OF AUTOMATION

- It is an electronics based activity which is carried out by humanbeings
- It is important for users and in accordance with the principles of library science
- Helpful in automation of library services
- Suitable for resource sharing and networking
- Early disposal of the routine library work
- Capable to transform a library to be more efficient and productive

COMPONENTS OF LIBRARY AUTOMATION

Objectives

It is important to know the objectives of a library where the automation activity is expected

Planning

Planning is an important component of library automation. It helps in achieving the objectives of a library

System Analysis

System analysis is needed before undertaking the work of automation in order to understand the needs of the library and meet the objectives with the available resources. The following points are considered while planning the library automation:

- Nature and objectives of a library
- Total collection of a library
- Nature of collection and usefulness
- Total strength of users
- Daily issue, return and reservation
- Number of multilingual documents available in the library
- Information services
- Networking and resource sharing
- Available human resource and future needs
- Internet and Intranet
- CD Net and Electronic Document Supply Service

Identification of main areas of automation

It is of utmost importance to understand the current needs of the library before undertaking the work of automation in order to understand the role that the various organs can play in their new setting. The work can be carried out in four stages as under:

Information Storage and Retrieval

It is the primary level work in library automation which

involves entry of bibliographical details to make available for on line cataloguing

House Keeping Work

In-house functions include all the work behind the screen such as acquisition, cataloguing, serials control, circulation, information services etc.

Networking Services

Under these services, library cooperation, online services, resources sharing and Internet applications are developed

Intranet and Multilingual Databases

In addition to the above services, Intranet-Multilingual Database and CD Net services are developed for the library.

Documentation of Automation Plan

The automation committee should consider a plan including the following points before proceeding on to computerization:

- Objectives of automation
- System Analysis
- System Design
- Requirements of system
- Level of human resources
- Financial resources
- Hardware requirements
- Software requirements
- Bibliography
- Record format
- Communication and exchange

Hardware Configuration

- Pentium 4 6MB RAM
- 4GB Hard Disk Drive

- 150MB Cartrisge Tape Drive
- Floppy Disk Drive
- BGA Colour Monitor
- 8Port Intelligent i/V Card
- X25 Card Drive Software
- Internal Modem

MANAGEMENT OF AUTOMATED LIBRARY

All functions of a library can be conveniently divided into the following two categories:

- Administrative and General works
- House Keeping and Routine work

Administrative and General Work

Under this category, computer can be applied for the following functions:

- Human resource management and development
- Database creation for employees
- Notification of library rules and service rules
- Maintaining records pertaining to leave, discipline, attendance
- Management of personal files
- Work related with library committees

House Keeping and Routine Work

Computer saves a lot of valuable time of employees in providing the library services by avoiding repetitive processes. The automation of the following functions is included in this category:

- Acquisition
- Classification and Cataloguing
- Serials Control
- Circulation

- Stock Verification

Acquisition

Acquisition process involves the following functions:

- Operation of library budget
- Receipt of approval from the various heads of departments
- Selection of books and other educational materials
- Verfication of bibliographical details
- Ordering of library materials
- Payment of bills
- Creation of orders on computer
- Activity for acqusition
- Transfer of details for classification and cataloguing

Budget Management

The following information is acquired under the budgetary management:

- Total library budget
- Departmental library budgets
- Budgets earmarked for special collections
- Amount of funds received from other sources
- Statement of expenditure of the other funds
- Statement of expenditure of the last years

Classification and Cataloguing

- Classification of documents according to the standardized scemes of classification
- Cataloguing of documents in accordance with the standard code of cataloguing
- Assignment of subject headings
- Preparation of book cards etc used in circulation
- Feeding of class Numbrs and cataloguing details in computers

- Display of new arrivals in the library

Serials Control

The Periodicals section is responsible for the following functions;

- Allocation of budget journals
- Approval of the list of journals on annual basis
- Action on recommendations of library committee and the heads of the departments
- Selection of journals suitable for subscription
- Verification of the cost and other details of journals through the list of publishers
- Ordering procedure
- Payment procedure
- Reciept of the subscribed journals
- Availability of the subscribed journals on OPAC
- Sending reminders for the unsupplied issues of journals
- Display of the titles of journals on weekly basis

Circulation

The automation of the circulation function of a library is one of the most difficult tasks. This is all because of the complications involved in the procedure. The following are the functions covered under circulation:

- To inform the users about issue, return and reservation of documents
- Providing information about the issue of documents to the users
- To retrieve documents, issue reminders to the borrowers and communicate information about the availability of documents
- To impose fine on the documents returned after the due dates

- To maintained statistics about the issued documents
- To inform users about the availability of new documents in their special fields

Stock Verification

In libraries, materials are shelved in sequences viz textbooks, reference collections, rare, reserved and non-book materials. The members have free access to them in most of the cases. As a result, documents are displaced and also lost sometimes. To ascertain the loss and disorder, stock verification is carried out after certain intervals. The Stock Verification involves the following functions:

- Preparation of lists of acquired documents according to the accession numbers
- Preparation of lists of the issued documents according to the accession numbers
- Comparision of the accession numbers of both the lists
- Listing of the documents not found in the issue record
- Listing of the lost document

For the abovementioned work, three computerized lists are obtained and one of them relates to the record of the missing ones.

Online Catalogue Searching

The following functions are undertaking under the online information search:

- Author
- Title
- Subject
- Class numberISBN
- Accession number
- Bar codes
- Key word

- Publisher
- Series
- All the above

In case of Internet search catalogues of any library can be searched through the Web whereas the Intranet provides information pertaining to the specified local area network only.

Reporting and Management System

Under the reporting function, the progress of the library in the past and also the planning for the future is viewed. The following are the main activities under this function:

- List of additions
- Peridical reports
- Subjectwise list of additions
- Serials progess report
- Present collection subjectwise
- Details of departmental libraries

Resource Sharing and Networking

- Preparation of union catalogues
- Online catalogue search
- E-mail
- Inter library loan
- Training and human resource development

Library Management

The following functions are covered under the library administration;

- Making of policies for library service
- Keeping coordination among the various sections of the library
- Stregthening library automation, networking, CD ROM and on line services

- Provision of budget for books, journals and the other educational materials
- Statement of expenditure
- Work details for the library staff
- Distribution of library publications
- Deciding standards for better library services
- Arrangements of training for the library employees

Reference Service

The main activities relating to the reference service in the library are;

- Awareness about the available print and electronic sources
- Identification of the proper source of information to answer a query
- Knowledge of the current sources of information
- Identification of reference tools
- Access to electronic databases available on CD ROMs and Internet
- Providing selective dissemination of information

Information Service

- Accessioning
- Summary
- Current awareness service
- Selective dissemination of information
- Preparation of list of books
- Online database search
- Information retrieval and communication
- E-mail
- Networking]
- Internet search services

FUNCTIONS OF LIBRARY MANAGEMENT SYSTEM

The following functions are covered under the library management sytem:

- Ordering of books and accessioning
- Cataloguing
- Circulation control
- Serials control
- Information management
- Community information service

Ordering and accessioning

The following are the responsibilities under this department:

- Collection of details regarding the books to be purchased
- Checking of duplication with the already available books
- Placing of order through Internet or by post
- Verification of pending orders and action
- Receipt of documents and payment of bills
- Budgetary control details about the available funds

Cataloguing system

The main purpose of cataloguing is to make available the details of the documents available in a particular library. The work is to be accomplished keeping in view the possibilities of networking and resource sharing with other libraries. For this work, professional competence is very necessary, otherwise a lot of changes have to be made in the database of the library.

ONLINE PUBLIC ACCESS CATALOGUE (OPAC)

OPAC is a computerized library catalog available to the public. OPAC may be designed for an individual library and consulted within its building or it may be made available outside the library through Intranet and Internet also. These days most OPACs are accessible over the Internet to users all over the world.

The following are the reasons for creation of the OPAC:

* Books that contain information on a particular topic may be shelved in several different areas of the library, in special collections, or even in different libraries altogether.
* Books are shelved in the library in call number order, so one has to be very familiar with the Dewey Decimal Classification System to find the small area devoted to topic.

Methods of Information Search

There are several ways to find materials in the online catalog. The most popular search options are:

- Search by Subject
- Search by Author
- Search by Title
- Search by Keyword

Subject search

It is most useful if you are looking for information on a topic or a person, but if you don' tknow the title or author's name.

* To find the best terms for the Search by Subject option , try the "Library of Congress Subject Headings" (LCSH) available at the Reference Desk.
* When searching for materials about a person, type the last name first.
* If you get no results, try similar words (synonyms).
* Discuss your topic ideas with your class instructor and with the librarian.

Search by Author

It is used for looking for works by a particular author, composer, artist, etc. Invert the author's name (type last name first, first name and middle initial last). For example, to find works by Edgar Allan Poe, enter: Poe, Edgar Allan (comma optional).

An author may be a person or an organization.

* For an organization, enter the full name of the organization. For example: American Academy of Arts and Sciences.
* OPAC, like most online databases, is not case sensitive, that means it doesn't care about capitalization (you could type: Poe, poe, or POE).

Search by Title

This option is tried to know the exact title or it's beginning. For example: discovering computers

* Omit any leading articles such as: "a, an, el, las, le, les, los, the, un, una, une," etc.
* You don't have to write the whole title, only first few words. For example, while searching for a book titled: "Never before, never again: The stirring autobiography of Eddie Robinson, the winningest coach in the history of college football" you may type only: "Never before" and achieve similar results.

Search by Keyword

It is the method to search the full text of OPAC records for terms that might appear in the author, title, subject, notes or even publishing information of the book you are looking for.

* Keyword searches are especially good for combining author and title searches if one does not know the complete name of the author and the full title.
* Use keyword search if you do not know the authorized subject heading for the term you are searching.
* Use search operators, such as AND or OR to combine terms representing different aspects of your subject to narrow or broaden your search. For example: SHAKESPEARE AND HAMLET.

DIGITAL LIBRARY

A digital Library is an assemblage of digital computing, storage, and communications machinery together with the content and software needed to reproduce, emulate, and extend the services provided by conventional libraries based on paper and other material means of collecting, cataloging, finding, and disseminating information. A full service digital library must accomplish all essential services of traditional libraries and also exploit the well-known advantages of digital storage, searching, and communication.

The concept "library" has been refined over several centuries. It would be injudicious to depart from what people expect merely because a digital service is replacing a material one. Except where explicit reasons suggest an improvement that is easily explained to ordinary users (e.g., in query services), library services should implement a familiar model.

The Digital Library is the "collection of services and the collection of information objects that support users in dealing with information objects and the organization and presentation of those objects available directly or indirectly via electronic/ digital means."

Scope of digital Library

Digital library is a concept that has different meanings in different communities. To the engineering and computer science community, digital library is a metaphor for the new kinds of distributed data base services that manage unstructured multimedia data. To the political and business communities, the term represents a new marketplace for the world's information resources and services.

- an organized data base of digital information objects in varying formats maintained to provide unmediated ease of access to a user community, with these further characteristics

- an overall access tool (e.g. a catalog) provides search and retrieval capability over the entire data base;
- organized technical procedures exist through which the library management adds objects to the data base and removes them according to a coherent and accessible collections policy." (Peter Graham, Rutgers University Libraries, 1997)

Digital libraries are a set of electronic resources and associated technical capabilities for creating, searching, and using information. In this sense they are an extension and enhancement of information storage and retrieval systems that manipulate digital data in any medium (text, images, sounds; static or dynamic images) and exist in distributed networks. The content of digital libraries includes data, metadata that describe various aspects of the data (e.g., representation, creator, owner, reproduction rights), and metadata that consist of links or relationships to other data or metadata, whether internal or external to the digital library.

Advantages of Digital Libraries

Many potential advantages of a digital library over a paper library are similar to those of any digital database over its paper counterpart:

- faster addition to the collection with better quality control
- improved search functionality and faster access to information found, and
- more freedom and reduced bureaucracy for individual users.

Achieving these advantage depends not only on efforts traditionally undertaken by computer scientists, but also on the highest quality enginee.

Characteristics of Digital Libraries

Following are the characteristics of digital libraries:

- users are usually elsewhere than the information they want.

and often wish to correlate things from several sources;

- whoever wants to use a library must show permission to do so;
- different patrons are permitted different actions and to see different parts of each collection;
- to find specific information, each user must understand the catalog structure;
- the catalog may describe items not actually held as part of the collection at hand;
- the catalog and the collected items are used differently and not necessarily housed in the same place;
- documents are cataloged with text descriptors and also with conventional properties, such as author names;
- documents contain cross references to other documents;
- document identifiers are different from document names; a document may have several names, one for each context;
- translations of a document may express essentially the same information, e.g., versions of classic literature in different languages;
- each stored item is valuable, often with part of its residual value owned by its authors or authors' assignees;
- part of the value provided by a library is the provenance information it holds for each item;
- items are put into libraries because, while each is thought valuable for future reference, the specific individuals who will read it and the times when this will occur are not known.

Requirements of Digital Libraries

Any organization like school, business, department, family, individual can create and manage its own library, and most individuals can access to many libraries. All libraries should do certain things similarly adhere to certain standards — so people do not need to learn new methods for each library and so information can be exchanged.

At the general level found in requests for proposals, in the trade literature, and in business publications, there is broad consensus on what services the digital library should have in 5-10 years. For a few of the generic components, such as storage subsystems and document markup languages and interpretation, detailed requirements analyses exist; typically they include hundreds of well-justified requirements. For most of the other generic components suggested earlier, similarly comprehensive requirements analyses are not available in the generally accessible literature.

To prioritize the requirements for academic and cultural DL services we must consider a range of objectives which will differ among different institutions. For some the premier objective will be improved accessibility to rare and valuable materials for scholars. For others, as in the TULIP project mounted by Elsevier in partnership with computer science groups at several universities, it will be easier information search by electronic publication of professional journals

Requirements for Catalogs

The radically new possibility for DLs is storage and dissemination of collected items. In contrast, digital catalogs have been in practical use for some time, and there is a considerable body of experience, both good and bad, or at least questionable [Ba94], and some standards in this area. Library cataloging is known to be difficult:

The preparation of a catalog may seem a light task, to the inexperienced, ant to those who are unacquainted with the requirements of the learned world, respecting such works. In truth, however, there is no species of literary labor so arduous and perplexing. The peculiarities of titles are, like the idiosyncrasies of authors, innumerable.

Requirements for Document Storage Services

An analysis done by IBM Research [GI90] identified several hundred specific requirements — too many to tabulate here. However, several broadly applicable elements emerged, and are summarized below because they typify what needs to be worked out for each library component class identified above:

- accessibility from all workstation
- application independence;
- catalog service from all kinds of operating system platforms;
- joining libraries to other databases;
- automatic capture and indexing;
- document managers;
- large and small items;
- low entry point, with growth to giant collections, maintaining performance;
- low installation and administration overhead;
- open subsystem
- standard interfaces and protocols;
- customer-defined data formats;
- support for all kinds of item storage;
- tools for "amateur" application programmers.

LIBRARY SOFTWARE PACKAGES

Library software of various types are readily available in the market now a days. The selection of a software depends upon the specific needs of the library where it is going to be used. There are the following three possibilities, which should be explored before deciding on the software:

- Development of software by the library professionals
- Contact by a software developing agency
- Study of the readily available software

Software development for library functions is a very difficult task. There are many problems which confront before and after the development of a software and it is because the complexity of the information procedures in the libraries. It is easier to develop the same for the other functions like accounts and inventory control. Therefore, it will always be better to opt for a readily available one.

Software fcr Library Services

Selection for a library software depends upon the specific needs of a library. The market is full with all types of software which are readily available. We are discussing below only a few of them which are in use at the national as well as international level.

- Softlink
- Horizon Information Management System
- VTLS
- Autolib
- Granthalaya
- CDS/ISIS
- Sanjay
- Trishna
- MINISIS
- LibSys
- SLIM++
- NextLib

SOFTLINK

Softlink is a package that is being used at international level with nearly 20 years experience, and almost 10,000 clients in 90 countries covering 10 major languages, Softlink International Limited is recognised as a world leader in the provision of library automation software. Softlink's core business is the development of technology to enhance the efficiency and effectiveness of library operations, catering for the needs of all types of libraries including Corporate, Commercial, and Special Libraries (e.g. legal and medical), Primary, Secondary, and Tertiary libraries, and community and educational resource centers.

Management module

This module provides:

* Cataloging
* Authority file maintenance
* General reports
* Utilities (housekeeping, map setup etc.)
* System administration facilities.
* Import/Export of data

In order to circulate a resource, its presence in the library must be registered and certain information recorded about it. This process is known as cataloging. When automating an existing library, the existing stock must be cataloged. Both Softlink Alice and Softlink Library provide a number of options for achieving this beyond simply typing in all the details for every resource. Most libraries automating for the first time use the Rapid Retrospective cataloging module. Thereafter, new acquisitions are cataloged as they are received. This may be achieved either through manual cataloging, or use of the Rapid Retrospective module.

The quality of the catalog determines the usefulness of the Inquiry facility, and hence of the system as a whole. The more ways, in which an appropriate resource can be retrieved, the more likely it is to be found and used. The level of utilization of appropriate resources is a good measure of the quality of service being provided by the library.

Cataloging

Softlink Alice and Softlink Library make cataloging easy,

with simple screens and authority file windows that can be browsed and updated during accessioning. This increases the efficiency of cataloging, and maintains the integrity and consistency of the catalog during data entry.

The information that can be recorded against each item is:

* Title
* Names (authors etc.)
* Edition details
* Publication details
* Collation
* GMD<
* ISBN (scanned in)
* Keywords
* Notes (unlimited length)
* Series
* Subjects
* Multimedia (images, video, sound, slide shows)
* Topics
* Suitability Levels
* NCA (National Curriculum Area)
* Country of Origin/Language

and for each copy:

* Location
* Classification
* Suffix
* Barcode
* Accession number
* Loan category
* Accession date
* Supplier

* Price
* Budget dissection
* Department

Not all of the above need to be entered. The only mandatory entries are title and GMD, for a catalog record, and barcode, accession date and loan category for a copy.

Classification can be done by Dewey Decimal, Library of Congress, or any other classification scheme.

Entering the title automatically causes the system to check against the catalog for duplicate or near-match titles. The system can automatically create a keyword for every significant word in the title, notes and edition fields if desired.

There are no limits on the number of names, subjects, series and keywords that may be added to a record. Authorities can be entered simply by typing the first few letters, which the system will use to search for and attach the full name from the appropriate authority file.

The system caters for cataloging multiple copies of individual titles, which may be shelved at one or multiple locations, collections of works and linked bibliographic items. A wide variety of material may be cataloged including video recordings, sound recordings, kits, maps, realia, equipment, resource boxes, rooms, World Wide Web sites, electronic documents, even playing fields. Should it be necessary to consult the catalog while entering data, the cataloger need simply click on the Inquiry icon to access this module.

Abbreviated Entry

A fast track input approach is also provided for a skeleton entry to be registered in the library. The user enters enough of the title to enable the resource to be identified, scans in the ISBN, and enters any copy information required (normally at least location, classification and circulation barcode).

Copies

Adding copy information to the catalog record is a simple matter of adding the barcode number of the copy and then filling in the necessary details. For multiple copies of the same title, a bulk copy function exists which automatically assigns barcodes and accession numbers to the copy records.

Linked Items and Resource Boxes

Often the situation arises where one resource contains others - such as a video recording with several programs on it, or a resource box with a related set of classroom resources in it. The system allows for the programs that make up the video recording to be cataloged as one resource and for each program to be searchable, through subject, title, keyword etc., in Inquiry. These are called linked items.

A resource box must be cataloged individually and all of the items contained in it must also be cataloged. Thus the box and/or individual content items may be accessed from Inquiry and the box with its contents may be controlled as a single item in Circulation. The system also allows for items in a resource box to be loaned and returned individually.

Notes

A free-text notes field of unlimited length allows for the addition of abstracts, notes and reviews. Keywords can be automatically generated for every word in the Notes field. This increases the accessibility of resources. The standard Windows "Cut" and "Paste" options can be used within the Notes when appropriate. With document scanning equipment, printed information, such as the publisher's blurb from the back of a resource, can be transferred into the Notes field in a form suitable for editing and keywording.

Multimedia

The Multimedia module allows images, such as photographs, diagrams, maps and text, to be attached to catalog records for display in Inquiry. Sound, video or film and slide shows, which are a combination of images and sound, can also be attached.

World Wide Web Sites and Electronic Documents

The Management module allows the cataloging of any site or specific page address from the World Wide Web. The cataloging process involves adding the title of the site, the address of the site and a GMD of WWW. Any relevant subject headings, notes and keywords are also added during the cataloging stage. When an Inquiry search results in a World Wide Web record appearing, Inquiry will display a 'Go to Web Site' button instead of the usual 'Copies' button. Upon clicking the 'Go to Web Site - button the patron is presented with the Web Browser which has been installed on the network or workstation. The patron will then be automatically taken to the cataloged site.

Electronic documents, such as word processing files, spreadsheets and databases may also be cataloged through Management. This gives the library patrons access to any electronic document, which is stored on the network, via the Inquiry terminal. For example, if a word processing document had been cataloged and consequently retrieved through Inquiry, a 'View' button would appear. If the 'View' button were clicked then the word processing software would be opened with the document able to be either viewed or printed.

Equipment

The catalog is designed to accommodate many different forms of media including audiovisual hardware and sports equipment. Equipment records carry additional inventory information such as:

* Make, model and serial number
* Engraved (Y/N)
* Storage location
* Staff member responsible

* Maintenance log

This information is usually confidential and as such is not available to borrowers from Inquiry.

Authority Files

The system contains authority files for all appropriate fields. Pop-up windows allow the authority files to be browsed on screen when cataloging, and for new entries to be added dynamically.

The following fields are controlled by the use of authority files:

* Title
* Names (authors etc.)
* Series
* Subject
* Publisher
* Supplier
* Location
* Budget Dissection
* GMD
* Department
* Topics
* Levels
* NCA (National Curriculum Area)
* Country of Origin/Language

In order to add data to these fields in cataloging, the first few characters need only be typed, and then a window will open displaying the closest entry in the relevant authority file. The cataloger may then select the exact heading required or, if necessary, add a new entry to the authority file directly. Functions to maintain the authority files exist outside of cataloging. The Windows environment allows these functions to be accessed during the cataloging process.

See and See Also references may be added into the subject authority file. It is also possible to automatically generate See references from any multiple-word subject heading. For example, when the subject heading "Art -History" is created, the cross-reference, "History - Art" wilt be created automatically. This means that resources with this subject heading will be retrieved via the word "Art" or the word "History", thus increasing accessibility.

A "stopped word" list is also supported, defining which words to ignore when automatically generating keywords from titles, notes and edition. Users are able to add to or delete from the list with ease.

Derived Cataloging

Softlink recognizes that cataloging can be carried out more rapidly by utilizing commercial or existing catalogs of bibliographic records.

Advanced facilities are available for data import from CD-ROM, other library packages, home-grown databases, bibliographic information providers, bookseller databases or any source of MARC (Machine-Readable Catalog) records. It is widely acknowledged that Rapid Retrospective represents the state of the art in retrospective cataloging. Rapid Retrospective is described in detail later.

Reports

The reporting capabilities in the standard modules are extensive, and are sufficient for most libraries. For more unusual requirements, customized reports are available, on request, for a minimal cost.

Printed Catalogs

Subject, author, title and series catalogs may be printed, either in full or abbreviated form. These may be tailored to individual departments, and can cover all stock, or only stock accessioned since a certain date. In this way complete or partial catalogs can be produced for a variety of purposes. An example of this might be for promoting the library to departments that make little use of it, or for planning projects with staff.

Data Validation Reports

Printouts of all authority files and general resources are available, arranged in alphabetical order. These can be selected by date range to provide either a complete listing, or a partial listing. An example of this might be a list of all of the resources that were cataloged in a particular month.

Other Reports

In addition a wide range of other printed outputs can be produced, including:

* Shelf lists
* Accession register
* Borrower cards
* Barcode labels
* Spine labels
* Catalog cards
* Borrower lists
* Statistics on item usage and borrower loans

All reports can be written to a nominated printer, browsed on screen, or written to disk in either text or rich text format for subsequent manipulation using desktop publishing, word processing, spreadsheet or database packages.

Utilities

A number of utilities are provided to make life easier for the librarian, for example changing the status of a batch of items to 'Disposed' can be effected simply by scanning their barcodes. A similar approach can be taken for changing the location of a set of books, selected from the main shelves, for featuring in a display collection.

Library Map

When a patron has selected a resource from the OPAC, they may click on the "map button" and a map will be displayed of the library with a blue dot representing their current position in the library and a green (available) or red (on loan) dot showing the location of the resource. The library map is setup and maintained via the Management module.

System Administrator Functions

The system administrator functions are also part of the Management module. The system has a very time efficient, simple and reliable method of backup and recovery. All other system administrator functions are capable of being performed by the library manager without requiring any special technical knowledge.

Functions are available for various procedures including running archives, recoveries, rebuilds and setting system security.

Inventory

A complete inventory processing system is provided. This allows an inventory of individual locations within the library to be carried out at any time. Items are best checked by using either a portable barcode reader, a normal reader attached to the computer via a long extension cable, or the normal reader, cable and computer moved round the shelves on a trolley. Entry of the items may be performed in any order using the barcode reader.

Sorting the shelves into classification order, ensuring that all loans are returned, and partial or complete closure of the library, are no longer requirements of stocktaking. Thus considerable time can be saved, and any inconvenience to users is removed.

A printed record of missing items (those that are normally stored in the checked location and are found to be not on the shelf and not out on loan) is produced. This contains full details of the items including cost. Items detected as missing have their status updated and the inventory date recorded automatically, in their catalog record. The operator has the opportunity to remove missing and disposed items from the catalog in a single process. During this procedure the user is asked to indicate the length of time that an item must have been flagged as missing before it will be removed from the catalog. A printout of all resources that have been removed from the collection is produced automatically.

HORIZON INFORMATION MANAGEMENT SYSTEM

This system delivers libraries capabilities in many areas:

* Anytime access
* Simplicity
* Customized interfaces
* Personalized preferences
* Delivery options

Horizon Launcher

Brings the whole Horizon system to your desktop as a single application. Improved navigation takes users directly to functions they need, less time is spent navigating menus. Horizon now functions as a multi-document interface (MDI) with each major function occurring as a window in the main Launcher frame. Launcher settings follow the user (by being tied to a user's login) instead of being tied to a particular workstation. Special launcher profiles can be created for specific functions, and profiles are fully customizable.

Staff Searching

The primary interactive link between staff and the library collection. It consists of user-oriented query functions for search and retrieval of bibliographic database records. Staff Searching interacts with the authority records and interfaces with multiple library subsystems, such as circulation, serials, and cataloging. It connects the system, local and wide area networks, and other computer systems via Z39.50.

Reports Manager

A simple new tool for standard reports, ready to use without the library staff having to know the database schema or SQL scripts and commands. Standard reports can be modified and saved for sharing with other library staff or other Dynix libraries.

Catałoging

provides tools that enable librarians to more easily maintain Horizon's bibliographic database. This module includes Z39.50 client software for interoperability, a MARC editor styled after a word processor, and a Best Seller/Hot Picks feature that flags the most popular items in the database.

Circulation

Simplifies check-in and checkout functions for your staff, as well as receipt-printer software, import/export of user data, notifications, a self-service checkout interface, a material handling interface, inventory control, and reciprocal borrowing. Also included in this module is Offline Circulation for backup functionality.

Serials Control

It has the capability to predict and receive publications. But it doesn't stop at prediction. Once the issue is received, your library can allow your users to search for the material either through Horizon Information Portal or have the item physically routed to the requester. Our Serials module has been fine tuned from predictions to claiming and more.

Acquisitions

enable your staff to order new items online and speed them into circulation via the X12, EDIFACT, and EDI ordering standards. Also included is an interface for obtaining electronic selections and use statistics.

VTLS

VTLS is the leading software in visionary technology for

libraries and is the premier tool in the market today for building and managing the digital resources of today's libraries.

Information is not only transmitted by words but also by photographs, slides, maps, posters, and videos, sound and movie just to name a few. By incorporating these into your digital collections, you are providing the public with a rich, new source of information to explore.

VITAL provides all types of institutions a way to broaden access to valuable resources that were once only available at one location to a select number of patrons. By eliminating the traditional limitations information seekers encounter, this technology grants equal access to materials for all, from professional researchers to recreational learners.

* Instant access to digital content anytime, from anywhere, to anyone with a web browser
* Tools to facilitate the digitization of all materials including, rare objects or historical documents
* Simultaneous access to diverse content and metadata through Fedora™ digital objects.

Based on Fedora™, the open source software and architecture upon which VITAL is built, VITAL provides every feature—storing, indexing, cataloging, searching, retrieving—required to handle large text and image rich content collections. VITAL takes advantage of technology standards such as XML, TEI, EAD and Dublin Core to easily describe and index an assortment of electronic resources.

VITAL builds on the Fedora™ repository architecture by providing VTLS developed work flow extensions, management utilities and enhanced searching capabilities. Using Fedora™ defined web services, VITAL provides a mechanism for your organization to create tools, enhance the functionality provided by VTLS, or leverage the open source community for future applications. Together, the package is known as VITAL.

As the only product of its kind on the market, VITAL

delivers a flexible and highly customizable solution for managing the digital resources of any type of information center.

VITAL Software and service options

At VTLS, we know that every institution's needs are unique—that's why we offer several different options for software and services.

1. The VITAL package
   * Fedora™ open source software (free)
   * VTLS software and hardware extensions, with features and work flows described above
   * VTLS installation, training, support, integration and documentation
2. The Fedora™ package
   * Fedora™ open source software (free)
   * VTLS installation, training, and support
3. A Hosted Solution where VTLS acts as an ASP service for either VITAL or Fedora™
4. VTLS Professional Digital Imaging Services and project consulting can be combined with any of the above to provide a solution tailored to your needs

VIRTUA

Virtua is an ILS (Integrated Library System) with visionary technology such as FRBR (Functional Requirements for Bibliographic Records), Update Notifications through SDI, User Reviews & Ratings—a peer review feature, and a Smart Device (PDA) interface to the catalog.

The Virtua ILS is the only system on the market that fully complies with the Unicode standard on both the client and server levels. Unicode is an integral part of Virtua's design. The system stores data natively in Unicode, a feature crafted for a shrinking world. With our system, users can import, catalog and display records in any language. Users can also change interface languages on-the-fly and store multiple scripts within the same MARC tag or sub-field.

Virtua is engineered for the flexibility and ease of use that library patrons and staff demand. Custom profiles can be created for each library and staff member, allowing or restricting access to over 600 functions throughout the system with the simple and intuitive Virtua System Client. Library staff may also customize the entire system by setting parameters in the System Client.

Scalability is one of Virtua's most attractive customer benefits. VTLS Inc. can provide a 4-user license or a 4,000-user license without compromising any of Virtua's functionality. Virtua's SLE - Small Library Edition is a multi-user system designed for a typical desktop or notebook PC that includes the Oracle Server, Windows client and the Chameleon Portal.

AutoLib

AutoLib - Integrated Library Automation Management Software has been designed, developed and promoted by M/s AutoLib Software System.

It has been designed and developed by a team of

- Library & Information Science specialists
- Database Administrators
- Software Developers and
- Network specialists

Designed to automate various activities of libraries in

- Universities
- Colleges
- Schools
- R&D Institutions
- Special Institutions
- Management Institutions
- Public Libraries etc. regardless of collection or size.

Available on various platforms

- Windows 95/98,2000 professional
- Windows NT/2000 server
- Novell Netware

Minimum Hardware Requirements

Server : Pentium III with 64/128 MB RAM, 10/20 GB HD FDD/CD-ROM/SVGA Monitor/LAN card and other accessories

OS : Windows NT 4.0 or Windows 2000 server

NODES : Pentium II/III/Celeron, 32/64MB RAM/4GB HD, monitor LAN card and other accessories

OS : Windows 95/98/workstation/2000 professionals

AutoLib - Integrated Library Automation Management Software Available versions

AutoLib - MS-Access version

AutoLib - MS-Access version with WEB enabled

AutoLib - MS-SQL version

AutoLib - MS-SQL version with WEB enabled

AutoLib - Public Library version

AutoLib - School Library version

Other Software

AutoLib - Digital Library

AutoLib - Article Indexing, Abstracting and Publishing(WEB module)

AutoLib - Journal Article Performance Analysis Reporter(JAPAR)

AutoLib Tools

Z39.50 software for searching remote database Export/ Import of data using ISO 2709 format using CCF/MARC tags Export/Import of data - to various database systems (text file/ Access/Foxpro/dBase/MS-SQL/Oracle)

dtSearch - a powerful text retrieval software from dtSearch Corpn. USA for Digital Library

AutoLib Software System is the authorized dealer in India for dtSearch products. For more details please visit dtsearch or send mail to autolib@yahoo.com

GRANTHALAYA

Granthalaya is an Indian package developed by INSDOC. It is based on MS DOS but is now available in UNIX and LAN versions also

Objectives

- To suit the requirements of different kinds of libraries.
- To promote IT in Library management at affordable price
- To provide maximum functionalities required by a librarian
- To suit the requirements of different kinds of libraries.
- To promote IT in Library management at affordable price
- To promote IT in Library management at affordable price
- To promote IT in Library management at affordable price.
- To promote IT in Library management at affordable price
- To provide maximum functionalities required by a librarian

Highlights

- Maintenance of members, groups, roles, basic information & receipts monitoring
- Periodical subscription, receipt, billing, payment & daily news paper monitoring.
- Accessioning the books, maintenance of selection committee list, picking the books required by the library from the list, billing & payments for books, stock verification
- Issue, return & renewal of books along with tracing of lost books.

- Searching books / periodicals on title, author, publisher or subject heading.
- Boolean search for books on title, author or publisher.
- Customized help on the package.

Security

- Access controlled through Login and password.
- Built-in privilege groups of users / operating staff.
- Access may be denied through membership module
- Bilingual Capabilities
- Works with NUDI 3.0 developed by Ganaka Parishat, Department of IT, Government of Karnataka and ISM 2000/ Leap office developed by CDAC. Can be customized to suit all Indian languages supported by ISM.

Other Features

- Web enabled query system supports search for books and other materials, request for new books, reader view about a book, List of books borrowed, readers statistics
- Technology
- Platform supported
- Works with Windows 98 / Windows XP / Windows 2000 Professional / Windows NT 4.0 / Windows 2000 Server.
- Back end Database: MS ACCESS / SQL Server.
- Bilingual Tool: NUDI 3.0/ISM 2000/ Leap Office 2000
- IDAMS for statistical data processing

CDS/ISIS

CDS/ISIS was developed by UNESCO in the year 1985 for information management in the libraries, information centers and archives at the national and international level. The software was originally written for a super computer, which was later on customized to be used on the other types of computers also.

CDS/ISIS is operational on MS DOSand Windows. It is

suitable for creating larger databases and the changes can be made in view of the local needs of libraries. CDS uses ISO 2709 for impor/export of data.

Hardware and Software Requirements

CPU-486 Processor at 40Mhz

(Pentium at 100Mhz or Higher)

RAM 8MB 1 Floppy Disk

1 Hard Disk (Min. 4MG Free)

1 VGA 640* 80 Colour Screen

(Super VGA 800*600 or Higher)

1 Printer, Windows 3.1 or Higher

CDS/ISIS is available in the following three versions:

- MS DOS Version
- UNIX Version
- Windows Version

SANJAY SOFTWARE

SANJAY is a package developed by NISSAT in collaboration with DESIDOC to help the libraries and centres in India to improve their house-keeping and service functions through automation. The package is totally menu driven and can be used even by non-professionals. The package was released for marketing in September 1995, and it has an installation base of many sites.

Main features of Sanjay Software are:

- Circulation Control
- Acquisition
- Online Cataloguing
- Report Generation

Hardware Needs

- PC XT or PC AT

- 32 MB RAM (minimum)
- 1 GB Hard Disk
- Monochrome or Colour Monitor
- Printer
- MS DOS 3-2 Version or above

LIBSYS

LibSys for library automation has been developed by a New Delhi based software company - Info-Tek Consultants Pvt. Ltd., engaged in providing software solutions for General Insurance and ERP/CRM since 1984. Its continuous growth for the last 12 years, has made LibSys a defacto standard for libraries in India. Its acceptance in global market further strengthens its popularity across the country as the most field proven library system in a wide spectrum of libraries with unmatchable depth in functionality and features.

With an open system architecture (3-tier) since its inception and its continuous transition from a host multi-user system to Client-Server implementation and finally a total web-based solution, makes LibSys an advanced multidimensional library system. A powerful and user friendly Web-OPAC along with Windows based OPAC, makes it an outstanding choice for a Library system.

LibSys handles Indian languages/scripts using ISM Publisher and GIST of C-DAC. There is an additional 'Unicode' support in LibSys that facilitates handling of both International and Indian languages/scripts

For a suitable platform for LibSys implementation - there are many possibilities such as WINDOWS (NT/2000/XP), UNIX (various flavours) and LINUX, giving a feel of open system for expandability and cross migration in future. Besides its own proprietary database handling capabilities, any preferred industry standard RDBMS such as SQL Server, ORACLE, MySQL etc. can be used as a back-end.

For a modern library having Electronic Surveillance Gate based security system installed, the SIP2 interface in LibSys supports various self check-out counters, Book drops stations, etc. based on RFID or any other advance technology. Adherence of LibSys to standards such as MARC and Z39.50 makes it suitable for cooperative networking and resource sharing. As LibSys can handle digital contents along with various multimedia files and electronic resources, implementation of a virtual library is a distinct possibility.

LibSys is an Integrated Library Management Software covering almost all the functions of a library in the following areas :

- Acquisition/Ordering
- Cataloguing
- Circulation
- Serials Control
- Article Indexing System
- OPAC (Online Searching of Bibliographic Information)
- Web OPAC

LibSys supports both print and nonprint materials. LibSys has various formats to describe each material type, using different fields with variable field lengths. It facilitates import/export of data in standard exchange format such as MARC as well as other formats. It provides on-line validation of input data prior to updating the database. Prompts and suitable messages are flashed when the data does not match and 'look-up tables' provides help as and when required. LibSys supports word based free text searching using Boolean operators. An efficient proprietory indexing feature substantially improve response time while searching for bibliographic information in large databases. The bibliographic database searching is integrated with the Circulation and Acquisition operations. In circulation operations, either bar-code or RFID technology may be employed for identification of both borrowers and materials. LibSys permits self check-out, book drop etc. based on SIP-2 standards.

LibSys has been written in 'C / C++'and 'Java' providing extremely user friendly interface during operations. Although LibSys is based on its own Bibliographic database, it is also available for environment using ORACLE (or SQL Server or MySQL) as back-end RDBMS. Full Graphical User Interface (GUI) front-end is provided for the windows client.

LibSys supports various electronic resources thus making it a modern system with virtual library implementation.Image and multimedia files can be integrated with LibSys search engine. They may be browsed in multi-windows interface with standard window features. Various formats handled by LibSys include Bitmap (.BMP), TIFF (.TIF), Wave (.WAV), Midi (.MID), Audio-visual Interface (.AVI), etc.

LibSys is providing the solution of a Union Catalogue to its users. Software is currently available to link these Union catalogues on-line.This facility of LibSys makes networking of libraries effective and promote the sharing of resources.

Presently LibSys is available as following two products:-

- A standard product with full fledged functionalities as usually required in universities, large academic institution, special libraries, public libraries, etc.
- A downsized product derived from LibSys4 for corporates, colleges and school libraries where some special functionality may not be requried.

However LSEase adequately meets the requirement of a modern growing library. Both LibSys4 and LSEase can be implemented in Client-Server mode providing complete range of features expected from any advanced library system. An effective workflow is provided through following integrated systems :- Acquisition / Ordering Cataloguing Circulation Serials Control OPAC (Online Searching of Bibliographic Information)

Following 'Add on' facilities are available in the standard LibSys4 and LSEase:-

- Making available OPAC on a browser of internet or intranetTo run the entire LibSys4/LSEase through a web browser. This Applet-Servlet implementation avoids loading of any software component on client machines
- Enables maintaining a mirror image of LibSys database on other server machine. Allows working on any database and simulatneously updates both the databases.
- Option provides handling data in unicode thus enabling support on various languages/scripts around the world including Regional languages in India.

Plateforms

There are many possibilities such as WINDOWS (NT/2000/XP), UNIX (various flavours) and LINUX, giving a feel of open system for expandability and cross migration in future. Besides its own proprietary database handling capabilities, any preferred industry standard RDBMS such as SQL Server, ORACLE, MySQL etc. can be used as a back-end.

SLIM++

SLIM++ is an integrated, multi-user, multi-tasking library information software for the Windows environment.

SLIM++ helps catalogue books, films, sound recordings, drawings, clippings, articles, reports, letters, pamphlets, serials publications... all those things that contain information so vital to your organization. SLIM++ cataloguing adheres to popular international standards. This means you can exchange data with the world. Retrieval of the data is simple, fast and efficient. Even a catchy phrase in the description of the catalogued item can be used for searching.

SLIM++ is designed and developed in modules to take care of complete functionality required for automating libraries. You can configure SLIM++ software for your library by selecting one or more of these standard and add-on modules.These modules exhibit features that make SLIM++ a top class software.

SLIM++ modules work on the same data from different nodes of a network. They can be installed independent of each other on different desktops. SLIM++ works just as well on a stand-alone machine as it does in a network of Computers. Moreover, your library can be browsed through the Internet / intranet with SLIM++.

NexLib - LIbrary Management System

NexLib is a full-featured library management system. It is Windows-based with simple point-and-click navigation; the system is easy and fun for library users and staff. NexLib is designed with a consistent, intuitive interface familiar to anyone who has used Microsoft Office. You can explore the entire system with just a few mouse clicks, yet behind the simple interface lies a powerful database engine capable of maintaining millions of records.

NexLib is designed to meet the needs of all information seekers. Academic researchers can search the entire library collections like, books, magazines, research reports, Company annual reports, CD materials etc. For the librarian, NexLib provides simple interfaces to catalog new books, manage users, create reports, and control budgets & acquisitions.

NexLib - Features

Search Module : The Search module in NexLib comes equipped with complex search capabilities. Users or an academic researcher, patrons will find the interface friendly, yet very powerful. Users can search the library or with few mouse clicks. Users can reserve books if they are not available. Search types include simple search by:

- title,
- author,
- keyword and

- subject

Librarians can create their own categories, such as materials for a certain course or books pertaining to a particular current event.

Classification: Search for books by classification and sub classification

Circulation Module

NexLib permits automatic notification of overdue. Librarians can perform almost any circulation task from one screen, including:

- Issues
- Returns
- Reserve
- Renew
- Advance Booking
- Reservation of Items by Users
- Request to acquire new items
- Collect or waive full or partial fines
- Renew all items issued to a user with a simple mouse click
- Issue items by hours/days/week/months
- Create an unlimited number of user types, such as Librarians,Faculty, Assistants, or Students, each with different privileges.

Cataloging Module

Cataloguers in school libraries and academic libraries alike appreciate the power and flexibility of the NexLib. Some of the Insignia Library Automation System cataloging features are:

- Predict Next due date
- Reader List
- Bind Serials
- Annual Reports

- CDs
- Audio & Video Cassettes etc

Acquisitions Module

NexLib Acquisitions module provides comprehensive collections control. Librarians can create budgets, allocate funds, and track them. The Acquisitions module is fully integrated with the Cataloging module. Some of the features of the acquisition system are:

- Acquisitions module is fully integrated with Cataloging module
- Keep track of funds
- Generate reports on orders and funds

OPAC - Online Public Access Catalogue

The Users in the library can search the database and find specific information online through the browser. The search facility also gives information about the availability of the item, including current status of individual copies of a title and reserve status. It also shows titles on order displaying current status in acquisition.

Online Catalogues

Online catalogue makes available following catalogues on-line:

- Title Catalogue
- Author Catalogue
- Subject Catalogue
- Classified Catalogue
- Keyword Search
- Publisher

Digital Image Management Module:

This module takes care of the management of the newspaper articles, research articles etc. Articles have to be scanned and image is assigned with certain parameters like brief description, keywords, date etc. through which the article can be searched in future.

Reports:

NexLib provides over 50 pre-defined reports covering all aspects of library management. Reports are divided into categories to make it easier to find the relevant report. These categories are: Users, Cataloging, Circulation and Miscellaneous. Reports and labels can be customized and viewed before printing.

6
Library and Information Networks

Network has become a very wide term now a days. It generally refers to the cooperative activity of man. There are as many networks in the society as are the fields of social activities. But the network we refer to here is about the coordination of the various information-providing agencies. Co-operation is a social activity as old as human civilization itself. The aim of any cooperation activity is to achieve what the members of the group can not achieve individually. So library cooperation or network may be defined as a combined effort of two or more libraries to share their resources for providing better services to their user community.

Networking for sharing the library and information resources can be traced to 200BC when Alexandria Library shared its resources with Pergamon Library. According to Kraus, there existed library co-operation among monastery libraries in the 13th century. There were exchanges of agreements among the universities of Lund, Abo and Greifswald as early as 1740. The other examples of library cooperation include a projected union catalogue of the libraries of Weimar and Jean and a proposal for a co-ordinated acquisition scheme for Walfenbuttel and Gottengen. The 'Catalogue of Manuscripts in various parts of India' complied by Whitney Stokes in 1868, and in 1863 Part I of Sanskrit manuscripts in private libraries of North-west provinces covering Varanasi was published. The first major union list entitled 'A Catalogue of Scientific and Technical Periodicals' was complied by Henry C.Bolton in 1885. With the advent of the 20th century, the Library of Congress started co-operative cataloguing projects and began working on the National Union Catalogue. Thereafter, in the 20th Century the compilations and publications of union catalogues of different types increased in number in most countries.

The first library cooperation activity in India is reported to be the Catalogue of Manuscripts complied by Whitney Stokes in 1868. Union catalogue development was one of major cooperative efforts in Indian libraries up to the 1960s. We can look at the following union catalogue development activities:

The 1960s also saw a large number of national seminars devoted to the concept of library cooperation. However, with the advent of computers in library work, a change occurred. It is reported that the first use of computer in library work for the production of the Union List of Serials in 1964 using the IBM/ 602 machine at INSDOC. Since then library automation has been a matter of primary importance in Indian Libraries. With the establishment of the National Informatics Center (NIC) in 1975 and the development of NICNET in 1977, networking and communication technology in India received a major boost. This as a whole had a major influence in resource sharing among various libraries and information centers through networks. In 1984, the working group of the Planning Commission. The 1990s are said to be the golden period of library networking in India. There has been a plethora of publications and seminars on library networking during this period. Today besides INFLIBNET, there are various local library networks in India such as ADINET, BONET, BALNET, CALIBNET, DELNET, MALIBNET, MYLIBNET, and PUNENET etc.

The efforts made for library networking in the 20th century began with the compilation of union catalogues, as no co-operation could be effective without the knowledge of the resources of other libraries. The scope of co-operations soon took big leap. It became diversified and incorporated the various activities of the libraries such as Abstracting and Indexing,

Acquisition, Bibliographic access, cataloguing, Circulations development, continuing education for staff and users, literature searching, management and accounting, microfilming, photo coping, processing, referral services, storage and union lists.

Resources sharing is sharing of library resources such as document collection, staff members, technical facilities and mechanical aids among the participating libraries on the basic principle of cooperation, "All for one and one for all". In this respect it is possible to consolidate the document collection of participating libraries, exchange their technical capabilities and share their services. In this way it is possible to share the resources to provide on access to the vast amount of library and information sources to a larger user community at the least-cost. The objective of resource sharing is obviously to make the greatest amount of best information available to the most users at the reasonable cost.

There has been a voluminous growth of published documents in the recent part. As a result no library in able to procure, process or store all documents that its users demand. According to Kent, it is difficult to anyone single library to acquire even one percent of the total document published in the world" due to one or more of the following reasons:

(i) Growth of Knowledge in different subjects

(ii) Rapid increase of literature and growth of publication

In the second half of the 20th century, the growth of new publication became unmanageable for traditional libraries. Its impact was felt primarily in major programs and later by the smaller libraries. In the field of Science and Technology alone about three million documents are published each year which includes articles, conference papers, books, technical reports and these the rate doubles every eight to ten years according to V.A. Kamath. There has been an alarming growth lately in journal articles.

Therefore some resource sharing is necessary between one

library and another library to acquire more information in a specific subject with low cost as published records are increasing at on incredible rate and their prices are keeping pace, is such circumstances library cooperation will assume a pivotal role and resources sharing will become the focal point of cooperation.

RESOURCE SHARING THROUGH NETWORKS

Earlier, the idea of resource sharing for a long time was restricted to the area of lending of books and periodicals. Now it has become diversified and incorporated the various activities of the libraries such as abstracting and indexing, acquisition, bibliographic access, Cataloging circulation, collection development continuing education for staff and user, literature searching management and accounting, microfilming photo coping , processing, referral services, storage and union lists. The resource sharing in modern times is helpful in the following four main activities.

The information on the web is growing and being updated every day. There are millions of web pages and there is a lot of great information. However, one of the most noticeable problems with the web today is the difficulty in finding a specific piece of information. Unlike a library, there is no central card catalog for the web and it follows no organizational standard. Instead, search tools are used to locate information on the web. For the most part, they are fast, easy to use and open 24 hours a day. A search tool performs searches of the Internet based upon input by the user. This input might include topics, keywords or phrases, or any other type of search criteria. Some of the difficulty in finding information is going away because the tools for locating information are maturing, becoming more powerful and sophisticated every day. Because of the enormous amount of information out there, search tools are indispensible.

There are numerous tools available for finding information on the web, and each of these operates somewhat differently. Some of the tools use a comprehensive approach and try to include all of the information on the web. Other tools only cover a narrow subject matter, for example, there is a tool specific for finding conferences sponsored by the Microsoft Corporation. The results of your search will depend on the type of search tool you are using. Because there is such a wide range of tools available and we cannot cover each of them, this module will focus on two representative tools

The past few decades have witnessed knowledge and information explosion the world over and inadequate financial resources to do the best in terms of dissemination of knowledge and information. Under these circumstances, resource sharing and cooperative functioning of libraries and information centres through networking becomes vital. Efficient resource sharing can be achieved by using recent advances in Information Technology, i.e. networking of libraries and information centres through Local Area Networks, Metropolitan Area Networks, Wide Area Network and so on.

Network of information/Resource sharing is to use the computer and telecom link for transmission of information or data from one library to another. Keeping this concept in view, various library networks have been established for cooperation and resource sharing among libraries. They have grown mostly during the last thirty years in different geographical environments in order to cater to the specific needs of users. In the United States, there has been a proliferation of them. Library networks in other countries are also growing. Several models have emerged that provide specific services. Not all networks conform to the essential functions of library networks. However, it is noted that the essential functions should include:

* promotion of resource sharing,
* creation of resource sharing tools like bibliographic databases such as union lists of serials, union catalogue of books, periodicals, bibliographic databases of articles and other types of materials such as CDs, Video recording, sound recording, theses, dissertations etc.,

* rationalization of acquisition,
* adoption of international standards for creation of records uniformly,
* delivery of documents, etc.

THE INDIAN SCENARIO IN RESOURCE SHARING

Economic pressures, growth of publications and emergence of subject specialization have compelled the libraries and information centres to think of sharing the information resources and optimizing the use of existing resources within India as well as from abroad through various networking systems. Some of the notable networks in India are NICNET, ERNET, SIRNET, INDONET and INET. In addition, there is a major initiative from the University Grants Commission called INFLIBNET, interconnecting universities, colleges and resource institutions countrywide.

National Level Resource Sharing

As stated earlier, INFLIBNET, a national level resource sharing of university libraries was set up in 1986 under Professor Yashpal Kapoor, the Chairman of UGC, INFLIBNET is a multiple functions/service network with focus on resource sharing and cooperation through computer communication links. It is very useful to all libraries and their readers. For this purpose, it is possible to create data banks in different subject fields, produce a number of bibliographical tools and information services. It is also possible to conserve a lot of library resource avoiding duplication at the national level.

But under the present conditions, it is not congenial to initiate a network of libraries at the national level, because all universities in India depend on the finance from central and state governments. The various universities have their own district characteristics based on factors such as geographical, linguistic and political. Each university library is following its own pattern and procedure in its routine work. For this reason, there is no uniformity and standardization. However, such a networking can be initiated in a limited environment, regional or state level.

State Level Resource Sharing

In India, formation of a network of university libraries in all states is possible only if the concerned administrative and professional staff and supporting agency make a sincere attempt in this direction. They should plan to co-ordinate programmes of all universities in the state to form a uniform academic calendar. They have to establish a body like Council of Higher Education to initiate a network of libraries in the state say KAULIBNET (Karnataka State University Library Network) in the interest of larger academic community. They should bring all the affiliated colleges within the fold of state level library network and extend the services to colleges.

It is not difficult to bring uniformity and adopt a standard procedure in all participating libraries within the state. After achieving the success in running the network at the state level, it is possible to link all such state level networks to the national level network. Further, it will not be difficult to link university libraries network with specialized networks in the field of library and information in India, using sophisticated modern technology and satellite facilities.

City Level Resource Sharing

Specialized library networks have come up for individual cities like DELNET, CALIBNET, MALIBNET, PUNENET, BALNET, ADINET, BONET, MYLIBNET, etc. These networks are meant essentially for providing a centralized database of library information to be accessed by its user libraries, mostly in a particular city for the purpose of resource sharing.

In the present day of limited resources, it is imperative that an integrated view of these networks and National Information Systems and Centres on the possibility of sharing resources among them should be taken to explore avoiding duplication of efforts, materials and resources and maximizing the utilization as they form the base for successful networking. Access through any network in the globe can be obtained virtually through INTERNET which is widely used international network.

INTERNATIONAL NETWORKS

Online Computer Library Center (OCLC)

Founded in 1967, OCLC is a nonprofit, membership, computer library service and research organization dedicated to the public purposes of furthering access to the world's information and reducing information costs. More than 45,000 libraries in 84 countries and territories around the world use OCLC services to locate, acquire, catalog, lend and preserve library materials.

Researchers, students, faculty, scholars, professional librarians and other information seekers use OCLC services to obtain bibliographic, abstract and full-text information when and where they need it. OCLC and its member libraries cooperatively produce and maintain WorldCat—the OCLC Online Union Catalog.

OCLC's objectives are to:

Establish, maintain and operate a computerized library network and to promote the evolution of library use, of libraries themselves and of librarianship, and to provide processes and products for the benefit of library users and libraries, including such objectives as increasing availability of library resources to individual library patrons and reducing the rate-of-rise of library per-unit costs, all for the fundamental public purpose of furthering ease of access to and use of the ever-expanding body of worldwide scientific, literary and educational knowledge and information. It is a unique cooperative venture, giving your library access to a wide range of services and databases, including WorldCat. Together OCLC member libraries make up the world's largest consortium.

OCLC's first offices were in the Main Library on the

campus of The Ohio State University (OSU), and its first computer room was housed in the OSU Research Center. It was from these academic roots that Frederick G. Kilgour, OCLC's first president, oversaw the growth of OCLC from a regional computer system for 54 Ohio colleges into an international network.

In 1977, the Ohio members of OCLC adopted changes in the governance structure that enabled libraries outside Ohio to become members and participate in the election of the Board of Trustees; the Ohio College Library Center became OCLC, Inc. In 1981, the legal name of the corporation became OCLC Online Computer Library Center, Inc. Today, OCLC serves more than 45,000 libraries of all types in the U.S. and 84 countries and territories around the world.

Products and Services

OCLC offers full-service online cataloging, simple copy cataloging, MARC record collections, offline cataloging, customized OCLC cataloging from your materials vendor, automated copy cataloging for materials purchased and custom cataloging services. It also administer the Dewey Decimal Classification system, the most widely used library classification system in the world.

Consortium of University Research Libraries (CURL)

CURL was established in 1983 to promote co-operation between academic research libraries in Great Britain and Ireland. The rich holdings of the CURL libraries are represented by catalogue records of varying types and quality, and there is a need to take the manual records, which are limited to local use, and make them universally available through electronic databases. This process is known in the library world as retrospective conversion.

The CURL database consists of approximately 18 million machine-readable catalogue records, of which 12 million have been contributed by its member libraries. In 1996 this database became accessible to members of the public through the CURL OPAC (Online Public Access Catalogue) which is available on the World Wide Web. However, the records of many collections within these great academic libraries, particularly those relating to older, scarcer material, remain hidden from view because they are still in manual form, and electronic access to these resources can only be achieved through the provision of machine-readable catalogue records.

In 1998, the Heritage Lottery Fund (HLF) agreed to provide some funding towards the cost of a feasibility study to investigate how public access to CURL resources could be widened through a programme of retrospective conversion of manual catalogue records to machine-readable form.

The aims of the feasibility study were:

* to detail which collections were appropriate to include in a retrospective conversion programme, taking account of local conversion projects already in progress, as well as the heritage value of collections
* to survey the manual catalogue records in CURL libraries, to assess the quality and form of the records and to consider the most appropriate methods for converting records
* to estimate the costs of retrospective conversion and suggest possible sources of funding
* to consider how readers would gain access to the wealth of books, pamphlets, maps and other heritage material which would be revealed by the electronic catalogue records.
* to The results of the study will form an important reference for the ddevelopment of business plans as the basis of bids to the HLF and other funding bodies for thc retrospective conversion programme.

This report forms the first stage of the feasibility study.

During the course of thise study, two major initiatives arose concerning retrospective conversion. The first was a commission to draw up a strategy for a national programme of retrospective conversion, carried out by UKOLN (UK Office for Library and Information Networking) and the National Council on Archives. Secondly, a major funding initiative arose in the form of a call for bids from the Research Support Libraries Programme (RSLP). CURL members were involved in various bids, both consortial and individual, and much valuable data was gathered which has been used to inform this study.

Thise study was undertaken by two consultants: Juliet Leeves (retrospective conversion options and methodology) and Stella Butler (funding and national initiatives), together with Anne Mealia, the CURL database officer, who collected and analysed the data from the CURL member libraries.

Methodology

Data collection for thise study was done in two stages. The first stage, carried out from October to December 1998, was a survey of all collections of printed materials in CURL libraries which still had manual catalogue records (see Appendix 2 for sample survey form). The second stage, carried out from January to March 1999, attempted to gather more detailed information about the collections by asking libraries to complete a template (see Appendix 3 for Stage 2 letter and template); this was followed up by a structured telephone interview to establish the suitability of the manual catalogue records for the different methods of retrospective conversion (see Appendix 4 for sample telephone interview form).

Mission

CURL's mission is to increase the ability of research libraries to share resources for the benefit of the local, national and international research community.

Vision

CURL will make a difference for researchers by helping to build the Distributed and Hybrid Research Library of the future.

Researchers, wherever in the world and whatever their disciplines, will be able to:

* Search, locate and request all resources, whatever their format, easily and quickly from the desktop
* Have quick and easy access to an increasing amount of electronic resources, both born-digital and digitised
* Have physical access to manuscripts, archives or printed items that have not been digitised and cannot be moved, wherever these are held
* Have other printed items from outside their own institutions delivered to them efficiently

CURL is committed to:

* Provide strong leadership to find research-centred solutions to common problems
* Influence change and provide a seedbed for innovative projects and services
* Provide practical tools for finding information
* Engage its membership to improve support for researchers
* Foster synergies through strategic alliances and collaborative partnerships that will benefit research support in the UK, Ireland and worldwide
* Help to shape the wider debate at national and international levels

The Consortium of University Research Libraries (CURL) has established a database for bibliographic records. This record retrieval service offers UKMARC records at competitive rates. The service can be accessed using telnet and ftp or via z39.50.

The database currently contains some 38 million records, and the number is growing constantly. The records include those from member libraries and also from LC (Roman script monograph records 1968- and CJK records) and from the BNB (1985-). As libraries progress their retrospective conversion programmes the number of records for older material and for non book material is increasing. The records are of good quality and CURL has established Bibliographic Standards for contributors and records are flagged to indicate standard.

The service is open to any non-profit organisation. There is a flat-rate for searching and no other charges. A month's free trial is available if required. Access is subject to signing licence agreements.

Other Database links and projects

* MARC21 Project
* National Online Public-Access Catalogue (COPAC)
* CURL feasibility study of Z39.50 technology
* CURL Database Project: A Feasibility Study for a National Programme of Retrospective Conversion of Catalogue Records
* CURL Minimum Standards for Bibliographic Records
* National Union Catalogue Feasibility Study

Library Information Networks (RLG) Research

Top of Form

Bottom of Form

The RLG Resources gives access to records of books, journal titles, manuscripts and archival material, music scores, maps, government publications, audiovisual material, art, and rare book auction catalogues and computer files. The material is contributed by over 200 research libraries, archives and museums, public and corporate libraries and learned societies. The RLG Resources include: - the RLG union catalogue for books (RLIN), artifacts and electronic material: Citation Resources (CitaDel), which includes a number of databasesand covers mostly journal articles, but includes sales catalogues (SCIPIO) as well as the English Short Title Catalogue.

The RLG individual databases listed below do not require a password if you are accessing on campus or accessing via dialup but DO need a password if accessing off-campus via an alternative ISP

Anthropology Plus: brings together into one resource the highly respected Anthropological Literature from Harvard University and Anthropological Index, Royal Anthropological Institute from the UK. Anthropology Plus provides extensive worldwide indexing of journal articles, reports, commentaries, edited works, and obituaries in the fields of social, cultural, physical, biological, and linguistic anthropology, ethnology, archaeology, folklore, material culture, and interdisciplinary studies. The index offers excellent coverage of all core periodicals in the field in addition to local and lesser-known journals. Coverage is from the late 19th century to the present

RLG's Archival Resources: provide centralized access for searching and retrieval of archival finding aids that have been encoded using SGML [Standard General Markup Language] and the emerging standard for Encoded Archival Description (EAD). The finding aids are indexed centrally at RLG but are supported in a distributed environment. Some reside on a server at RLG, others are located on other servers around the world. Archival Resources also includes access to RLG's AMC (Archival and Mixed Collections) file. AMC provides researchers with timely and comprehensive access to brief, high-level information for nearly half a million collections of manuscripts and archives, and has greatly enhanced the dissemination of information about the holdings in repositories around the world.

Index to Periodical Literature: The only comprehensive American index to the current periodical literature of architecture and design. The Avery surveys more than 2000 US and foreign journals, 75 percent of which are not indexed in any other source. It covers not only the international scholarly and popular literature, but also the publications of professional associations, US state and regional periodicals, and major serial publications in the architecture and design of Europe, Asia, Latin America, and Australia.

Art History Bibliography: The most comprehensive and up-to-date art history bibliography available, this file covers European and American art from late antiquity to the present, indexing art-related books, conference proceedings, dissertations, exhibition and dealer's catalogs, and articles in more than 2,500 periodicals from 1973 to the present.

This file covers Mexican-American topics and the broader Latino experience of Puerto Ricans, Cuban Americans, and Central American immigrants; it indexes all types of materials including journal articles, books, and newspaper articles published from the 1960s to the present, with selective coverage dating back to the early 1900s.

Descriptions and holdings information for letterpress materials printed in England or its dependencies (in any language) or in English (anywhere in the world) from 1473 to 1800.

Humanities & Social Sciences: An index to multilingual, multidisciplinary information in the humanities, social sciences, economics, religion, the history of art, and literature from 1984 to the present.

Scholarly evaluations of books, book chapters, articles, and conference papers in the field of Latin American studies published worldwide from 1990 to the present, indexed by the Hispanic Division, Library of Congress.

The definitive international bibliography for the history of science, technology, and medicine and its influence on culture from pre-history to the present. Journal articles, conference proceedings, books, book reviews, and dissertations from 1975 to the present are indexed in this file, which combines the Isis Current Bibliography of the History of Science, Current Bibliography in the History of Technology, the Bibliografia Italiana di Storia della Scienza and the Wellcome Library for the History and Understanding of Medicine.

The only online index to art periodicals that were published in the United States during the 19th century. Since entire journal contents are indexed — articles, art notes, illustrations, stories, poems, and advertisements — the index is a valuable source of information on popular culture and industry, as well as artists and illustrators, painting, sculpture, drawing, photography, architecture and design, exhibitions and sales, decoration, and collecting.

This file cites and abstracts books, manuscripts, dissertations, and articles from more than 19,000 periodicals covering Slavic studies and social sciences published primarily in Russia, the republics of the former Soviet Union and countries in Eastern Europe from 1986 to the present. Records are provided by INION: the Institute of Scientific Information on Social Sciences, Russian Academy of Sciences.

RLG Cultural Materials: is a collaborative effort from RLG member institutions, bringing together primary source materials in high-quality digital form. It contains maps, photographs, objects, documents, art, sound, and motion. Archives, libraries, and museums from around the world are making their treasured collections available through RLG Cultural Materials. The content reflects the richness of the human experience through time, high-quality digital versions of ancient maps, medieval manuscripts, handwritten letters, drawings, paintings, sound recordings, books, and moving images ? from prestigious memory institutions. Bringing these exceptional materials together encourages new kinds of multidisciplinary research. This database has separate password

The RLG Serials File: is a comprehensive database of primarily textual material such as journals, magazines, periodicals, newspapers, monographic series, some conference proceedings, annuals, yearbooks, annual reports, looseleaf, and electronic journals. Some formats and materials issued serially such as maps and computer files may be included.

INDIAN NETWORKS

Information and Library Network (INFLIBNET)

Information and Library Network (INFLIBNET) is regarded as a landmark in the information scenario of higher education. It is the brainchild of Prof. Yashpal, an eminent scientist and the former Chairman of the University Grants Commission. Incepted in the year 1988, INFLIBNET became operational in 1991 and got the status of an autonomous body in 1996.

INFLIBNET is now an Inter-University Centre of the University Grants Commission (UGC) of India. It is a major National Programme initiated by the UGC with its Head Quarters at Gujarat University Campus, Ahmedabad. Initially started as a project under the IUCAA, INFLIBNET is involved in modernizing university libraries in India and connecting them as well as information centres in the country through a nation-wide high speed data network using the state-of-art technologies for the optimum utilisation of information. INFLIBNET is set out to be a major player in promoting scholarly communication among academicians and researchers in India.

Objective of INFLIBNET

The objectives of INFLIBNET as envisaged in Memorandum of Association are:

* To promote and establish communication facilities to improve capability in information transfer and access, that provide support to scholarship, learning, research and academic pursuit through cooperation and involvement of agencies concerned.
* To establish INFLIBNET : Information and Library Network a computer communication network for linking libraries and information centres in universities, deemed to be universities, colleges, UGC information centres, institutions of national importance and R&D institutions, etc. avoiding duplication of efforts.

Functions of INFLIBNET

In order to fulfill the broad objectives, INFLIBNET will:

* Promote and implement computerisation of operations and services in the libraries and information centres of the country, following a uniform standard.
* Evolve standards and uniform guidelines in techniques, methods, procedures, computer hardware and software, services and promote their adoption in actual practice by all libraries, in order to facilitate pooling, sharing and exchange of information towards optimal use of resources and facilities.
* Evolve a national network interconnecting various libraries and information centres in the country and to improve capability in information handling and service.
* Provide reliable access to document collection of libraries by creating on-line union catalogue of serials, theses/ dissertations, books, monographs and non-book materials (manuscripts, audio-visuals, computer data, multimedia, etc.) in various libraries in India.
* Provide access to bibliographic information sources with citations, abstracts etc. through indigenously created databases of the Sectoral Information Centres of NISSAT, UGC Information Centres, City Networks and such others and by establishing gateways for on-line accessing of national and international databases held by national and international information networks and centres respectively.
* Develop new methods and techniques for archival of valuable information available as manuscripts and information documents in different Indian Languages, in the form of digital images using high density storage media.
* Optimise information resource utilization through shared cataloguing, inter-library loan service, catalogue production, collection development and thus avoiding

duplication in acquisition to the extent possible.

* Enable the users dispersed all over the country, irrespective of location and distance, to have access to information regarding serials, theses/dissertations, books, monographs and non-book materials by locating the sources wherefrom available and to obtain it through the facilities of INFLIBNET and union catalogue of documents.
* Create databases of projects, institutions, specialists, etc. for providing on-line information service.
* Encourage co-operation among libraries, documentation centres and information centres in the country, so that the resources can be pooled for the benefit of helping the weaker resource centres by stronger ones.
* Train and develop human resources in the field of computerised library operations and networking to establish, manage and sustain INFLIBNET.
* Facilitate academic communication amongst scientists, engineers, social scientists, academics, faculties, researchers and students through electronic mail, file transfer, computer/audio/video conferencing, etc.
* Undertake system design and studies in the field of communications, computer networking, information handling and data management.
* Establish appropriate control and monitoring system for the communication network and organise maintenance.
* Collaborate with institutions, libraries, information centres and other organisations in India and abroad in the field relevant to the objectives of the Centre.
* Create and promote R&D and other facilities and technical positions for realising the objectives of the Centre.
* Generate revenue by providing consultancies and information services.
* Do all other such things as may be necessary, incidental

or conducive to the attainment of all or any of the above objectives.

Activities of INFLIBNET

Database Development and Management

* Provide reliable access to document collection of libraries i.e. Union Catalogues etc.
* Provide access to world wide bibliographical information.
* To maintain consistency and quality in databases created by the participating libraries
* Evolve standards, uniform guidelines, methods, and procedures, both for data capturing as well as Hardware and Software.

Major Activities

Development, managing and updating of Union databases is one of the major activities of this group. Eight databases have been developed and are continuously growing. Following is the list of databases:

- Books - Represents holding of participant libraries under the programme
- Theses - Doctoral theses submitted to various Indian universities till date
- Serial Holdings - Holdings information of various university libraries about the serial
- Current Serials - Currently subscribed journals by the universities
- Secondary Serials/CD-ROMs
- DDC Serials - Currently subscribed journals by the six universities identified as DDC
- Experts - Useful data about specialists in various disciplines
- Research Projects - Information about ongoing projects

NISSAT Project - Experts Database (Science & Technology)

Group also proposes to create and develop other databases of national importance viz.

- Patents
- Manuscripts
- Technical Reports
- Non-Books Materials

Standards and Formats required for creation of Databases

1. Guidelines for Data Capturing a user manual

To maintain consistency and quality in databases prepared by the libraries and INFLIBNET, INFLIBNET Centre had constituted a taskforce consistency experts in this area. This taskforce has brought out a 100 pages documents entitled GUIDELINES FOR DATA CAPTURING : A USER MANUAL. This documents is prepared based on Common Communication Format (CCF), 1992 edition and same has been given participating libraries for adoption. Taskforce also studies other standard required for this activity and according recommended that the following may also be used

1. Anglo American Catalogue Rules. Edition 2nd revised
2. Library of Congress Subject Heading

2. SOUL Guidelines for Data Capturing: A user manual for books

This is designed to be a handy manual to create records in SOUL. The user guide lists all bibliographical elements covered in the SOUL, with complete description of each field and subfields. It also provides guidelines as per AACR - 2 as to how to render the information in each field and subfield with examples.

Creation and Maintenance of Authority File

INFLIBNET is suggesting libraries to use Library of Congress Subject Headings as LCSH as a standard for providing subject headings, INFLIBNET is going create and maintain the authority files of names and subject headings in the machine readable form and it will be linked with the Union Catalog and Library Automation S/w SOUL developed by INFLIBNET.

A few more standards required for the participating libraries and INFLIBNET Centre are being developed.

Infrastructure

Well equipped laboratory with latest Pentium/RISC computers running on different operating systems like DOS, Windows 95/2000

Development tools: CDS/ISIS Ver. 3.08 (DOS version)

RDBMS: Databases were loaded on Microsoft SQL Servers on SYBASE Adaptive server.

Database Research and Development

Creation of union databases of books, serials, theses etc has been one of the major objectives of INFLIBNET and the Database Research and development group has been setup to address the problems involved in the development, maintenance, updating of these union databases. Development of software tools for converting data from one format to another, effective retrieval and managing the databases are the major areas of work undertaken by this group. Future planned activities include research and development of retrieval software for multilingual, multimedia and full text databases. Distribution of databases through the medium of CDROM is also going to become a thrust area for database research and development group.

Major Activities

* Database design, analysis and technical support.
* Assisting participating libraries in database development.
* Development of utilities for database creation, conversion and maintenance in different formats like CCF and MARC 21 etc.

* Development of retrieval software for CD-ROM based bibliographic Databases.
* Development of Utility tools for Retrospective conversion of union catalogues.
* Development of software tools for Multilingual Database of union catalogues.
* Administration (routine jobs like backup, tuning and implementation of security policies etc) of Union Database servers in the Centre.

Future areas of research and development

Further research and development in the areas of

- Retrieval software for CDROM databases
- Retrieval software for multilingual databases
- Retrieval software for textual and non textual databases
- Software for effectively managing union database systems
- Retrieval software for union databases
- Software for automatic backup, performance tuning
- Algorithms for effective searching and sorting and compressing data.

Infrastructure

Well-equipped lab with latest Pentium/RISC computers running different operating systems like Windows 95/98/2000/XP, LINUX, HP UNIX.

Development tools: Microsoft Visual studio, SDK.

RDBMS: Microsoft ACCESS, Microsoft SQLSERVER 7.0/2000, ORACLE 8i/9i,SYBASE Adaptive Server.

E- Education

E-Education Group is concerned with the R & D and keeps abreast with latest technological changes in the area of computer technology. This group was established sometime in August 2001 and is responsible to implement Web-Based Training (WBT) to technocrats and Professionals. Various e-learning training courses will be launched with the help of HRD group of the Centre. This group will provide the necessary tools and technologies to deliver the e-learning courses.

This group is promoting R & D activities in area of e-learning. One of the major objective of this group is to collaborate with Universities/colleges for setting / managing e-learning lab for various training/e- courses. Consultancy is provided for starting the e-learning activities and also to selecting the H/W, Software combinations etc. Guidelines and suggestions for effective and optimized use, administration, maintenance and timely starting the Web-Based Training are also can be obtained from the Group.

Major Activities

* The Group is concerned with all the technical and non-technical issues related to e-learning in general and Web Based Training in particular.
* Plan, evaluate, implementation, review of e-learning policies, models, soft wares and technology.
* Setting up e-learning Lab at INFLIBNET premises.Development of retrieval software for CD-ROM based bibliographic Databases.
* Exploring various options regarding e-learning.
* Preparation of analysis, and minimum critical resources.
* Development of various disaster scenarios and formulation of a framework for the plan coverage.
* Assessment, preparation and recommendation of system requirements for e-learning set up.
* Analysis of proposals from Techno-major (e-learning vendors) and recommendations for selection of the solution.
* Discussions with technocrats on technical and feasibility issues.

* Planning, preparation and recommendations for e-learning preparation work and infrastructure for the set up.
* Preparation of road map for e-learning activities for the coming next few years.
* Further area of research and development
* Implementing e-Learning at all levels at INFLIBNET.
* Collaboration with subject-matter-expert from colleges/ universities for contents to be made available free to academic communities from content sever at INFLIBNET
* Setting up and starting e-learning software R & D facility equipped with state-of-the art technology at the centre.
* Providing consultancy and Guidance to the R & D Institutions/ universities / colleges wishing to work with INFLIBNET.
* Design and Development of e-learning Model.
* Knowledge Management techniques and sharing, manage knowledge with other national organisations.
* Exploring technology to implementing Digital Library (DL) and Knowledge Management (KM).

HUMAN RESOURCE DEVELOPMENT

To enhance the skills of University Library staff for implementation of INFLIBNET Programme, following training courses are conducted.

One month Training Programme

This is mainly meant for operational staff of libraries. They are given exhaustive training on application of computers to library and information services. Eighteen such programmes were held covering most of the universities, and around 350 persons have been trained.

On-site Training

Staff from INFLIBNET Centre visited 31 universities, and

conducted training for the library staff members for a week initiating automation process.

ILMS Training

Ten Librarians from different universities spent a week at INFLIBNET to solve their problems in using ILMS.

SOUL Training

Soul was installed at 66 Libraries and onsite training of one week to the library staff was provided at each site.

CALIBER

It is an annual convention held every year in collabration with a university in different region on a theme related to library automation. Nine such conventions have been held so far.

Works Resource Sharing through Network

Workshops

Six workshops for senior level staff viz. University Librarians and Deputy Librarians were conducted.

Networking of university libraries present networking environment

Currently libraries funded under the programme are advised to subscribe to one of the following networks, depending on the availability in the respective locations:

* ERNET
* VSNL
* NICNET
* Other ISPs

Wide Area Network

It is planned to setup a Wide Area Network "UGCNET" linking more than 170 universities and other acedemic institutes in the country.

Local Area Network

INFLIBNET Centre has suggested all the funded universities to set up LANs using HUB/SWITCH and CAT V cables within their libraries for successful installation of SOUL software. Since SOUL is based on client/server architecture, It is essential that the server and all other nodes be connected by LAN.

INFLIBNET Centre desires that each university should establish a LAN in it's campus linking all the departments including library.This LAN in turn will be connected to the WAN.

Library Management Software:

For the automation of in-house functions of participating university libraries, INFLIBNET Centre has developed a user friendly state of the art GUI based software named ' SOUL' SOftware for University Libraries. This is based on Client/Server Architecture. It uses an robust RDBMS as back end tool. This works on Windows and Windows NT environment with a number of new features.

LIBRARY SOFTWARE MANAGEMENT

Utility Softwares:

Following utility softwares developed at the Centre are available to the universities on request.

* To search the data from union databases (OPAC).
* Catalogue card generation.
* Duplicate checking of records.
* Customised software for Books, Theses, Serials.
* Data Conversion from Dbase, Foxpro and text file to ISO-2709 format.

Major objective of this group is to develop software for Library automation and other supporting tools for library automation. This group is also involved in supporting all other activities of the center by providing adequate software help time to time. The mission of this group is to provide technological support to all activities of the center with software developments using latest technologies and available development tools.

Major Activities

Development, managing and updating of Union databases is one of the major activities of this group. Eight databases have been developed and are continuously growing. Following is the list of databases:

* Development of SOUL
* Incorporation of Various Bibliographic standards in SOUL
* Constant Update of Current version based on user requirements
* Trouble Shooting and Customer support for SOUL users

Future Plans

* Development of fully web based library management system
* Incorporation of Multilingual Interface (To be developed by Database R & D Group) in SOUL
* Incorporation of Data Conversion Utilities (To be developed by Database R & D Group) for conversion of Various Bibliographic format including MARC and CCF in to SOUL
* Development of MARC 21 based database creation tool.

Infrastructure

Working Platforms of this group:

Operating Systems

Windows 95,Windows 98,Windows NT 4.0, Windows 2000 RDBMS MSSQL Server 6.5,MS SQL Server 7.0, MS SQL Server 2000, Sybase 11.5,Oracle 9i

Development Tools

PowerBuilder 6.0, Microsoft Visual Studio 6.0,Microsoft

Visual Studio. Net (beta), Oracle Internet developer suite.

WEB DEVELOPMENT

Organization of vast information present on the Centre's website and making the website a resource gateway and a knowledge hub, to the user community is one of the main objectives of the INFLIBNET Centre. The web development group setup in promoting the access to the information in the field of research and academic pursuit by using latest web technologies is working towards in implementing this objective. The major areas of work undertaken by this group are to select, organise and present the quality resources of the Centre in a meaningful way that will be useful for the user community.

Major Activities

* INFLIBNET Site design and updating.
* Promoting the website of the centre and provide a complete tracking reports of users accessing the website.
* Maintenance of various web services running at the site.
* Identifying the Hardware, Software requirements in improving the Centre's Infrastructure with the latest available technologies.
* To install and provide support for the available software at the Centre and advice the participating libraries with regard to hardware and software requirement.
* Bringing out SOUL software CD's for all the versions i.e. SOUL network version, SOUL Standalone version & SOUL Demo version.

Future areas of development

Setting up an Intranet for managing the internal information of the Centre.

Infrastructure

Well equipped with Pentium-IV systems running windows 98/2000 and Linux operating systems. The web server is hosted on a Pentium-IV system and is likely to switch over to a rack-mount machine. There is one CD writer to burn the SOUL software CD's.

This group has been created for promoting R & D activities in area of Networking and Quality management. Major responsibility of this group is to manage, maintain and timely update the campus wide Network. One of the major objective of this group is to coordinate with UGC-NETWORK, the proposed wide area network connecting all academic institutions under University Grants Commission for setting/managing data centre for various databases of INFLIBNET, Indian universities, Information Centres. This group is working progressively for implementing Total Quality Control (TQC) for in-house developed softwares. Training /workshop in the area of network management, security design and state-of-the-art technologies for library professionals across the country is being initiated by the group. Consultancy work in the area of networking, network security of universities/colleges library is also going to become thrust area of this group.

Major Activities

- LAN/WAN Setup and maintenance at INFLIBNET.
- Assisting Universities/colleges for Campus LAN.
- Design network security policy.
- Network Traffic management.
- Network resources allocation to the other groups.
- System administration, configuration and tuning.
- Database administration and tuning.
- Disaster recovery plan for e-resources.
- System maintenance at Centre.
- Testing and Quality control of software developed at the centre.
- Guidelines, suggestions and standards to all development groups for maintaining quality.

Future areas of research and development

Further research and development in the areas of

- Upgrading Local Area Network (LAN) with FC backbone, Layer-2, Layer-3 switches.
- Collaboration with UGC-NETWORK for setting / managing data centre for various databases of INFLIBNET, Indian universities and Information Centers.
- Setting up network R & D and quality control Lab. equipped with state-of-the-art technology at the Centre.
- Offering consultancy service to the universities / colleges for computersing the libraries including H/W, Local Area Network (LAN).
- Designing the Network security and disaster recovery plan for data servers.
- Knowledge sharing with different national and international organization.
- Promoting Linux operating system in universities.
- Insuring implementation of different standards for software development and management.
- Software testing using advanced software available in the market.

Infrastructure

Well-equipped server lab. with P3 and P4 Servers running on Windows NT/ 2000 Advance Server. Separate mail server is running on Linux. Network is protected by firewall running on Linux. Centre has 128 kbps-leased lines Internet connectivity. Currently LAN at Centre is based on Radio Modem, CISCO 2610 router, hubs. New high End RISC server is being added to the existing infrastructure.

INFONET

Indian Universities constitute one of the largest higher education systems in the world. With 325 universities/institutions,

15000 affiliated colleges, 100.00 lakh students and 4.27 lakh teachers; it is a great challenge to ensure effective coordination and communication.

Fast changing curricula and frequent introducing of new subjects impose a great demand on the system in general. Indian Universities need to be given the required thrust to entire the third millennium with a leading edge.

Technology is a driving force in the contemporary education systems. University Grant Commission has launched an ambitious programme to bring about a qualitative change in the academic infrastructure, especially for higher education. Under this initiative UGC is modernizing the University Campuses with State-of-the-art campus wide networks and setting up its own nationwide communication network named UGC-Infonet.

ERNET India, scientific society under the Ministry of Communications and Information Technology, in partnership with the University Grants Commission is setting up UGC-Infonet. Under this programme it is proposed to use information and communication Technology (ICT) and Internet to transform learning environment from a mono-dimensional one to a multi-dimensional one. UGC-Infonet will be a boon to the higher education systems in several ways:

- UGC-Infonet will become a vehicle for distance learning to facilitate spread of quality education all over the country.
- UGC-Infonet will be a tool to distribute education material and journals to the remotest of areas.
- UGC-Infonet will be a resource for researchers and scholars for tapping the most up-to-date information.
- UGC-Infonet will form a medium for collaboration among teachers and students, not only within the country but also all over the world.
- UGC-Infonet will be an Intranet for University Automation.

- UGC-Infonet will encompass entire University Systems for most efficient utilization of precious network resources.
- UGC-Infonet will establish a channel for Globalisation of Education and facilitate the universities in marketing their services and developments.

Intranet for Universities

Availability of Reliable and Stable network infrastructure will facilitate increased usage of computers in the University Campuses. Campus Management will be more efficient and student friendly. Interlinking of the universities will expand the reach of students and faculty to other universities providing them with better avenues for wider horizontal growth.

UGC-Infonet will establish a seamless link between the UGC and the universities. This will help to provide a more accurate and up-to-date picture of the Universities, while at the same time it will enable universities to have timely information about the various schemes of the UGC. Consequently, this will bring a qualitative change in the UGC-Universities interaction. The huge and multifaceted Indian Education Systems would achieve greatest efficiency through e-governance of UGC.

Technology Partnership

Information Technology is evolving at a rapid pace worldwide to cater to the need for providing information in any form, at any anywhere. The trend is to set up networks, which are device independent, thus enabling flexibility of access, and also meet the requirements arising out of codependence technologies. Regular technology inputs would be required to upgrade the network infrastructure to ensure delivery of upcoming applications and contents to the education and research community in the country. UGC and ERNET have come together to meet the challengers that may face the education community with respect to real time information.

Implementation Methodology

The UGC-Infonet will be overlaid on ERNET Infrastructure in a manner so as to provide assured quality of service and optimal utilization of bandwidth resources. The network will be run and managed by ERNET India. The project will be funded by UGC with 100% capital investment and up to 90% of recurring costs. Towards this end, a MoU has been signed between UGC and ERNET India for implementation of UGC-Infonet and also for long-term technology partnership. A joint technical and tariff committee, consisting of leading experts in the country has also been setup to guide and monitor the design, implementation and operations of UGC-Infonet. INFLIBNET, an autonomous IUC of the UGC, would be the nodal agency for coordination of the UGC-Infonet and facilitate linkage between ERNET and the Universities. In the long run, each University will become a hub for the colleges affiliated to it.

Network Architecture

UGC Infonet is based on open IP platform, employing state-of-the-art technologies like IP or TV, enabling on-line response to queries. Open system architecture will ensure support for current and future applications. Users from educational Institutions would enjoy high data rates while accessing Intranet and Internet resources.

Main features of the UGC-Infonet are:

- Scaleable Architecture to grow from Universities to affiliated Colleges
- Nation-wide Terrestrial Backbone using Fiber Optic links
- Integrated Satellite WAN supporting broadband and SCPC VSAT technology
- Comprehensive Network Management Systems for overall monitoring of the network, down to each and every device.
- Linkage with other Academic and Research Networks all over the world.

- Data security and virus protection using firewalls and Intrusion Detection Systems
- Dedicated Data Center for Web hosting, e-Journals and Mail Boxes.
- Mirror sites spread all over the country for content hosting.
- Broadband Multimedia and Video Channels for Distance Learning

Data Center

A data center with large server capacity is being set up for the UGC-Infonet., Content of common interest will be maintained at this data center. Each University will have the option of hosting their website and the journals subscribed through University Consortia.

The data center will be:

- dedicated for the UGC-Info Net
- comprising of Email, Web, News and Proxy Servers
- protected with firewalls and IDS
- co-located with Satellite Hub
- within single hop access to the Universities over VSAT
- hosting a Portal on Higher Education in India

Electronic Subscription of Journals

With globalisation of education and competitive research, demand for journals has increased over the years. Due to insufficient funds, libraries have been force to cut subscriptions of journals.

UGC has turned towards the Internet to cover the gap between demand and supply by way of e-journals that can be subscribed online. Most of the journals are available in electronic form.

UGC is also exploring the possibilities of alliances with publishers for adapting a consortia-based approach for e-subscription of journals. These journals will be available over

UGC-Infonet to all the universities. Much of the new research publications are also available on the net as free ware, thereby, making quality information accessible to a wider academic scholar base spread across the country at an affordable price.

Connectivity Options for the Universities

UGC-Infonet is overlaid on ERNET Infrastructure including a nation wide terrestrial backbone and a complimentary satellite Wide Area Network (WAN). As such ERNET can provide a complete range of connectivity options to the universities depending upon their location and bandwidth requirements. Since terrestrial media offers greater scalability and performance, efforts will be made to connect the universities on terrestrial media. Alternately a Satellite connection will be provided through VSAT.

Digital Leased Lines

In the localities where telecom network is well developed, dedicated leased lines will be hired from basic telecom service providers. Such links are primarily for 64 Kbps and 2 Mbps speeds. Since fiber optic connections facilitate better connectivity, efforts will be made to bring the fiber links as near to the universities as possible. Most of the universities have the potential to become hubs of communication for affiliated colleges. Therefore, basic service providers will be locating their terminal within the university premises.

The universities, located within 30 kms of the ERNET PoPs, will be provided with dedicated radio links operating from 64 Kbps to 2 Mbps speeds. These links require line of sight clearance between the network node and the concerned university. Radio links are very reliable and their operational cost includes only maintenance of the equipment and Radio Link a nominal license fee.

Satellite based Wide Area Network

ERNET operates a Satellite based Wide Are Network

(SATWAN) using C-Band transponder on INSAT-3C. SATWAN hub, located at Bangalore, supports Broadband VSATs with up to 45 Mbps shared bandwidth and Single Channel Per Carrier (SCPC) VSATs capable of providing up to 2 Mbps dedicated bandwidth.

Broadband VSAT

Most of the remote universities will be served using Broadband VSATs. These VSATs operate in a shared bandwidth mode for optimal utilization of the precious satellite resources. Since Internet traffic is asymmetric in nature Broadband VSATs are optimized to receive high bandwidth (shared beam of up to 45 Mbps) and relatively smaller capacity for outgoing traffic (shared channel of up to 307 Kbps) from a University.

SCPC VSATs

Single channel Per Carrier (SCPC) VSATs will be used for establishing dedicated tow-way channels of 64 Kbps to 2 Mbps from Hub. SCPC VSATs are ideal for those universities which are located in remote areas but wish top host their own internet server for providing access to their information through internet all over the world.

Campus LANs at Universities

Infrastructure at the University campus is also critical to take full advantage of the UGC-Infonet. Campus LAN technology is evolving rapidly and many universities may not have the expertise to setup the most modern and cost effective LANs. ERNET India has participated with many institutions in the planning and implementation of their campus computing facilities. The expertise generated thus will be extended to the Universities so that every university can have a state of the art infrastructure.

Network Access Center

For maximum benefits of UGC-Infonet, Universities should preferably set up a campus wide network and ensure uniform access all over the campus. Wherever campus LAN is not in place, it is suggested that the university sets up a network access center, which is open to all students at the university. This will work on lines similar to the terminal in traditional computer centers.

Network-Trained Manpower

Trained manpower is one of the most critical resources for successful implementation of high-tech programmes like UGC-Infonet. ERNET India has setup a modern training laboratory to train network system managers and users of UGC-Infonet. Technical staff from each of the participating universities will be trained to take maximum advantage of the infrastructure.

University Grants Commission

The University Grants Commission (UGC) is a statutory organisation established by an act of Parliament. This is a national body for the coordination, determination and maintenance of standards of University education. The UGC serves as a vital link between the Union and State Governments and the institutions of higher training. In addition to its role of giving grants to universities and colleges, the UGC also advises Central and State Governments on the measures necessary for the improvement of university education. It also frames regulations on various issues like the minimum standards of instruction and minimum qualifications of teachers, on the advice of subject specialists and academicians with whom it frequently interacts in connection with the formulation, monitoring, and evaluation of programmes.

294 Universities/institutions in the country are directly under the preview of UGC. The universities are uniformly spread all over the country from metropolitan cities to very remote areas.

Implementation and operation of UGC-Infonet will be coordinated by INFLIBENT, an autonomous Inter-University Center of the University Grants Commission of India. INFLIBENT is providing a variety of services to the academic community of the country and is helping libraries in their automation efforts. About 142 University libraries are on the way to computerization.

ERNET

ERNET India, and autonomous scientific society under Ministry of Communications and Information Technology, is providing Internet access to Education and Research community in the country for over 10 years. ERNET is a nation-wide terrestrial and satellite network with points of presence located at leading education and research institutions in major cities. ERNET infrastructure is a judicious mix of satellite and terrestrial networks ideally suited for the Education and Research community in the country.

ERNET has pioneered the Internet revolution in the country. Way back in 1986 ERNET started as an R&D programme of the Government of India and UNDP, with the objective of enhancing the national capabilities in the area of computer communications and networking. After successful completion of the R&D phase, ERNET became an Autonomous Scientific Society under the then Department of Electronics (now Department of Information Technology), to provide the best network resources to the Indian academic community. Marching towards this goal, ERNET India is participating with UGC for implementation of the UGC-Infonet.

Apart from providing computer network infrastructure for the academic community ERNET is playing a role of total service provider for various institutions. ERNET provides High End education in the area of computer networking, undertakes R&D for evolving newer solutions and also assists universities in establishing their in campus infrastructure. Content provision is a major thrust area for ERNET. ERNET has designed and made operational many portals to supplement the information for students and teachers alike.

In this era of globalization and hyper-competition, the

concept of teaching has under gone sea change. Learning and dissemination of information is becoming more important. Internet based education and e-learning are the trends of the day. In what it is described, as the first effort of its kind in the country, the then Department of Electronics had initiated a project "ERNET" with the funding from UNDP. The objective was to create expertise R&D and education in the country in the area of networking and Internet in the country. ERNET is dedicated to the above objective for the last 15 years.

Today ERNET is largest nationwide terrestrial and satellite network with point of presence located at the premiere educational and research institutions in major cities in the country. Focus of ERNET is not limited to just providing connectivity, but to meet the entire needs of the educational and research institutions by hosting and providing relevant information to their users. Research and Development and Training are integral parts of ERNET activities.

Developing Library Network (DELNET)

Delnet started as a network of libraries in Delhi in 1988 and was named as Delhi Library Network. It is the first operational library network in India. It was initiated as a project of the India International Centre with the financial and technical assistance by National Information System for Science and Technology (NISSAT), Department of Scientific and Industrial Research, Govt. of India. It was registered as a society in June 1992 under the Societies Registration Act of 1860 and is currently being promoted by the National Informatics Centre (NIC), Planning Commission, Govt. of India and India International Centre, New Delhi.

Delhi is growing as a major centre of information resources in India. These resources cater both to the specialized and the general users. They are located in activities, information and documentation centres, institutional libraries, research libraries, government libraries, public libraries, department libraries besides the libraries of the universities, colleges and schools.

During the recent years, increase in information has led to increase in the demands of the users. It has been noticed that in this area of information explosion, libraries in India are generally ill-equipped to handle and retrieve information effectively, the financial resources and the space requirement for housing library collection are limited in almost all of the libraries. No a single library can afford to house every necessary document even in the area of its interest. Resource sharing, thus assumes great importance at this juncture the option left with the forward looking librarians has been to promote the sharing of resources by automation and networking. With this objective, in January 1988, the India International Centre initiated efforts for the establishment of Delhi Library Network (Now Developing Library Network).

The following are DELNET's main objectives:

* to promote sharing of resources among the libraries by developing a network of libraries, by collecting, storing and disseminating information and by offering computerized services to the users.
* to offer guidance to the member libraries on cataloguing database services, circulation, acquisition, serials control, online services, selection of hardware and software, etc.
* to coordinate efforts for suitable collection development and reduce unnecessary duplication wherever possible.
* to establish a referral centre, to monitor and/or facilitate catalogue search and maintain a central online union catalogue of books, serials, and non-book materials of all the participating libraries.
* to facilitate and promote delivery of documents manually and mechanically.
* to develop specialist bibliographic database of books, serials and non-book materials.

* to develop a database of projects, specialists and institutions.
* to possess and maintain electronic and mechanical equipment for fast communication of information and delivery of electronic mail.
* to coordinate with other regional, national and international networks for exchange of information and documents.
* To undertake facilitate and provide for the publication of newsletters/journals devoted to networking and sharing of resources.

Membership

At present, DELNET has **over five hundred** libraries as its members, including both institutional and associate-institutional members: in India 235 and outside India 8.

Fees Details: Following are the fees details for its members Admission Fee : Rs.5,000

Institutional membership : Rs.7500/- per year (For libraries with 10,000 or more book collection)

Associate institutional membership : Rs.10,000/- per year (For libraries with less than 10,000 books)

Overseas Institutions : Admission fee : US $100/-

Annual Membership fee : US $500/-

The membership is progressively increasing and includes universities, diplomatic missions, college, government department, institutions and public libraries. Some institutions from far off places like Shimla, Bhopal, Punjab, Andhra Pradesh, Lucknow and Pondicherry in India have also joined DELNET as members. DELNET's membership has increased from 103 in Feb'99 to 243 to date (August, 2001).

DELNET Activities/Services

(I) Promotion of Database Creation

For effective networking, standard bibliographic data

should be available in machine readable form with the libraries. So, efforts were made from the very beginning to promote the standardization of databases in the DELNET libraries. Experts were sent to the libraries to solves day-to-day problems. A panel of experts was seeing maintained for this purpose. Regular meetings of the librarians and computer specialists were organized to discuss mutual problems and the areas of cooperation. Nevertheless, there have been some libraries in Delhi that took keen interest in database creation on their own. But the practice of regular meetings for database creation and resource sharing continue. DELNET provides technical assistance to member libraries in the following areas:

* creation and maintenance of bibliographic databases
* serials controls
* user services
* hardware and software requirements
* union catalogue preparation
* current awareness and SDI services
* authority data compilation
* subject profiles construction
* abstracting services
* inter-library loan and user services
* document transfer/copying facilities
* access to local, national and international databases

II. Resource Sharing

DELNET saved foreign exchange worth Rs. 10 million by rationalizing subscriptions to foreign periodicals during 1991, 1992 and 1993 through resource sharing. This was mainly achieved in the fields of physical science, medical science and agricultural sciences. It is hoped that in the years to come, DELNET would be able to save more foreign exchange for India through sharing of periodical resources. In 1991, a courier service was started on contract basis will a private agency for inter library lending among the participating libraries but it was not very effective. Later, DELNET has introduced its own courier service with the financial help of NIC. The service is well used.

III. Standardization

A standardization committee of DELNET has been meeting from time to time. The standardization committee takes into account the following areas:

* Communication format for interchanging bibliographic data
* Input output format
* Bibliographic description : Mandatory and optional data elements
* Classification scheme and subject headings
* Thesaurus
* Authority files
* Language scripts into roman script
* Forms of heading
* Identification numbers, codes and abbreviations
* Data input for abstracting and indexing
* Search/command language

It was noticed that colon classification, universal Decimal classification and Dewey Decimal classification were mostly used in Indian libraries and therefore, it would be almost impossible to impose a standard classification scheme on all libraries. It was decided to use Dewey Class Number. As searching by class numbers was done by very few librarians, it was decided that the participating libraries could search by the classification numbers or they could pass on such requests to DELNET central office for necessary action. With regard to the standardization of subject headings and to usage DELNET recommends the use of LCSM. Specialized libraries may use additional thesauri that are available in each major discipline such as social sciences, humanities and science and technology.

IV. Online databases:

DELNET has around twenty databases available online for its users. These are:

* Union Catalogue of Books : UCF
* Union Catalogue of Books : MARC Format
* Union List of Current Periodicals
* Union Catalogue of Periodicals
* Database of Periodic Articles
* Indian Specialists Database
* CD-ROM database
* Union list of Video recordings
* Union List of Sound Recordings
* Union List of Newspapers
* Union List of Serials of Management Libraries
* Union Catalogue of Hindi Books
* Multilingual Books : Sample database
* Urdu Manuscripts Database
* Database of Theses and Dissertations
* DEVINSA Database
* Serials : Petroleum and Natural Gas
* Books in-Print Database
* Jain Database
* Directory of Libraries

The Other Services

ILL Online

DELNET members can place their inter-library loan requests through our ILL online facility, which is available on the union catalogue of books database. The member requests appear on the main server, which are monitored by DELNET staff at regular intervals and the books are acquired and supplied to the requesting library through the courier. Photocopying charges for journal articles etc. and courier charges for sending books to member libraries outside Delhi are extra.

DEL-LISTSERV

DELNET has created a Listserv service called DEL-LISTSERV to provide the current awareness service to users and allow the member libraries to receive the latest daily information from the INTERNET automatically in the form of electronic mail. The following listservs have been created and are available online through DELNET:

* **Net-happenings** – This Listserv appraises the users about the latest new sites along with their web addresses on the INTERNET and has proved to be a major source of information for the users on the INTERNET.
* **Med-clips** – This medical clippings listing discusses the various topics of medical interest like AIDI, cancer, etc. and is informative in nature.
* **IFLA** – This Listserv allows the users to get the latest information from the International Federation of Library Associations and Institutions, which includes the issues of concern to library and information professionals.
* **LIBJOBS** – Through this Listserv, the library professionals are able to find out daily, the jobs/vacancies available throughout the world.

Book : New Arrivals

This is a new service through internet giving a list of recent publications in all subjects. The service covers education, management and physical sciences. Other subjects can be introduced on demand.

Book Reviews from INTERNET

This is an INTERNET service of reviews of latest published

books covering different subjects. The service covers in the field of Arts and Music, INTERNET and military history. From time to time, other subjects will come into this fold.

Current Contents

This service gives the current contents of the latest issues of journals. It is particularly useful for rationalization of periodicals and resources sharing in member libraries.

Index to Hindu

DELNET has started offering Index to Hindu online to its members. Indexed news items are available on the system covering different periods of the Chennai edition. More updates and archival data is being added into the system regularly.

Retro-Conversion

DELNET offers retro conversion facilities to the libraries through specialized agencies and also facilitates the use of modern tools such as CO-ROM's and online facilities for retro-conversion.

Referral Services

DELNET maintains a referral centre that provides reference facilities to participating libraries. The referral centre also looks after the access to the central databases and monitors access to international databases.

Document Transfer/Copy facilities

DELNET provides the facility for transferring or copying of the documents to its users.

Training Programmes

DELNET conducts training programmes in the use of DELNET services, software, E-mail, AACR II and LC subject headings, Internet, etc. from time to time. Information about future training programmes is available on request.

Lectures and Workshops

DELNET organizes lectures by networking specialists working in different parts of the world. The lectures are open to members, specialists and users in general. DELNET also organizes national workshops, seminars and meets on library networking from time to time. DELNET had organized National Annual convention on Library and Information Networking (NACLIN) in 1998 & 1999.

Newsletter

DELNET publishes a newsletter in order to spread the message and increase the awareness about library networking in India. Through this Newsletter, DELNET communicates to its members the progress, it is making in various fields. The Newsletter is also a forum for communication on the advances, achievements and needs of the libraries and their services.

VI. INTERNET

Electronic Mail

DELNET provides RENNIC Email facility to its member libraries, which is introduced by National Informatics Centre. This gives them access to both national and international E-mail users and also to INTERNET users. DELNET Email reaches the libraries, institutions and individuals in India as well as abroad having E-mail connection. Email is being used not only for communication between institutions but also for inter-library-loan requests.

Subscription rates for E-mails are as follows:

RENNIC of NIC : Rs. 2750/- per year for 5 MB data transfer

Full INTERNET (TCP/IP) connectivity

DELNET is providing full INTERNET SLIP/PPP dial up access at a concessional rate of Rs. 8,500/- per annum for Rs. 500 hours of connect time through NIC to the member libraries.

Also the shell account facility for INTERNET access is available for Rs.4,000 per annum for 500 hrs of connect time. A number of DELNET member libraries are already availing these facilities. These rates are subject to change by NIC.

Web Page

DELNET has a web page (http://www.delnet.nic.in/) on INTERNET . This enables all INTERNET users the world over to know about DELNET and its activities. The web page also includes a list of Member-libraries along with their E-mail addresses. The Web page is being updated from time to time.

VII. PRODUCTS

DELSIS

A major breakthrough has been achieved by DELNET with the launch of DELSIS, a powerful library networking software. DELSIS (DELNET System for Information Services) is an integrated modular system, which supports DELNET online databases.

It has been developed by DELNET on a Relational Database management System called BASIC plus, a product of Information Dimension Inc. of USA, which has been provided to DELNET courtesy National Informatics Centre, New Delhi. It handles not only the Online Public Access Catalogue (OPAC) but also has the administrative tools for building up the union catalogues on BASISplus. It provides powerful and extensive facilities for online enquiries for books, serials, biographical details about the specialists and supports the cataloguing of books in Indian languages.

Features of DELSIS:

* DELSIS is a user friendly menu driven package
* Its versatile options allow the users to retrieve the information quickly.
* It contains the modules for Online Public Access Catalogue

as well as the modules for the creation of databases e.g. addition, deletion, inserting of records etc.

* The Online Public Access Catalogue (OPAC) components of DELSIS can meet the needs of the users, irrespective of whether the user has little computer experience or is familiar with using computers to perform various library tasks.

DEL-WINDOWS

DELNET has released the DEL-WINDOWS version 1.0 after the successful creation and implementation of DELSIS Unix version. It is an efficient tool for creating and retrieving bibliographic databases and catalogues.

DEL-WINDOWS can convert the simple PC into a powerful management information system. Some of the **salient features** are:

* It is simple and easy to use. The novice library professionals and end users can interact with the software without any prior training.
* It is user-friendly with adequate windows-menus for data inputting and search capabilities.
* It provides the option for creating the bibliographic records either using ECF or the MARC format.

DELSEARCH

DELNET has opened a new chapter in the information retrieval procedure by devising a new database access mechanism through DELSEARCH. It is an off-line remote database access system through E-mail. It is the first of its kind and is the most economical and user-friendly remote database access system. It helps institutions, information specialists, research scholars, librarians and users interested in bibliographies and tutorial information on South Asia. It allows them to search the DELNET union catalogues through E-mail and is a great tool for research scholars. The software is developed on UNIX platform and allows the users to send their search requests through E-mail. As soon as the query is received by the system in the form of an E-mail, the respective databases are searched for the query word and the results are returned to the addressee immediately. The searching of the database does not require any human intervention and the searches are done by the system automatically.

The Future of DELNET

The future of DELNET is very promising. Its membership with India and outside India is going to take a quantum jump. The DELNET databases are growing in number and size and as a variety of information on South Asia is becoming available through DELNET, it is expected that all institutions outside India specializing in South Asian studies to take DELNET membership. DELNET databases are going to be accessible through INTERNET which will made accessibility very fast. INTERNET users in India are increasing and it will increase DELNET presence in different parts of India. DELNET has already created software, viz. DELDOS and DEL-WINDOWS for creating MARC records.

These software will so on be developed to perform library operations as well. There developments are likely to give more revenue to DELNET and provide justification for more and more libraries to join DELNET. As a resource, it is hoped the DELNET will grow faster as a service based resource sharing model in India.

Calcutta Library Network (CALIBNET)

It was the first library network visualized and started by NISSAT. At a meeting in 1986 in Calcutta, DSIR initiated action for preparation of a feasibility study for networking about 40 libraries in Calcutta. CALIBNET now is a society under West Bengal Societies Registration Act 1961 and responsible for Calcutta Library Network, a project sponsored and supported by NISSAT. NISSAT also contributed to the development of MAITRAYEE software package based on INGRESS 5.2 for

CALIBNET. This package was developed through CMC Ltd. And given to CALIBNET. So far, no data has been created in machine readable from using MAITRAYEE. At present, CALIBNET has become a centre for CD-ROM databases.

Objectives

CALIBNET has made significant studies towards fulfilling its dual **objectives:**

Launching its library network programs, facilitating remote online access to the holding data of Calcutta libraries and other specialized databases as well – a significant step towards bibliographic resource sharing amongst Calcutta libraries; and

Providing electronic access to globally available information, imbibing its information centre approach.

Both are essential for advanced learning and scholarship. In the process, CALIBNET aims at covering a wide panorama of information end-user interests, with diffusion of new electronic information technology as the primary concern.

Software Developed and Library Network Launched:

Intense in-house research and development efforts have now achieved the Library Network capability by three significant studies:

* A multi-user storage and retrieval software **'SANJUKTA'** to support CALIBNET's centralized Database (CDB) and to provide online access to its from remote locations.
* A conversion software package **'PARAPAR'** to support interchange of bibliographic data between USMARC, UNIMARC and CCF files and also from non-standard formats to standard ones.
* Evaluation of a centralized Database (CDB) of holdings data of Calcutta libraries, and specialized databases as well.

These apart, CALIBNET'S pioneering study and research led to its publication of the "Guidelines for Implementation of

UNIMARC in Indian Libraries". This will be an invaluable aid for the national database development programme under consideration, that favors adoption of UNIMARC format.

With the support of SANJUKTA, the centralized database hosted on CALIBNET server and located at the Network Service Centre, can be accessed and searched online by any one from a remote location, provided one is equipped with a computer, a telephone, a modem and a password from CALIBNET. The efficacy of SANJUKTA has been tested by successful remote logging of the CALIBNET server at Jadavpur, hosting the CDB from a workshop venue at Great Eastern Hotel, Calcutta. Online access to the locational information of bibliographic resources via the CDB and sharing up such resources amongst the libraries of this metropolis is now a reality.

The capability of PARAPAR was established through exercises and tests on sample records furnished by a major library in New Delhi and conducted in-house at Calcutta at their instance and eventually demonstrated at a workshop-cum-meeting in New Delhi.

The Centralised Database

Since library network capability has been established, the most crucial and indispensable activity is to develop the basic resource – the Centralized Database (CDB), that constitute the very backbone of any library network – by inputting the holding data of Calcutta libraries. The centralized database, launched only recently, currently held around 30,000 record covering:-

* conference documents held by Calcutta and contiguous libraries.
* social science management and economics, behavioral sciences, quantitative methods, computer science, etc. including predominantly journals held by management libraries in South Asia libraries of Indian Statistical Institute and the Indian Institute of management, Calcutta and

* Index to contents of serials published by Asiatic Society in previous two centuries.

Library Network

The Centralized Database (CDB) is the bedrock of CALIBNET and its development essentially calls for a cooperative movement, whereby each library par rakes in the movement by contributing its own holdings data to be incorporated in the CDB and thereby enrich it. The CDB needs to be now augmented by inputting holdings data of as many libraries as possible and getting the data continuously updated. Optimum coverage of libraries, which alone will progressively transform the CDB into a truly resourceful online searchable central pool of Calcutta's bibliographic holding data, is now on with the cooperation of libraries.

The participating libraries

The responses from institutional libraries are very encouraging. The libraries of following institutions have extended co-operation by way of furnishing their respective machine-readable database and current journal subscription lists:

1. Calcutta University
2. Jadavpur University
3. Indian Statistical Institute
4. Indian Institute of Management
5. Central Research Institute for Jute and Allied Fibres
6. Anthropological Survey of India
7. Botanical Survey of India
8. Geological Survey of India
9. Zoological Survey of India
10. Bengal Engineering College (a deemed university)
11. National Atlas and Thematic Mapping Organization
12. Bose Institute
13. University College of Medicine (Calcutta University)

These are being now inputted into the CDB. In coming years, holding data of many more libraries are expected to go into the CDB. Priority is being accorded to holding data relating to current journals subscribed and new additions from January 1, 1999.

Electronic Access to Global Information

In addition with its library network programme, CALIBNET has added to itself under to information centre approach, a new dimension that of a purveyor of global information, a phenomenon that now pervades international information market.

With online access to Internet and in-house CD-ROM resources, CALIBNET can explore a wide spectrum of the knowledge base and cooperate and professional enterprises, and meet the information requirements of researchers, academics and other scholars, professional and any other practitioners engaged in a wide gamut of subject interest.

CALIBNET Services/Activities

(i) On-demand Information services

CALIBNET has several attractive information packages:

* **Confile Service** – CALIBNET's Confile service reaches at one's desk contents of any journal of one's choice out of over 20,000 high-impact journals. Libraries can now prune their journal subscription list or even forego subscribing to new ones, when budgetary constraints so demand, and still get expressed to their contents from ConFile. ConFile helps libraries in economizing on journal subscription and reducing the drain on precious foreign exchange resources.
* **Caliborder** – On demand, caliborder offers the requisite back-up service by way of delivery of full text of any article and even patents.
* **ConAlert** – Through ConAlert service CALIBNET gives

current and tailored bibliographic information. One can leave with CALIBNET just keywords defining his subject interest and get at regular intervals, the current information related to his interest at his desk.

* **RetroFile** – This service offers latest status and trend of research on any specific topic.

ConFile, ConAlert and RetroFile, in combination, offers the latest information and advances in the entire spectrum of the subject interest.

(ii) CALIBLINK :

A special feature of CALIBNET is the Caliblink, a email connectivity (from its ERNET hub) installed and working fine at four institutions.

(iii) Institutional Resources Development Services :

Some of the key institutional resources development services offered are:

(a) Retrospective conversion of existing card catalogue in libraries into computerized local databases via electronic mode by down loading from international databases;

(b) Consultative services on LIS automation

(c) Manpower development for operating and manning automated LIS environment through a wide range of graded training programmes, and customized courses for individuals or group at client's site.

(iv) SANJUKTA & PARAPAR Software

SANJUKTA

A multi-user storage and retrieval software has been developed in-house to support CALIBNET's Centralised Database and to provide online access from remote locations. SANJUKTA has been designed and implemented by A Mukhopadhyay, Technical Consultant, CALIBNET and his associates based on MOD+, a software he developed earlier to support management of small/medium-size libraries.The software has been developed, using 4 GL Code and designed to provide the user with options and flexibility in generating records, organizing and searching information viewing the search outputs, and interchanging data files with external databases with least manual interference.

PARAPAR

A conversion software package, PARAPAR has been developed in CALIBNET to support interchange of bibliographic data between USMARC, UNIMARC and CCF Files and also from non-standard formats to standard ones. Its primary objective is to convert data files, received from the participating libraries in variant formats, into a ISO-2709 compliant implementation through which the files are merged into the centralized Database of CALIBNET.

(v) Guidelines for Implementation of UNIMARC

It has been brought out by CALIBNET to provide the library professionals in India with a working tool for developing their databases in a mutually exchangeable format. The document has been prepared in 1994, based on UNIMARC Manual (1987), by A Mukhopadhyay, Technical Consultant, under a project sponsored by the National Information System for Science and Technology (NISSAT), Department of Scientific and Industrial Research, Government of India. The guidelines have made an attempt to take care of the special requirements of the Indian libraries. They are expected to serve the Indian libraries in upgrading their databases to the international standard.

Immediate Focus

(i) Indian Resources Database

Development of Indian Resources Database on historical value covering manuscripts and rare books, and personal collections, has already been initiated with porting on the CDB and index to serials published by Asiatic Society during the last two countries.

(ii) CALIBNET on INTERNET

The design of CALIBNET web page is complete and is available on the Net . The web page(http://www.calibnet.org/) facilitates access to bibliographic information resources available through hosting of CALIBNET's centralized database. The **CALIBNET web site** provides:

a. Active link to access
   - Indian Library and Network Resources
   - Overseas Library Resources on India, including rare documents – printed and manuscripts.
   - Worldwide Library Catalogues
   - National Libraries of the world
   - Newspapers and journals
   - Electronic Reference tools
   - Factual Information sources
   - Book Trade Databases

b. Varied CALIBNET programs for
   - On-demand Information services
   - Electronic-mail connections
   - Consultative services for Library Automation
   - Manpower Development
   - R&D in IT Application

3 LIBRARY AUTOMATION

The automation of university libraries is a pre-requisite for networking and resource sharing. INFLIBNET Centre, through UGC, has been providing the required support to universities in phases.

Till 1999-2000, 123 universities have been given initial grant of Rs. 6.5 lakhs each to develop infrastructure for automation. By the end of IXth plan period, rest of the universities will also be included. After installation of the systems, further financial support is provided for the first five years to take care of recurring expenditure.

These Libraries on receipt of initial grant sign a Memorandum of Understanding with INFLIBNET. An integrated software for the automation of in-house functions called SOUL has been developed. It has been well received by the University Libraries. SOUL has been installed at 15 Libraries. Many more libraries have shown desire to procure and install SOUL.

Currently libraries funded under the programme are advised to subscribe to one of the following networks, depending on the availability in the respective locations:

- ERNET
- VSNL
- NICNET
- Other ISPs

Wide Area Network

It is planned to setup a Wide Area Network "UGCNET" linking more than 170 universities and other acedemic institutes in the country.

Local Area Network

INFLIBNET Centre has suggested all the funded universities to set up LANs using HUB/SWITCH and CAT V cables within their libraries for successful installation of SOUL software. Since SOUL is based on client/server architecture, It is essential that the server and all other nodes be connected by LAN.

INFLIBNET Centre desires that each university should establish a LAN in it's campus linking all the departments including library.This LAN in turn will be connected to the WAN.

7
INDIA AND INFORMATION TECHNOLOGY

INTRODUCTION

India remained a centre of greatt civilizations of the world through out the ages. It's contribution to mathematics, medical sciences, astronomy and political science is unparallel. Mathematics being the "mother of all sciences" was one of the most potential discipline for technical knowledge to grow. The natural resources of the country, specially its high yielding land always remained a sources for prosperity.

India is primarily an agriculture based country where 60% of the population is engaged in farming. About 25% of its workers are engaged in service sector. The country is rapidly transforming to information society and the millions of its information workers lead lifestyle similar to information workers in the advanced countries. Their number is escalating day by day bringing a sea change in its culture specially the urban elite. Although the percentage of information workers in the Indian society is very low still their collective strength is more than the information workers in Japan and about the same number in the United States.

The overall roads and highways scenario in India has also witnessed major improvements over the last few years. Most cities and fist and second tier towns are connected and interlinked to each other. Major investments have gone into the development of highways, both on the side of the central and state Governments. Clearly, the Indian Government has understood the importance of infrastructure to industries such as IT and created a conducive environment for its development and expansion.

Credit for India's rapid growth in the IT sector goes to the availability of a robust infrastructure telecom, power and roads in the country. Relevant telecom facilities are an important prerequisite for the success of the software industry and over the years, the Government has taken steps to ensure that telecom remains a priority area.

Similarly, regular, reliable, uninterrupted power, a major necessity for running IT software and services businesses, has also received substantial attention from the Government. Recent steps to privatize the distribution of power and bring in greater efficiencies and customer centricity in the market, have been welcomed by the ICT industry.

The communication technologies including its various applications in telecommunication such as radio, television, cable, satellites, Internet etc are driving the social shift toward the information society. These technologies are converging today in order to form new ones and making their separate identity difficult. Computer has affected them the most with its application in almost all the areas of information collection, storage and dissemination.

Computer is undoubtedly the key technology in an information society. The United States has led the way in computer era but the other countries are equally making headways in it. The first computer of the world ENIAC was developed in the year 1945. Funds were made available by the U. S. Department of Defence and it was used for military purposes. ENIAC cost millions of dollars to build, took up a lot of space and was initially used for number-crunching tasks. The worlds' first main frame computer used vacuum tubes for its millions of switches.

The first computer in India was acquired by the Indian Statistical Institute, Calcutta in 1955. Additional computers in the country were purchased from IBM. By 1972, there were 172 computers and three-fourth of them were made by IBM. Microcomputer was developed as a result of miniaturization of the computer in the early 1970s using semiconductors. Microcomputer was later converted into personal computer.

Computer revolutionized the world of information technology with telephone and Internet. It gave birth to an array of information technology products and services which changed the national as well as the international landscapes. India being a vast country full of its human resources and having the second largest number of English speaking people in the world has made rapid strides in the field of information technology. Below we discuss some of the premier IT institutions of the country being confined to the Information related service aspects of these organizations.

DEPARTMENT OF INFORMATION TECHNOLOGY (DIT)

Vision

To make India an IT Super Power by the Year 2008.

Vision Objectives

- Creation of Wealth
- Employment Generation
- IT led Economic Growth
- Role of the Department of IT
- Pro-active facilitator
- Pro-active motivator
- Pro-active promoter
- Spread of IT to masses and
- Ensure speedy IT led development

FUNCTIONS OF DIT

Policy matters relating to Information Technology

- Promotion of knowledge-based enterprises.
- Development of electronics and coordination amongst its various users.
- All matters relating to the personnel under the control of the Department.
- Coordination of requirements relating to electronics processing equipment(computers).
- All matters pertaining to silicon facility.
- All matters concerning computer based information, technology and processing including hardware and software, standardization of procedures and matters relevant to international bodies such as IFP, IBI, ICC.
- Promotion of the Internet.
- Promotion of E-Commerce.
- Promotion of Information Technology education and Information Technology based education
- National Informatics Centre.
- Electronics and Computer Software Export Promotion Council.

International Cooperation and Trade

IT Industry, Information Technology and in particular the Software Industry is one of the fastest growing sectors of the Indian economy with more than 2000 companies. It is host to established IT companies such as IBM, Intel, Microsoft, Oracle, Cisco, Sun, HP, Alcatel and also to many innovative companies with leading edge capabilities in their respective fields like Juniper, Dell, Compaq, Cerent Tellabs. It has its own homegrown leaders i.e. Infosys, Wipro Satyam, TCS and Pentafour.

Objectives

India's progress in Information Technology, more significantly in Computer Software, has been recognized globally. Over the last decade, the Indian IT industry, particularly the software sector has been growing by leaps and bounds. Industry revenues in the software sector have grown more than ten folds from a mere US$ 50 million in 1988-89 to US$ 5.7 billion in 1999-2000. The major destinations of Computer Software exports from India are - USA, West Europe and Japan. The Ministry of Information Technology has set a target of US$50 billion for software exports by 2008. To achieve these targets, the Ministry of Information Technology has initiated several concerted efforts. A key component of this has been focused International Initiatives through the official mechanisms like Joint Commissions, Joint Working Groups, meetings exclusively on IT with important countries like US, Japan, France, China etc. The objective of these mechanisms is that the Governments in both the countries, acting as facilitators, would bring the industries on both sides together on a closer platform for forging business ties. These interactions would help in capitalizing on complementarities and opportunities offered by each other.

Partnering with India

The Indian IT industry and in particular the software industry is vibrant and successful. It is one of the fastest growing sectors of the Indian economy with more than 2000 companies. It is host to established IT companies such as IBM, Intel, Microsoft, Oracle, Cisco, Sun, HP, Alcatel and also to many innovative companies with leading edge capabilities in their respective fields like Juniper, Dell, Compaq, Cerent and Tellabs. It has its own homegrown global leaders in Infosys, Wipro, Satyam.TCS and Pentafour.

While the mainstay export software areas such as professional services and projects add upto more than 80% of the dollar revenues, the domestic software has a share of close to

49% in products and packages. The Indian strengths include e-commerce, multimedia applications, communication software, ASIC design and mission critical software.

India has:

- a software and computing services sector with the highest compound growth rate globally for the last five years in a row
- a thriving indigenous software industry which includes many innovative companies
- a skilled and flexible English-speaking workforce with multilingual capabilities
- an enabling and facilitating regulatory framework
- an established tradition of research and innovation in both academiaand industry
- an advanced and competitively priced telecommunication infrastructure with Convergence being built in at a very rapid pace
- a venture capital sector that actively invests in IT start-ups
- a Government that positively welcomes inward investment and believes in helping create wealth
- economic and political stability.

India is the partner to world's IT markets

Many global IT companies having established their bases in India, draw on the world-class research and development skills in Indian Institutes (IITs/IISc etc.), particularly in such areas as parallel computing, artificial intelligence and embedded design software. The Institutes themselves are active partners and many collaborate with the industry to help generate revenues from technology development.

Strong Industry Growth

Top 20 Software Exporters

S.No.	*Company Name*	*Total Export During 1999-2000 (in million US $)*
1	Tata Consultancy Services	370.67
2	Wipro Ltd.	226.52
3	Infosys Technologies Ltd.	189.06
4	Satyam Computer Services Ltd.	144.11
5	HCL Technologies Ltd.	137.59
6	NUT Ltd.	119.95
7	Silverline Technologies Ltd.	94.52
8	Pentamedia Graphics Ltd	84.57
9	Pentasoft Technologies Ltd.	76.74
10	Patni Computer Systems Ltd.	64.13
11	IBM Global Services IndiaPvt Ltd.	56.41
12	Mahindra British Telecom Lid.	51.08
13	DSQ Software Ltd.	50.04
14	l-flex Solutions Ltd.	42.11
15	Tata Infotech Ltd.	41.50
16	Zensar Technology Ltd	40.26
17	Cognizant Tech. Solutions India Ltd.	39.86
18	Biria Soft Ltd.	35.65
19	Polaris Software Lab Ltd.	31.76
20	L & T Information Technology Ltd.	30,31
	Total	1926.94

%AGE SHARE IN TOTAL SOFTWARE EXPORT 51.23%

Based on ESC Statistical Year Book 2000

Since 1995 the Indian software and computing services

industry has grown at the compound annual growth rate of 56.3%. This trend is expected to continue in the Third Millennium. By March 2001 end the combined turnover of the IT and software services companies in India would have touched almost US $ 10 billion with exports touching US $ 6.24 billion and profits expected to continue and also to increase by more than 30 percent year on year. India's total systems and applications software market share alone is predicted to increase to around 60 per cent by 2001. As it is India's software exports total uptc more than 13 percent of exports in 1999-2000. In 3 years, the broad IT and communications sector is expected to contribute in excess of 10 percent of Indian GDP.

The key point here is the strong positioning and the credibility enjoyed by Indian software in the largest software market of the world. Here India exports more than 60% of its software. The export itself is across a broad range of the software sector.

Indian Electronic Industry

Electronics and Information Technology is the fastest growing segment of Indian industry both in terms of production and exports. Today, the electronics industry is completely delicensed with the exception of aerospace and defence electronics, and alongwith the liberalization in foreign investment and export-import policies of the entire economy, this sector is attracting considerable interest not only as a vast market but also as potential production base by international companies.

In recent times, 'software development and IT enabled services' have emerged as a niche opportunity for India in the global context. The Government is taking all necessary steps to make India, a Global Information Technology Superpower and a front-runner in the age of Information Revolution. The Government has announced promotion of Information Technology as one of the five top priorities of the country and constituted a National Task Force on Information Technology and Software Development.

To cater to information needs in the field of electronics of the Industry, Entrepreneurs, Planners and Decision-Makers; Data Bank and Information Division (DBID) of Department of Information Technology has developed and maintains a large integrated information base called "LIPS Information System". It covers production, exports, foreign collaborations, manufacturers, other macro level statistics relating to Indian Electronics Industry.

DBID has also brought out a comprehensive book - "Guide to Electronics Industry in India". This Guide covers a wide range of information such as manufacturers directory, product directory, export product directory, time series data on production and exports, production trends, electronics units in states, etc.

It also publishes monthly techno-economics journal "Electronics Information and Planning " intended to serve the government, the industry and the users by providing information neccessary for healthy promotion of electronics applications, electronics industry development and innovations, policies, and data. The journal has a wide readership among the industry and users.

It also brings out "Annual Report of Department of Information Technology (downloadable)" every year. The Annual Reports contains eight chapters viz., Overview, Industry Profile, Technology and Application Development, Human Resource Development, Infrastructure, Societies, Public Sector Units, and Promotional Matters.

Electronic Production

Indian Electronics and IT Industry Production Profile: 2002

Information and Communication Technology (ICT) today permeates almost every sphere of human endeavour. Investment in ICT has the largest multiplier effect rippling through the economy than any other sector. Apart from the R&D and Information Infrastructure initiatives, many countries are benchmarking the success of their e-Governance initiatives in terms of the resultant increase in the competitiveness of the country. In fact the World Information Technology Report and Global Competitiveness Report emphasize on a country's IT and network readiness as important parameters to catapult it into a knowledge based economy.

The Indian software and services industry has grown significantly during 2002-03, a period marked globally by a fall in ICT sector revenue, a major drop in IT spending by customers and overall sluggish market conditions. The software and services industry has emerged as one of the fastest growing sectors in the Indian economy with a growth rate of over 26 per cent during 2002-03 and turnover of US$ 12.7 billion (Rs. 59,900 crore) and exports of US$ 10 billion (Rs. 47,500 crore).

Indian IT software and services industry is expected to account for about 2.4 per cent of India's GDP and 20.4 per cent of exports during 2002-03 and is projected to account for 7% of India's GDP and 35% of exports by 2008. The Nasscom McKinsey Report 2002 (June 2002) has stated that despite the current slowdown, the Indian IT services (ITS) and IT enabled services (ITES) industry is poised to meet its long-term export potential of US $57-65 billion. The Indian IT Enabled Services sector has emerged as a key driver of growth for the Indian IT Industry. This segment is poised to grow very rapidly, world-wide, over the next few years.

Larger Indian companies focused on moving up the IT value chain, by offering services, such as system integration, package implementation, IT outsourcing and IT consulting, as well as targeting new verticals, such as utilities, healthcare and retailing, in addition to the traditional financial services, telecom equipment and manufacturing industries.

The Indian ITES-BPO industry has grown by about 65 per cent during 2002-03. The total export revenues of the Indian IT-enabled services industry are projected at Rs. 11,700 crore, up from Rs. 7,100 crore in 2001-02. The growth of the Indian ITES-

Electronics Production				*(Financial Year)*		
Item	*1997-98*	*1998-99*	*1999-2000*	*2000-01*	*2001-02*	*2002-03*
1. Consumer Electronics	7,600	9,200	11,200	11,950	12,700	13,800
2. Industrial Electronics	3,150	3,300	3,750	4,000	4,500	5,550
3. Computers	2,800	2,300	2,500	3,400	3,550	4,250
4. Commn. & Broad. Eqpt.	3,250	4,400	4,000	4,500	4,500	4,800
5. Strategic Electronics	900	1,300	1,450	1,750	1,800	2,500
6. Components	4,40	0 4,750	5,200	5,500	5,700	6,600
Sub-Total	22,100	25,250	28,100	31,100	32,750	37,500
7. Software for Exports	6,500	10,940	17,150	28,350	36,500	47,500
8. Domestic Software	3,470	4,950	7,200	9,400	10,874	12,400
Total	32,070	41,140	52,450	68,850	80,124	97,400

BPO market has been facilitated by key business drivers-cost, need to focus on core competencies, high attrition, all of which match with India's strengths. India has maintained its global competitiveness offering the best combination of cost-quality-scalability versus competing offshore destinations such as the Philippines and China.

Indian IT software and services industry is expected to have provided employment to 650,000 IT professionals by March, 2003. It is estimated that out of the 650,000 knowledge workers, almost 205,000 are working in the IT software and services export industry; nearly 160,000 in IT enabled services; 25,000 in the domestic software market and over 260,000 in user organizations.

Electronics & IT Production

The software and services industry continues as one of the fastest growing sectors in the Indian economy with a growth of over 26 per cent during 2002-03 and turnover of US$ 12.7 billion (Rs. 59,900 crore) and exports of US$ 10 billion (Rs. 47,500 crore). Inspite of global fall in ICT sector, the export of Indian software and services is likely to witness a growth rate of about 30%.

Consumer electronics sector has bounced back during 2002-03 and is estimated to achieve a production level of Rs. 13,800 crore as compared to Rs. 12,700 crore in the year 2001-02, thus achieving a growth rate of 8.7%. The colour TV production has shoot up to 75 lakh units during the year 2002-03, against 60 lakh units in the previous year. VCD/MP3 player sales have witnessed impressive growth and have been of the order of 5 million units.

Indian colour TV picture tube manufacturers have made huge investments for manufacture of pure flat picture tubes. The production of CPTs has increased to over 75 lakhs during the year 2002.

The sale of personal computers has also increased to about 20 lakhs in numbers during the year 2002-03 as compared to over 16 lakhs in 2001-02. The production in computer and instrumentation industry is not matching growth in demand. The strategic electronics sector has shown a growth of about 39 per cent. Prices of colour TV and computers have also come down in consonance with the worldwide trend.

The production and growth trends during last 5 year have been as follows:

Year of Production	*(Rs. Crores) Growth*
1997-98	32,070 20.4
1998-99	41,140 28.3
1999-2000	52,450 27.5
2000-01	68,450 31.3
2001-02	80,124 16.4
2002-03	97,400 21.6

Consumer Electronics

Consumer electronics is the largest sector of electronics hardware industry and accounts for almost 37 per cent of the total electronics hardware production. Consumer electronics sector is estimated to achieve a production level of Rs. 13,800 crore during 2002-03 as compared to Rs. 12,700 crore in the year 2001-02, thus achieving a growth rate of 8.7 per cent. The Colour TV segment, which contributes over 60 per cent of the turnover of the Consumer electronics industry, has witnessed impressive growth of 25 per cent over the previous year. The total production of colour televisions was reported at 75 lakh units during the year 2002-03. Within this, the market for flat colour televisions has grown by approximately 100 per cent over the previous year. More and more companies have introduced flat television which are available with a variety of different features like increased sound output, woofers, picture in picture (PIP), video games and the 29 inch television being upgraded from 50 to 100 Hz. During the year 2002-03, production of flat CTV is estimated at 400,000 units.

Mega sporting events like FIFA World Cup Soccer in June 2002, ICC Champion trophy in September, 2002 and the Cricket World Cup in early 2003 have increased the off-take of colour TV sets. The availability of quality software (television programmes) and cheap software and hardware (compact disc and CD players) have also boosted the sales of colour TV set. Exports of CTV set have also registered a significant growth in the current year.

B&W televisions registered a negative growth even this year as the production is estimated to have dropped to 31 lakh units from the level of 38 lakh units in previous year. Due to decreasing volumes and low margins, the organized sector is losing interest in this product category.

During the year 2002-03, audio products have also witnessed high growth with sales of music systems with VCD/AD and MP3 compatibility gaining momentum. With the introduction of MP3 and reduction in prices of audio CDs, the market for CD based audio system have increased. More DVD units are coming up and with availability of software on DVD, the trend is slowly moving towards DVD based system. This has resulted in drop in demand for mono and stereo based system by at least 20 per cent. During the year 2002-03, VCD/MP3 player sales have been of the order of 50 lakh units.

The microwave Ovens production has witnessed steady growth with a number of new players entering this product segment. Production during 2002-03 is estimated at 2,50,000 units. With increase of volumes, microwave ovens are becoming more affordable.

Production of Major Consumer Electronics Products

(Production in Lakhs Nos.)

ITEM	*2000-01*	*2001-02*	*2002-03*
B&W TV	42	38	38
CTV	57	60	60
Radio Receive	60	60	60
Tape Recorder & Combinations	140	140	140
VCRs/VCPs	3.2	27	25
Electronic Watches	160	183	175
Electronic Clocks	246	236	240

Electronic Components

The impressive growth experienced by CTV industry during the year led to rapid increase in the market for colour picture tubes (CPT). Two new lines for CPT also went into production. As a result, CPT production is expected to increase from 56 lakhs numbers in 2001 to around 75 lakhs numbers in 2002, leading to growth of 34 per cent. The production of B&W picture tubes declined further due to fall in the production of B&W TVs. B&W picture tube manufacturers have been forced to slash the prices. The components like PCB, connectors, Ferrites, CD-R, etc., showed a positive growth. The total production of components has increased to Rs. 6,600 crore in 2002-03, a growth of 15.8%, over production in previous year.

COMPONENTS Production	*2000*	*2001*	*2002*
CPT (lakh nos.)	55	56	73
B/W Tube (million nos.)	43.3	40.5	41
PCBs (Rs. crore)	505	512	563
Connectors(Rs. crore)	212	213	300
Semiconductor Devices(Rs. crore)	356	352	322

The export of electronic components is expected to rise to Rs. 2,500 crore during the year, a growth of 12% over previous year. The components with major share in the export are floppy diskettes, CD-R, semiconductor devices, PCBs, connectors, ferrites, CPTs, etc.

The demand of surface mount components, display devices, micro-electronic, opto-electronic devices, etc., continued to be met by imports due to limited non-existent manufacturing base in the country.

Due to availability of cheaper imported components, the profit margin of component manufacturers continued to be under pressure.

Computer Industry

Computers are at the core of every IT application, which in turn are having a profound impact on the business processes and life styles. During the year 2002-03, production in this sector was Rs 4,250 crore, showing a growth of 20% over the last year.

Products being manufactured in the country include personal computers, servers, workstations, supercomputers, data processing equipment printers, digitizers, networking products such as modems, hubs, etc., and add-on cards. The production in the PC segment is dominated by P-4 Processors. Other processors are gradually entering the market reflecting, perhaps, the need for low-cost computing solutions. Inkjet printers dominated the printers segment.

The PC sales during the year is expected to have crossed 20 lakh nos. The increased off-take was due to higher consumption by industry verticals and e-governance initiatives taken by the Central and State governments.

More and more government Departments / Ministries at the Center and the State level are publishing information on the web. Interactive services like downloadable forms, online feedback, public grievance submission and other similar services are being made available through the Internet. On-line

Government services provided over Internet are related to dissemination of information such as public exam results, Government forms, tender notices, information about Government Departments, etc. By March 2003, the Internet penetration was estimated to be 0.37% of the population.

The PC population is estimated to be over 8.0 million nos. The penetration of computers in commercial and domestic segments in the country is approximately in the ratio of 80:20 respectively.

Computer Software

India's main competitive advantage in software and services is its abundant, high quality and cost effective pool of skilled knowledge workers. Today, India is a magnet for software clients because of its vast resource of skilled software manpower. The Indian ITES-BPO industry has grown by about 65 per cent during 2002-03. The total export revenues of the Indian IT-enabled services industry are estimated at Rs. 11,700 crore, up from Rs. 7,100 crore in 2001-02. The growth of the Indian ITES-BPO market has been facilitated by key business drivers-cost, need to focus on core competencies, high attrition, all of which match with India's strengths. India has maintained its global competitiveness offering the best combination of cost-quality-scalability versus competing offshore destinations such as Philippines and China.

The software and services industry has emerged as one of the fastest growing sectors in the Indian economy with a growth of over 26 per cent during 2002-03 and turnover of US$ 12.7 billion (Rs. 59,900 crore) and exports of US$ 10 billion (Rs. 47,500 crore).

During 2002-03, Indian software majors have managed to leverage on existing customer relationships to generate additional business and made a concerted effort to tap geographies outside strongholds such as the United States. A number of Indian software and services companies are also now addressing other high potential markets such as Europe and Asia Pacific.

Larger Indian companies focused on moving up the IT value chain, by offering services, such as system integration, package implementation, IT outsourcing and IT consulting, as well as targeting new verticals, such as utilities, healthcare and retailing, in addition to the traditional financial services, telecom equipment and manufacturing industries.

As budgets tighten across the world and corporate resort to drastic cost-cutting, global majors are under pressure to offshore to cheaper locations. India is an ideal location and has the added advantage of traditionally plying in the non-discretionary space of corporate IT spend. Corporate enterprises are not the only companies taking advantage of Indian talent; virtually every single or large global systems integration firm is rapidly expanding its footprint in India.

Since the inception of the IT industry in India, players within the country have been focusing on quality initiatives, to align themselves with international standards. The industry has set in place processes and procedures for offering world class IT software products and services. The focus on maintaining high quality has lead to an increasing number of companies getting assessed at key quality standards. As of December, 2002, India has 48 companies at SEI CMM Level 5 assessment. The quality maturity of Indian software and ITES-BPO industry can be measured from the fact that already 254 Indian software and ITES-BPO companies have acquired quality certification.

The domestic software market size continues to grow at a marginally lower rate, as compared with software services exports. The Indian domestic software market is estimated to have grown by about 14 per cent during 2002-03, due to a slowdown in IT spending by the banking sector and manufacturing sectors.

The Enterprise Portals market in India is still in its development stage. The segments leading to the adoption of EP applications in India are manufacturing, retail banking and financial services, telecom, IT services/call centres, insurance, and state government and government agencies. Service is becoming the key to differentiation and this is driving coporates to adopt CRM solutions. Some of the prominent telecom players in the Indian market that have gone in for these solutions are Bharti, BPL, and Orange.

The banking segment is a key user of software products and services in the domestic market. The major areas in which banks have undertaken IT related investments include computerization of branches, VSAT based networking among branches, installation of ATM networks, systems related to handling of credit/debit cards and facilities for internet banking.

A number of large companies in the manufacturing sector have made significant investments in IT. These companies have focused on acquiring IT products, development of customized applications and integration of systems in order to improve their competitive positions. Privatization of State Electricity Boards and distribution sector has led to greater use of IT in billing and transmission applications.

During the last two years, a number of initiatives have been taken at the Central and State Government levels to computerize departments and administrative functions. Various government departments have earmarked between 1-3 per cent of their budgets on improving their IT infrastructure. At the central level, the focus of IT investments is likely to be primarily on revenue services (such as income tax, excise, and customs), citizen services (such as issue of passports) and information dissemination. At the state level, the main area of IT investments is likely to be computerization of land records, citizen records, and payment of taxes.

Indian IT software and services industry is expected to have provided employment to 650,000 IT professionals by March, 2003. It is estimated that out of the 650,000 knowledge workers, almost 205,000 are working in the IT software and services export industry; nearly 160,000 in IT enabled services; 25,000 in the domestic software market and over 260,000 in user organizations.

Control, Instrumentation and Industrial Sector

In manufacturing enterprises, more test and measuring system will be networked directly to back office business systems, whereas factory floor test are used for product monitoring, quality control results are analyzed in the back office to find ways of improving quality and yield. This lead to development of efficient, cost effective power and energy management instrumentation. Technology available within the country is at reasonably matured level.

In control instrumentation and industrial electronics, ultrasound equipment and uninterrupted power supply are major export items. In industrial electronic products group, mixed performance was observed.

Energy meter product group has an upswing for the second consecutive year with sales touching about Rs. 272 crore in current year.

This segment of the electronics industry continue to face more or less the same type of adversities as in the previous year. Low volumes, fragmented capacities, low pace of growth in infrastructure projects and unbridled competition particularly in the lower/ medium end/product segments have remained the major bottlenecks in the growth of industrial electronics sector. The domestic production in this sector of the industry is estimated to be around Rs. 5,550 crore for the year 2002-03.

However, there have been two distinctly positive signs of improvement in the core infrastructure sector. The steel industries in general have been showing better results and investment decisions for automation packages are coming up. Similarly, a well meaning APDRP (Accelerated Power Development and Reforms Programme) of the Ministry of Power has also opened up better opportunities for the industrial electronics sector in this area. Demand for Computerized Energy Management Systems, various Process Control and Drive Systems for steel plants and SCADA / Distribution Automation technologies, Automatic Meter Reading Technologies, Energy Auditing System, etc., for the power sector have been slowly picking up in recent times and are expected to grow further in the coming year. Products or systems continue to be supplied in the Indian market essentially through large scale imports including the core hardware and software. Local manufacturing and building up of indigenous strength on design and manufacturing processes remain in a low scale.

Communication & Broadcasting Sector

The thrust areas in this sector are Convergence, Communication and Broadband technologies which include the next generation wireless technologies such as 3G/4G, access technologies, broadband products based on IEEE 802.11a, b and g standards. The broadcast sector covers digital broad-casting of audio and video, IP telephony, broadband access, digital compression, etc.

The Department's proactive role in promoting the growth of Internet in the country led to the opening of Internet telephony in the country with effect from April 2002. Further, the Department played a key role in delicensing of the 2.4-2.4835 GHz spectrum applications in a contiguous campus. This will help in delivery of broadband content to remote Indian villages in a cost effective manner.

The production of communication and broadcasting equipment, during the year 2002-2003 is estimated to be Rs 5,600 crore as compared to Rs. 4,500 crore during 2001-02.

Strategic Electronics

The strategic electronic sector covers the area of satellite based communication, navigation and surveillance systems, navigational aids, sonars, underwater electronic system, infra-red based detection and ranging system, disaster management system, internal security system, GPS based vehicle tracking systems, etc. The bulk of the requirement in this sector is being met by the defence PSUs, a number of new units such as WIPRO, Reliance, Satyam, Larsen & Toubro, ASPL, Zen Technologies, Security Defence Systems, etc., from the private sector are contributing to this sector.

The production in the strategic electronic equipment during the year 2002-03 is estimated to be Rs.2,250 crore as compared to Rs.1,800 crore during the year 2001-02.

Electronics Exports

During the year 2002-03, electronics exports are estimated to be Rs. 53,500 crore, as compared to Rs. 42,300 crore in 2001-02, showing a phenomenal growth of over 26 per cent. The computer software and services exports are estimated to rise from Rs. 36,500 crore during 2001-02 to Rs. 47,500 crore during 2002-03, implying a growth of 30 per cent.

Electronics Production (Calendar Year)

Item	*1998*	*1999*	*2000*	*2001*	*2002*
1. Consumer Electronics	9,000	11,000	11,880	12,300	13,580
2. Industrial Electronics	3,280	3,750	3,970	4,480	5,400
3. Computers	2,200	2,500	3,350	3,520	4,180
4. Commn. & Broad. Eqpt.	4,400	4,000	4,450	4,450	4,800
5. Strategic Electronics	1,270	1,400	1,730	1,750	2,330
6. Components	4,650	5,100	5,500	5,650	6,510
Sub-Total	24,800	27,750	30,880	32,150	36,800
7. Software for Exports	10,500	16,000	27,000	34,000	44,000
8. Domestic Software	4,700	7,000	8,800	10,600	12,000
Total	40,000	50,750	66,680	76,750	92,800

Targets for the Year 2008

Opportunities in Software Sector by the Year 2008
(McKinsey Report)

Software Sector	*Total Market Exports*
IT Services	$ 28-30 billion $ 28-30 billion
Software Products	$ 8-11 billion $ 8-11 billion
IT Enabled Services	$ 21-24 billion $ 21-24 billion
Domestic Market	$13-15 billion
Total	$ 70-80 billion $ 57-65 billion

IT Industry by the year 2008

Employment Generation Year 2002-03

IT Exports 35% of India's Total Exports in 2008 from 20.4% during 2002-03

Share of IT Software & Services Industry in GDP Likely to be 7% of GDP in 2008 from 2.4% of GDP during 2002-03

Hardware Production Projections for Tenth Plan

Rs. Crore	*Realistic Scenario*	*Optimistic Scenario*
01-02	32,750	32,750
2002-03	39,500	41,600
2003-04	45,000	50,500
2004-05	52,000	61,500
2005-06	60,000	74,700
2006-07	69,000	90,900

Electronic Export

During the year 2002-03, electronics exports are estimated to be Rs. 53,100 crore as compared to Rs. 42,300 crore in 2001-02, showing a phenomenal growth of 26 per cent. The computer software and services exports have increased from Rs. 36,500 crore during 2001-02 to Rs. 47,500 crore during 2002-03, implying a growth of 30 per cent

Electronic Exports (Rs. Crores)

Item	*1997 -98*	*1998 -99*	*1999 -00*	*2000 -01*	*2001 -02*	*2002* -03
1. Consumer Electronics	600	400	300	648	700	750
2. Industrial Electronics	200	160	200	500	950	1,400
3. Computers	1,250	400	240	1,250	1,800	550
4. Commn. & Broad. Eqpt.	100	70	50	550	150	500
5. Strategic Electronics	10	10	10	-	-	-
6. Components	840	760	600	1,840	2,200	2,400
Sub-Total	3,000	1,800	1,400	4,788	5,800	5,600
7. Computer Software	6,500	10,940	17,150	28,350	36,500	47,500
Total	9,500	12,740	18,550	33,138	42,300	53,100

Foreign Collaboration

The Foreign Collaboration details can be found in EIIS Package.

EIIS Package

The data pertaining to production, exports, approvals, foreign collaborations, manufacturers and product directory and other macro level statistics related to electronic industry are maintained in an information system, called, 'LIPS Information System' by the Data Bank and Information Division (DBID) of Ministry of Information Technology. The time-series (itemwise and unitwise) production and export data is available since 1981. The manufacturer and product directory provides latest and reliable information and serves as a Buyer/Seller Guide. It provides manufacturer's information such as address (both office/ factory), telephone, telex, fax,email, website, name and designation of the top executive, year of establishment, brand, manpower employed, sector, product range and export product range, etc. It also provides manufacturers and exporters for a given product.

This package comes in a self-extracting archive. Click on

the link and then click Open on the browser dialog box to install immediately, or click Save As to install at another time.To extract and install after saving the file, simply run the downloaded executable file.

Electronic Governance

The advent of Information Technology as a highly leveraged enabling tool for delivery of services in the public and the private sector has by now been universally recognised. This has redefined the fundamentals and has the potential to change the institutions as well as the mechanisms of delivery of services forever. It is in this context that the issues of Smart Governance – Electronic Governance needs to be analysed.

Quite obviously, therefore, the objective of achieving Electronic Governance (EG) goes far beyond mere computerisation of stand alone back office operations. It means to fundamentally change as to how the Government operates and this implies a new set of responsibilities for the executive, legislature and the citizenry. The effort should aim to bring about a social catharsis which needs to be orchestrated in a comprehensive, concerted and planned fashion.

DIT Initiative

A new division –

'Electronic Governance Division' has been set up in the Department of Information Technology as an initiative to accelerate the usage of Information Technology in all spheres of Governance.

The E-Governance division examines the practical implications of IT related issues in the Government with the aim of improving services to the citizens. The goal is to reach beyond current efforts to "reinvent government," by identifying breakthrough strategies that rethink the core value of key government services, improve service delivery, reduce costs, and redefine administrative processes.

DIT Initiatives and major Policy Issues:

Centre for E-Governance

Department of Information Technology has set up a Centre for E-Governance at DIT. The objective of the Centre is to showcase existing tools and applications in e-Governance and also serve as a forum for government officials, legislators, industry, and various other key players to come together, discuss, learn and explore issues of shared importance. The Centre also helps identify/develop applications of immediate concern to the various Central Ministries/Departments and the State Governments. The Centre showcases e-governance projects developed and implemented by different States.

The primary activities of the Centre are:

a) To showcase the best practices in the area of Electronic Governance which would encompass technology, processes as well as public policies;

b) Conduct programs for creating awareness among decision makers in the Central and State Governments;

c) Demonstrate the feasibility of Electronic Governance to decision makers through workshops, demonstration programs, video/tele-conferencing etc.

d) Help the Central and State Governments in defining and implementing process and policy changes; and

e) To enrich the repository of best practices through continuous interaction with subject matter experts from India and abroad.

National level workshop on E-Governance.

For effective implementation of E-governance it is necessary that there is a political ownership. It is proposed to organize a high level national seminar under the chairmanship of Prime Minister. Important opinion makers from the political leadership and citizen forums will be invited for this conference wherein the issues related to Electronic Governance are debated with the aim of getting a strong national consensus to implement the same.

Establishing E-Governance Website

DIT has setup an E-Governance Website http://egov.mit.gov.in/·for dissemination of public information at DIT.

Identify key projects of relevance for E-Governance and develop technology pilots as demonstrators.

Steps Taken by State Govenrments

EG Initiatives in States/Ministries/Departments

Ministry of Textiles

Ministry of Parliamentary Affairs

Ministry of Chemicals And Fertilizers

Ministry of Civil Aviation

Ministry of Environment & Forests

Ministry of Finanace

Ministry of Labour

Ministry of Tourism

Ministry of Communication

Ministry of External Affairs

Ministry of Informaion and Broadcasting

Ministry of Power

Ministry of Surface transport

Ministry of Science & Technology

Steps taken by various Departments in the area of E-Governance

Department of Agriculture

Department of Posts

Department of Space

Steps taken by various States in the area of E-Governance

Andhra Pradesh Haryana Chandigarh

Gujarat Karnataka Kerala

Lakshwadeep Maharashtra Orissa

Pondicherry Punjab Rajasthan

Sikkim Tamil Nadu Tripura

Uttar Pradesh West Bengal

This list is not comprehensive but indicative of the initiatives being undertaken by various

State Governments/Central Ministries/Departments

Government portals of different Countries

USA	UK	Canada
Singapore	China	Australia
Ireland	Israel	France
Netherlands	Germany	Tasmania
Finland	Estonia	Italy
Sweden	United Nations	

E-GOVERNANCE RELATED PROJECTS

Projtcs.htm

Projects undertaken by TCSProjects undertaken by CMC

Projects undertaken by C-DACProjects undertaken by IQ Virtuals

Technologies from SHONKH Projects undertaken by ORACLE

Projects undertaken by IBM Projects undertaken by NIC

Projects undertaken by MBTProjects undertaken by TCIL

Centre for e-Governance

As part of the increased thrust on e-Governance, Ministry of Communications & Information Technology, Department of Information Technology, Government of India, has set up a Centre for e-Governance (CEG) at its premises – Electronics Niketan in New Delhi. The Centre, first of its kind in the country, showcases several e-Governance applications and solutions that have been successfully deployed in various states, and offers such other services like technical consultation, proof of concept and thematic presentations. Conducting programmes for creating awareness among decision makers in the Centre and State Governments and helping them in defining and implementing process and policy changes for effective e-Governance are other important objectives of the Centre.

The primary activities of the Centre are:

* To showcase the best practices in the area of e-Governance
* Conduct programs for creating awareness among decision makers in the Centre and State Governments.
* Demonstrate the feasibility of concepts in e-Governance to the decision makers through workshops, demonstrations video/teleconferencing etc.
* Help the Central and State Governments in defining and implementing the process and policy changes.
* To enrich the repository of best practices through continuous interaction with subject experts from India and abroad.

The Centre would also draw upon leading companies, technical institutions and business partners in India and abroad and help initiate projects to address specific needs. The Centre would further strive to establish strong links with similar institutions worldwide to enrich the repository of best practices through continuous interaction and participation. The foreign Delegations or Visitors are also shown the facility that has been created at the centre. The Centre was formally inaugurated on 15th August 2000.

Minimum Agenda for E-Governance in the Ministries / Departments of the Central Government

* Each Ministry / Department must set up LANs and provide PCs with necessary software up to the Section Officer level.

* 100% training of all staff who have access to and need to use computers for their office work should be ensured.
* Each Ministry / Department would start using the Office Procedure Automation software developed by NIC with a view to keeping a record of receipt of dak, issue of letters, as well as movement of files in the department.
* Pay roll accounting and other house-keeping software should be put to use in day-to-day operations.
* Notices for internal meeting should be sent by email to the officers and also put up on online notice boards of the Ministry / Department.
* Ministries / Departments should use the Web-enabled Grievance
* Redressal Software developed by Department of AR & PG.
* Each Ministry / Department should have its own website.
* All Acts, Rules, Circulars should be converted into electronic form and, along with other published material of interest or relevance to the public, should be made available on the internet and be accessible from the Information and Facilitation Counter.
* The websites of Ministries / Departments / Organisations should specifically contain a section in which various forms to be used by citizens / customers are available. The forms should be available for being printed out or for being completed on the computer itself and then printed out for submission. Attempts should also be made to enable completion and submission of forms online.
* The Hindi version of the content of the websites should be developed simultaneously, as far as possible.
* Each Ministry / Department would also make efforts to develop packages so as to begin electronic delivery of services to the public.

* Each Ministry / Department should have an overall IT version or strategy for a five year period, within which it could do detail specific action plans and targets (including the minimum agenda) to be implemented within one year.

Centrally Sponsored Scheme

Government of India has taken up several measures to promote e-Governance and use of Information Technology in the Central and State Governments. The Planning Commission constituted a Working Group on Convergence and e-Governance for the Tenth Five Year Plan (2002-2007).

National Informatics Centre (NIC)

The long-term objective of the National Informatics Centre, as approved by the Planning Commission, Ministry of Finanace and the Electronics Commission, is 'to establish the feasibility of a system for the provision of detailed information to government ministries and agencies to assist them in making decisions relating to the country's economic and social development planning and programme implementation'. (Annual Report of the Department of Electronics, Government of India, 1977-'78,p172.)

NIC was set up with the objective to promote economic, social, scientific and technological activities, and also for macro-economic adjustment programme of the Government, through the applications of IT.

Objectives

The long-term objective of the National Informatics Centre, as approved by the Planning Commission, Ministry of Finanace and the Electronics Commission, is 'to establish the feasibility of a system for the provision of detailed information to government ministries and agencies to assist them in making decisions relating to the country's economic and social development planning and programme implementation'. (Annual Report of the Department of Electronics, Government of India, 1977-'78,p172.)

NIC was set up with the objective to promote economic, social, scientific and technological activities, and also for macro-economic adjustment programme of the Government, through the applications of IT.

Mandate

As laid down in the Annual Reports of DOE 1976-'77 and 1977-'78, NIC was given the mandate to provide this informatics service to various user agencies in Government play a promotional role in creating appropriate information systems in Governmentact as a focal point for developing, managing and operating information system in Government act as a focal point for development of methodologies for designing and implementing national information systems and data management techniques act as a focal point for maintaining inventories of primary data and computer-based systems for data collection and dissemination train users in information systems, data management and computing techniquesTen information systems were planned for development by NIC in the following sectors:

Agriculture

Construction and Transport

Education and Manpower

Energy

Finance

Industry

Small-Scale Industries

Socio-Economic Index

Trade and Media

Government Archival Information

With this, NIC embarked on a gradiose mission to develop various national data bases for use in planning and deceision making by the government.

Evolution

Starting as a small programme under an external stimulus by an UNDP project in early 1970s, NIC started functioning in 1977 and since then it has grown incrementally and later exponentially as one of India's major S&T Organisation promoting Informatics-led Development, which has helped to usher in the required transformation to cope with the trends in the new millennium.

NIC has played an important role of an active catalyst and facilitator in informatics development programme in Governments at the national, state and district levels, during the last 26 years which made them take policy decisions to create knowledge societies – societies that can exploit knowledge to derive competitive advantage using the opportunities provided by digital technology. NIC has been instrumental in adopting Information Technology and Communication Technology to reach out into India i.e. by implementing IT applications in Social and Public Administrations.

ORGANIZATIONS

Profile

The organizational set up of NIC encompasses its Headquarters at New Delhi, State Units in all the 28 State capitals and 7 Union Territory Headquarters and District centres in almost all the Districts of India. The Organization employs a large pool of efficient technical manpower.

At the NIC Headquarters, a large number of Application Divisions exist which provide total Informatics Support to the Ministries and Departments of the Central Government. NIC computer cells are located in almost all the Ministry Bhawans of the Central Government and Apex Offices including the Prime Minister's Office, the Rashtrapati Bhawan and the Parliament House.

Headquarters

NIC Headquarters is based in New Delhi. At NIC Headquarters, a large number of Application Divisions exist which provide total Informatics Support to the Ministries and Departments of the Central Government. NIC computer cells are located in almost all the Ministry Bhawans of the Central Government and Apex Offices including the Prime Minister's Office, the Rashtrapati Bhawan and the Parliament House. Apart from this, NIC has various Resource Divisions at the Headquarters which specialize into different areas of IT and facilitate the Application Divisions as well as other NIC Centres in providing state-of-the-art services to the Govt.

National Informatics Centre,
A-Block, CGO Complex,
Lodhi Road,
New Delhi - 110 003, India
Telephone : 91-11-4361133
Fax : 91-11-4362628

State/UTs

At the State level, NICs State/UTs Units provide informatics support to their respective State Government and at the District level lie the NIC District Infomatics Offices.

District Centres

At the District level, NIC District Units provide effective informatics support to the Development, Revenue and Judiciary administration of the District.

Please click on any of the State/UT given below to get contact information about the concerned NIC District Units

SERVICES

Computer Aided Design

For survival in the rapidly changing technological environment, competitive marketing and rapid obsolesce, it has become a need for the Indian industries and organizations to switch to the latest design techniques for their products. NIC provides specialized Computer Aided Design (CAD) services to industries in the field of Engineering, Automobile and Civil Structures Design. NIC also utilizes one of world's best software packages, called SESAM, for the design of large engineering structures, including those for offshore oil platforms. The SESAM Package, originally imported from Norway, has been extensively modified by NIC to suit the customized needs of the Users. NIC also provides Consultancy Support to big companies for setting up their own CAD Centres and also in the area of Analysis and Design. It also provides extensive training to the personnel of the User Organizations.

Computer Aided Paperless Examination System

Capes at National Informatics Center (a premier IT organization of Govt. of India) provides an extremely effective automated, multi-user software to help organizations to meet their varied examination needs with a competitive edge.

Capes ensures scientific, rational method for conducting the examinations in addition to the requisite confidentiality and security features. Its GUI based Software with Twin Architectures, for Web and Client/Server environment provides cost, time & administrative benefits for examinations with 50 or more candidates specially.

The Knowledge & Skill Test with its comprehensive and constantly updated question bank helps assess and retain the best talents in industry while the computerized Typing Speed Test helps clients monitor and judge accurate performances.

Our mission is to make CAPES a premier technology enabled Recruitment/ Examination software solution in the IT world.

Computer Aided Telephony Interface

The Computer Telephony Solutions by NIC is a solution for Public Interface.

A CTI (Computer Telephony Interface) or IVRS (Interactive Voice Response System) application is one where the caller dials a given telephone number and the computer plays the part of an operator giving out the information requested, in recorded or synthesized voice.

The Computer is configured to accept calls with the help of dedicated CTI software and hardware required on the CTI server computer for their application. The calls are placed from any standard telephone instrument. The CTI Computer server accepts both pulse dial and tone dial instruments. For best results, Tone dial instruments are preferred. Since the telephone can dial out numbers only, the application is limited to the numerical usage only.Information from Database can be played also.

There are no limitations to the voice used for answering the system. It purely depends on the service provider as to what language he wants and gets a suitable voice to record the voice prompts. The synthesized voice is available only for American English

Internet Services

Internet has evolved into one of technology's greatest democracies, permitting the passage of all kinds of information carries crossing with full freedom. NIC has taken upon itself the ask to make sure that India becomes an active member of the 'Global Village' as created by the INTERNET.

The Internet services of NIC are provided through NICNET, NIC' s satellite based computer communication network.

The range of Internet Services being provided by NIC includes:

* Electronic mail
* WWW Browsing
* File transfer Facility
* Remote Login

* Directory Services
* Gateway to SMTP/UUCP

Mathematical Modeling and Simulation

In order to propagate and promote, the scientific decision making as a, process, full fledged division, taking care of the following major activities for the government departments (central and state as well as public sector undertakings) is operational in NIC Headquarters from its inception.

Mathematical Modelling & Simulation Division has developed infrastructure facilities and expertise in the area of computer aided modelling techniques using state-of-the-art quantitative quantitative and simulation techniques besides development of   Business Intelligence (BI) applications and providing consultancy and trainings.

For planning in a dynamic economic environment and choice among strategic option(s), the use of quantitative, qualitative ,management and simulation techniques for a scenario generation has been well established and been used worldwide. Computer Aided Model(s) and Decision Support System(s) DSS have been widely used by planners, policy makers, administrators and academicians for strengthening the decision making as a process. Computer systems linked with powerful computer communication network have further increased the utility and operationalization of such systems world wide.

Multimedia Services

The Multimedia Technology has helped the presentation of information in the most interesting, comprehensive and organized manner. NIC realized the potential of Multimedia years ago and was amongst the first in India to get down to the task of introducing and developing the technology in the Country. The Organization promises to offer attractive and cost-effective solutions to all your diverse multimedia needs. The range of Multimedia Services offered include the development of following :

The training divisions of NIC are duly equipped with hi-tech multimedia systems and state-of-the-art lecture/convention halls. The facilities include the capacity to conduct four training programmes simultaneously with a man-machine ratio of 1:1 in practice sessions. Regular Training Programmes to update the skills of the in-house staff are also held throughout the year. Apart from these, NIC also conducts, customized training sessions for specialized groups such as Civil Servants, International teams visiting India, Armed Forces personnel etc. The training centres of NIC are located at the Head Quarters in Delhi, at the Regional Centres and at all the State Centres.

Videoconferencing

Videoconferencing is changing the way companies do business. It is bringing decision-makers together, face-to-face, wherever they are, across the country or around the globe. Experts from remote locations can interact with each other in real time. It is bringing education and training to corporations and to students around the world. By providing strong lines of visual, graphical and multimedia communication, Videoconferencing opens the lines in every area - business, government, educational institutions and healthcare facilities.

With 9 years of experience in Videoconferencing Technology, National Informatics Centre's technical expertise is unmatched in the country. NIC is currently providing videoconferencing services from 206 cities in India including all north-eastern state capitals over its high speed satellite based network called "NICNET". This is the largest videoconferencing network in India, spread across length and width of the country. The advantage of using satellite based communications is that it can deliver high speed data and provide videoconferencing at remote locations, which were earlier not easily accessible.

NIC is also providing Videoconferencing services from many Central and State Government Ministries using ISDN lines.

"Anytime Any Where Videoconferencing Services" of

NIC, using Portable VSAT and portable Videoconferencing, is widely being availed by various NICNET users. This service can be utilized to provide temporary Videoconferencing service for conferences, exhibitions, seminars, and other important events.

NIC's VC Service has been made available as a paid service at the rate of Rs. 3240/- per hour for a point-point Video Conferencing.

WWW Services

After the commercialization of Internet, World Wide Web is experiencing a revolution of unmatched magnitude. In India too, hundreds of organizations are launching their websites daily. NIC provides value added services in this area to facilitate Govt. Sector in India to have an effective presence on the Net.

Equipped with the latest state-of-the-art Multimedia work stations and chosen professional in the field of conceptualization, visualization, graphic arts,script writing, web & multimedia authoring and programming, NIC strives to provide a competitive solution to all your web needs.The entire gamut of web services include:

Web site Design & Development

Web page Hosting & Maintenance

Review of Web Sites

Enhancement of Existing Web Sites

NIC maintains state-of-the-art web servers at its Headquarters which currently hosts around 2000 web sites providing extensive information about various aspects of the Indian Government. NIC has also set up a state-of-art Storage Area Network (SAN) in its data center at Delhi. This high capacity SAN is being used as storage infrastructure for Web Sites, Portals, Citizen Services, Databases,

E-Mail and other Internet services.

NICNET SERVICES

NIC has established a nationwide ICT Network – NICNET – with gateway nodes in Central Government Departments, 35 State/UT Secretariats, and in almost all 603 District Collectorates, for IT services. The Government has designated the nation-wide Computer-Communication Network, NICNET, as the Government Network.

NICNET was designed and implemented by NIC using state-of-the-art satellite-based computer communication technology. Keeping in view the wide geographic spread of the country, ranging from Islands in the Indian Ocean to the highest Himalayan Ranges, the design of NIC NET, which is one of the largest VSAT Networks of its kind in the world, ensures extremely cost effective and reliable implementation.

In Mahe, NICNET has now been operational since 1994 and has become an integral part of Office of the Regional Administrator and large no of Government Departments, providing information exchange services. NICNET services include file transfer, electronic mail, remote data base access, data broadcast, EDI. The installation Direct PC & FTDMA technology started the internet facility in NIC, Mahe which helps general public to access important information quickly especially examination result and competitive exam results.

E-governance initiatives

PAYROLL

As a part of the office automation, Payroll system has been implemented in following Government Departments in Mahe.

1. Office of the Regional Administrator
2. Office of the Chief Educational Officer
3. Office of the Dy. Collector, Revenue
4. Police department

5. Health Department
6. Government Higher Secondary Schools, Mahe
7. Government Higher Secondary Schools, Palloor
8. Government Higher Secondary Schools, Pandakkal
9. Mahatma Gandhi Arts College
10. Public Works Department

COMPUTERIZATION OF EXCISE DEPARTMENT

The Software for issuing Import Permit, Export Permit and Transport Permit for Excise Department, has been implemented since the beginning of the NIC. The computerization helped the department speedy dispatch of Permits with in a limited time frame.

COMPUTERIZATION OF TRANSPORT DEPARTMENT

The Software for Issuing Lerner's License, Driving license and Registration of Vehicles is implemented in NIC, Mahe.

LAND RECORDS COMPUTERIZATION

Computerization of Land Records for Sub Taluk Office, Mahe has been successfully completed. The Software in Bi-lingual (English & Malayalam) has been installed in NIC, Mahe. Data Entry , Verification of Data and Updating for all villages has been completed. The Settlement Register and other Reports has been generated in pre-printed stationery.

EMPLOYMENT EXCHANGE COMPUTERIZATION

The registration of employment seekers, renewal of registrations, additional entries of qualifications and experiences obtained subsequently. Submission of candidates list to employers. Employment market information compilation and submission of statistical data. Generating Registration Identity Card to public in pre printed stationery. Verification of Renewal status, Seniority status, correctness of data entered already in respect of registrants etc, are the major attraction for the computerization.

CERTIFICATE COMPUTERIZATION IN SUB TALUK OFFICE

Issuing different Certificates like Community certificate, Nativity certificate, Income certificate etc of Sub Taluk, Revenue Department has been computerized.

LAN BETWEEN NIC AND OFFICE OF THE REGIONAL ADMINISTRATOR

A Multi Lingual terminal has been installed at Regional Administrator's Chamber through Dialup Modem Connection using EPBX lines. This Facility helped Regional Administrator to transmit\Receive urgent E-Mails to\from Government of Pondicherry and other Departments\Ministries.

COMPUTERIZATION OF OLD AGE PENSION SCHEME

The Pension scheme of Social Welfare Department has been computerized. This System generates Anganwadiwise Acquittance for distribution of pension to the Old Age widows/ Handicapped persons. Acquittance for Plan Schemes and Non-Plan Schemes generate separately. Monthly consolidated and statistical reports needed for the dept. are also prepared. Continuous return/Expire cases were taken care by the system. Prepares statements for these cases.

NIC SUPPORT TO MAHE ADMINISTRATION DURING GENERAL ELECTION

Updating the data every TWO hours on the polling day by logging directly into the Server at Pondicherry through NIC NET. The reports like Region wise. Polling Percentage, Constituency wise Polling Percentage and Booth wise Polling Percentage of UT disseminated to General Public, Mahe. The Reports like FORM A08, FORM 20 has been generated for Election Office. Transmitted the Flash News, VIP Tracks, and detailed Track forms to Election Server, NIC HQ, New Delhi through NIC NET for DoorDarshan. After installing necessary computer system and peripherals at counting place, round wise election result from counting place has been displayed on Board at various places in Mahe for General Public.

Databases available on NICNET

Medlars

DISNIC

COURTNIC

GISTNIC

For the purpose of research, projections, etc.,academicians, researchers, and professionals require data. NICNET also caters to these needs by providing a variety of databases. Some of them are :

Medlars in INDIA

Medical Literature Analysis and Retrieval Systems(MEDLARS) created by National Library of Medicine(NLM) of National Insti- tutes of Health,Bethesda,USA, comprising 28 databases is the most extensively used biomedical information system in the world.The information provided by this system extends to literature, pub- lished and unpublished,in all areas of medicine including dentistry, nursing, cancer, AIDS,toxicology,population and health planning and administration.

Medical Literature, Analysis and Retrieval Systems (MEDLARS) in India is the 17th International centre, that provides instant access to biomedical database through an arrangement with the National Library of Medicine, USA. The database is designed for meeting the information requirements of doctors, medical reasearchers and students alike.

The National Informatics Centre(NIC) New Delhi has been designat- ed as the Indian MEDLARS Centre(IMC). MEDLARS services are pro- vided by NIC NICNET. This network is accessible from all 450 computer centres of NIC. NICNET provides linkages to international networks, using which IMC has directly been linked to the National Library of Medicine and can access all MEDLARS databases.

One of the most important database of MEDLARS is MEDLINE which covers articles from over 3500 journals from 70 countries in the field of general medicine including nursing,dentistry and pre-clinical sciences.

Medline data from 1986 onwards is available on a minicomputer at NIC, New Delhi. A menu driven bibliographic retrieval software,BRS/SEARCH is used to search this database. This data- base is directly accessible to NICNET users.MEDLINE data prior to this as well as information from all other MEDLARS databases is available on request from IMC.

Some of the services offered by Indian MEDLARS Centre are :

Online access to MEDLINE and AIDS databases.

Information from other NLM databases.

Interactive access to CDROM databases.

Online search of Catalogue of Biomedical Periodicals.

District Information System(DISNIC)

DISNIC programme facilitates the development and analysis of databases (both spatial and non- spatial) for decision support in 27 sectors. These include education, industry, agriculture, cooperative, microlevel planning etc. This NICNET based programme is operational in about 460 districts in the country Implementation of DISNIC programme facilitates development planning and responsive administration right from grass root level.

CourtNIC

COURTNIC is a user friendly information system designed to provide information on the pending cases of Supreme Court of India to a wide range of users. The information made available on the COURTNIC includes listing information,status & position of a case filed in the Supreme Court of India, complete daily case list and retrieval through lower court details. This information is made available from all NIC-High Court computer centres on NICNET.

JUDIS

JUDIS is a comprehensive on-line caselaw library.It contains all reportable judgements of the Supreme Court of India from 1950 onwards. JUDIS provides a facility to find relevant precedents to a case on virtually any subject that is dealt by Supreme Court of India, and it is a powerful citation : case citations can be very easily found through JUDIS. JUDIS is accessible from any of the 650 nodes of NICNET.

GISTNIC

GISTNIC (General Information Service Terminal - National Informatics Centre) is an on-line database service of NICNET. GISTNIC offers on-line information retrieval services from its wide ranging static and quasi-static areas such as Indian Economy monitor, IMF databases, 1991 population Census Database, Village Amenities Database, Rural Technology Database, Tourist Guide of India, District Profiles, University and College directory of India and a Database on Traditional Sciences and Technologies of India.

NIC has taken up the task of creating and disseminating a computer based database on traditional sciences and technologies of India as a part of the rural technologies databases covered under the GISTNIC(general informations service terminal-national informatics centre) project of National Informatics Centre. The GISTNIC database on traditional sciences and technologies of India has been classified into about 10 major subject areas like :

* Traditional Indian Medical,Health Care,Yoga and Other Related systems.
* Traditional Indian Architecture ,Building Materials,Town Plan- ning and Construction Methodologies.

* Traditional Indian Metallurgy,Mining,Geology and Material Sciences.
* Traditional Indian Textile and Handloom Technologies.
* Traditional Irrigation,Water Resource Management,Hydrology and Ground Water Management Methodologies of India.
* Traditional Indian Agriculture ,Agronomical methods, Practices and Implements.
* Traditional Skills,trades,professions,arts,crafts & handicrafts.
* Ancient Indian science & technology.
* Traditional and Ancient Indian management administration, economic, social and political systems and sciences.
* Miscellaneous and General.

GISTNIC may be accessed from the following sites.

telnet 164.100.12.8 (Pentium machine at Hyderabad)

telnet 164.100.10.80 (Pentium machine at New Delhi)

For further details please contact :

CCA

Trust in electronic environment through digital signatures PKI Framework under the IT Act

Central to the growth of e-commerce and e-governance is the issue of trust in electronic environment. The future of e-commerce and e-governance depends on the trust that the transacting parties place in the security of transmission and the content of communication.

Creating trust in electronic environment involves assuring the transacting parties about the integrity and confidentiality of the content of documents along with authentication of the sending and receiving parties in a manner that ensures that both the parties cannot repudiate the transaction. The paper based concepts of identification, declaration and proof are carried through the use of digital signatures in electronic environment. Digital signatures, a form of electronic signatures, are created and verified using Public Key Cryptography that is based on the concept of a key pair generated by a mathematical algorithm, the public and private keys.

The Information Technology Act, 2000 provides the required legal sanctity to the digital signatures based on asymmetric cryptosystems. The digital signatures are now accepted at par with handwritten signatures and the electronic documents that have been digitally signed are treated at par with paper documents.

The IT Act provides for the Controller of Certifying Authorities (CCA) to license and regulate the working of Certifying Authorities. The Certifying Authorities (CAs) issue digital signature certificates for electronic authentication of users.

The CCA certifies the public keys of CAs using its own private key, which enables users in the cyberspace to verify that a given certificate is issued by a licensed CA. For this purpose it operates, the Root Certifying Authority of India (RCAI). The CCA also maintains the National Repository of Digital Certificates (NRDC), which contains all the certificates issued by all the CAs in the country.

CCA at the root of the trust chain in India.

CERT in

The Indian Computer Emergency Response Team (CERT-In) has been established by the Department of Information Technology to be a part of the international CERT community. It has a mandate to respond to computer security incidents reported by the entire computer and networking community in the country alongwith creating security awareness among the Indian cyber-community.

laboratory has a small permanent senior research staff that is independent of the associated academic institutions, and researchers who have short-term appointments of three to five years; students; and researchers from sponsoring organizations, including companies and NGOs.

Language Technologies

Prime Minister's Message TDIL Initiatives

Information Technology has brought about the revolution that has transformed commodities, people and their relations. Our sages envisioned the world as a Global Village: "Vasudhaiv Kutumbkam". That vision is poised to become a reality as communities and countries network and join up. What we need is the right mindset to impel us towards the state of "Sarve Bhavantu Sukhinah".

The opportunities that today's knowledge economy offers enable us to make the knowledge and innovation available far and wide, without any barriers of nationality, language, culture, caste and creed. IT with such a humanitarian perspective will lead to a society where peace and harmony obtain. I hope that with the success of the Technology Development for Indian Languages Mission programme, India will emerge as a pioneering hub of multilingual computing and provide appropriate technology solutions for overcoming linguistic and cultural barriers, and thereby ensure knowledge for all.

Community Information Centre

ArunachalPradesh

Assam

Nagaland

Manipur

Meghalaya

Tripura

Mizoram

Sikkim

The main project was inaugurated on 17th August 2002 with the dedication of 457 CICs to the people of the North-East by Hon'ble Minister for Communications and Information Technology and Parliamentary Affairs, Shri Pramod Mahajan in Guwahati.

The following table gives a summary of the magnitude of the project :

State	*Districts*	*Blocks*	*Pilot*	*Main*
1. Arunachal Pradesh	15	56	2	54
2. Assam	23	219	15	204
3. Manipur	9	33	2	31
4. Meghalaya	7	32	2	30
5. Mizoram	8	26	2	24
6. Nagaland	11	52	2	50
7. Sikkim	4	40	2	38
8. Tripura	4	29	3	26
Total	81	487	30	457

Infrastructure and Management

Each Centre is well- equipped with infrastructure including one server machine, five client systems, one each of a VSAT, Laser Printer, Dot Matrix Printer, modem, LAN hub, TV, Webcam and two UPS (1KVA, 2 KVA).

Each CIC has two CIC Operators (CICOs) for managing the centers and providing services to the public. CIC operators in all states have been trained on networking equipment and software applications available at their sites.

The project is a joint effort by Department of Information Technology (DIT) under Ministry of Communications and Information Technology (MCIT), National Informatics Centre (NIC) and the State Governments of the North-Eastern states.

DIT has funded the project and has the responsibility of

overall monitoring and management. NIC is the Implementation agency. Application Software development and Training of CIC Operators are a part of NIC's responsibilities. The State Governments were entrusted with the mandate of site selection, preparation and maintenance, manpower recruitment and identification and creation of content for various services/ applications to be delivered through the CICs

Project Implementation and Monitoring

In addition to the CIC Cell at DIT and the CIC group at NIC Headquarters, the project has been executed with the contribution of NIC's State Informatics Officers (SIOs) and District Informatics Officers (DIOs) who have liaised with the state government authorities and the vendors delivering and installing the equipment at the CICs. Eight State coordinators have been appointed at NIC Headquarters to facilitate implementation at the local and central levels.

The CIC group at NIC, New Delhi has developed a comprehensive information system for the CICs wherein every aspect of the progress of the project is remotely monitored. The delivery, installation and operation status of all hardware and software is logged into this site by the SIOs and CIC Operators themselves, including post-installation malfunction of machines and applications.

The CIC group holds review meetings, twice a week, over Video Conference, with the SIOs of the North-Eastern states, vendor representatives both in Delhi and in Guwahati and Calcutta, State Coordinators and officers from other NIC divisions associated with the project such as SATCOM division. Chat sessions are held everyday between staff from CIC group and SATCOM division at Headquarters and the CIC Operators at remote sites for troubleshooting. A Visual Monitoring system is in place whereby CICOs can send images captured with the Web Cameras to Delhi for attendance and general observation. TVs have been provided at each site to disseminate educational programmes through Doordarshan and IGNOU in addition to general entertainment which is anticipated to attract visitors to the CICs.

The establishment of the CICs has been an arduous and very challenging task.

Services

Basic services to be provided by CICs include Internet Access and E-mail, Printing, Data entry and Word processing and Training for the local populace. In addition, several citizen-centric or Government to Citizen(G2C) services are to be delivered from the CICs. Some such services are

- Birth and Death Registration
- Service Facilitation Centre (e-Suvidha) wherein different types of certificates issued by Block and District administrations like SC/ST, Marriage etc can be disseminated through CICs
- Prices and other market information of Agricultural produce
- Information on Educational opportunities
- Job portals etc.

The number of visitors varies between 20 to 100 a week depending on location of CIC. Many CICs report over 150 visitors/week.

Utilization of CICs

Training

Training of the local population on the fundamentals of using computers and the imparting of basic working knowledge is a major activity in the Community Information Centres.

Project Sustenance

Many of the CICs, already operational, charge nominal amounts from users for services which helps them to meet day-to-day running expenses such as consumables, stationery, fuel for the Genset etc.

DIT/NIC will continue to provide manpower support to the CICs for five years and NIC will provide technical and maintenance support for this period. DIT/NIC will continue to provide satellite connectivity after five years. The Community Information Centres will then be handed over to the respective state governments. The state governments are required to evolve a viable business model to make the CICs self-sustaining during these five years. The private sector may collaborate with government for effective service delivery.

Substantive revenue generation has been achieved by many CICs such as Golaghat, Assam and Gangtok, Sikkim which pays the salaries of the operators from this revenue.

Future Plans

It is proposed to use the Community Information Centres for E-edutainment in the future. A select bouquet of channels could be telecast through the VSAT based network as TVs with other associated infrastructure is already available at the CICs. Other future prospects are the provision of connectivity to Schools,Hospitals and Post Offices in major habitats.

BHARAT SANCHAR NIGAM LIMITED (BSNL)

BSNL is the 5th largest network in the world, second largest among emerging economies (after China). It has 39 million line telephone network including mobile phones. Annual growth rate of 22% in basic telephone service and over 100% for cellular and Internet services. BSNL expects Increase in teledensity from 4% to 7% by 2005 and 15% by 2010.

Approx. 75 million telephone connections to be added by 2005 and 175 million by 2010.

Investment requirement of US$ 37 billion by 2005 and US $ 69 billion by 2010.

Private participation allowed in all types of telecom and IT enabled services. License granted on non-exclusive basis for basic, national long distance, international long distance, Internet, V-Sat services, etc.

Foreign equity participation permitted in the telecom service sector which varies from 49% to 100%.

Huge market for all types of telecom equipments for both wire line and wireless, Internet, radio trunking, call centers, etc.

Foreign direct investment of up to 100% permitted for the manufacturing of telecom equipment.

Investments potential across a wide spectrum of telecom services.

Data source : Indian Telecommunications Statistics 2002.

Human Resource Development

With a corporate philosophy that considers Human Resource as the most prized assets of the organization, it's natural for BSNL to continually hone employee skills, enhance their knowledge and their expertise and their aspirations to fruition. Even as BSNL goes about conducting its business activities, it lays emphasis on constant enhancement of knowledge and skills through regular training programmes.

Bharat Sanchar Nigam Limited has a vast reservoir of highly skilled and experienced work force of about 3,57,000 personnel.

We believe that our staff, which is one of the best trained manpower in the telecom sector, is our biggest asset.

We believe that our future depends on our staff who provide services to our valued customers and stay in touch with them.

To meet the technological challenges, employees are trained for technology up-gradation, modernization, computerization etc in BSNL's training Centers spread across Country. These centers are properly equipped with the requisite infrastructure facilities such as Lecture rooms, modern audio-visual aids, libraries, hostels etc.

To apex training centers of BSNL i.e: Advance level Telecom Training Center (ALTTC) at Ghaziabad and Bharat Ratna Bhimrao Telecom Training Center at Jabalpur are

Service using FWT

In this case, there is a small box fitted with a small antenna at the subscribers premises and a normal telephone instrument is connected to the box. There is no wire connection as in conventional telephone.

Service using Hand Held Terminal (WLL-M service)

In this case, subscriber can carry a small handset of CDMA technology. There is no antenna or any other equipment at subscribers premises. Subscriber will get the service for major part of greater Kolkata stretching from Bhatpara, Chinsurah in the north to Budge-Budge, Harinavi in the south. In the east-west direction it works from Barasat in the east to Uluberia in the west.

Why Choose BSNL'S TARANG CDMA Mobile

BSNL's WLL Tarang service is the most reliable and affordable service giving you the best of both fixed line telephony & Mobile telephony.It offers host of value added services at virtually no cost to our esteemed suscribers.Customer may get the handset by paying premium approx. Rs. 20/- per month only for the comprehensive policy taken for the cost of handset.

Tarang WLL-M

It offers you a host of value-added services:

Voice-mail service: 24 hour personal call answering service

Call waiting: allows you to receive an incoming call while already engaged in one call

Call hold: allows you to put a current call on hold and make a second call

Call divert: allows you to divert calls within your SDCA

3-way call conferencing: allows a conference between 3 persons from your mobile handset

CLIP (Caller Line Identification Presentation): enables

you to view the number of the calling person when you receive a call

CLIR (Call Line Identification Restriction): enables you to block presentation of your own number on a called person's phone

Internet be accessed from WLL-FWT line

Dynamic STD/ISD locking.

Data / Fax transmission (upto 14.4.kbps).

Morning alarm / Hotline

Voice Mail Service

Short Message Service (SMS)

Group Messaging

National Roaming

Call forwarding

Corporate Virtual Private Network

Call conferencing

Friend and Family Talk

Call waiting and Call holding facility

Unified Messaging Services: This provides Voice mail, FAX, e-mail, text to voice services on your mobile phone. So stay in touch with your nears and dears by means you like the most.

Wireless Application Protocol (WAP): Surf WAP enabled websites on Internet using this service.

List of cities where BSNL mobile service starts in the first phase

Details of the state-wise plans for countrywide coverage of the BSNL Mobile service

Internet

BSNL is India's no. 1 Internet service provider with more than 7.5 lakh subscribers, providing Internet service throughout the entire country (except in New Delhi and Mumbai)under the brand name of "Sancharnet". Sancharnet provides free all India roaming and enables it's users to access their accounts, using the same access code (172233) and user ID from any where in the Country. In order to make Internet available through out the length and breadth of the Country Internet Dhabas are being commissioned at all the Block Headquarters. BSNL has also started DIAS and Account free internet access(CLI based) facility on few select cities recently.

BSNL has launched "SANCHARNET CARD" recently. The Sancharnet Card" is a prepaid Internet Access Card with following features for customers:

Self-register for internet access with your choice of userid

Renew your existing Sancharnet Account

Wide Range of Internet Access Packages

Web-hosting service is also provided by the BSNL. It allows customers to host their static or dynamic web-sites on BSNL servers. Web hosting service provides basic features like Web-space (Data Storage) on servers for hosting HTML pages with browser supported MIME types, Primary or Secondary Domain Name Hosting, Server Side Scripting: Perl, Java Servlets, JSP, Database Access(MySQL), Email Access and Web-email, Multiple Email IDs as per the plan, Ftp access for uploading and downloading pages as per the plan, Continuous usage billing for Web, Messaging and FTP etc.

Call your nears and dears abroad at very cheap rates availing Internet telephony services of BSNL named 'Web Fone'. Click here to see complete details about this service>>

BSNL Internet subscribers (Sancharnet users) can see their account information i.e. hours used/left, change passwords and see their e-mails on BSNL Sancharnet website www.sancharnet.in

MPLS BASED VPN SERVICE

BSNL's IP Backbone using MPLS Technology:

Keeping pace with the technological trend to provide latest and varied value added services to its customers, BSNL harnesses IP Infrastructure based on MPLS Technology to offer world class IP VPN services. MPLS is an acronym for "Multi Protocol Label Switching".

MPLS VPN is a technology that allows a Service Provider like BSNL to have complete control over parameters that are critical to offering its customers service guarantees with regard to bandwidth throughputs, latencies and availability. The technology enables secure Virtual Private Networks (VPN) to be built and allows scalability that will make it possible for BSNL to offer assured growth to its customers without having to make significant investments. BSNL would now be geared to provide Bandwidth on demand, Video Conferencing, Voice Over IP (VoIP) and a host of other value added services that could revolutionize the way a corporate business works!

MPLS based VPNs reduce customer networking complexity, costs and totally do away with the requirement of in-house technical work force. Rather than setting up and managing individual point-to-point circuits between each office using pair of Leased Lines, MPLS VPN customers need to provide only one connection from their office router to a service provider edge router.

BSNL has tied up with various Networking solution providers to provide end-to-end solution to its valued customers, including Customer End (CE) routers and other networking components.

What advantages does MPLS VPN have over other Technologies:

BSNL's primary objectives in setting up the BGP/MPLS VPN network are:

(i) Provide a diversified range of services (Layer 2, Layer 3 and Dial up VPNs) to meet the requirements of the entire spectrum of customers from Small and Medium to Large business enterprises and financial institutions.

(ii) Make the service very simple for customers to use even if they lack experience in IP routing.

(iii) Make the service very scalable and flexible to facilitate large-scale deployment.

(iv) Provide a reliable and amenable service, offering SLA to customers

(v) Capable of meeting a wide range of customer requirements, including security, quality of Service (QOS) and any-to-any connectivity.

(vi) Capable of offering fully managed services to customers.

(vii) Allow BSNL to introduce additional services such as bandwidth on demand etc over the same network.

ISDN

ISDN Has emerged as a powerful tool worldwide for provisioning of different services like voice, data and image transmission over the telephone line through the telephone network. ISDN is being viewed as the logical extension of the digitalization of telecommunication network and most developed countries are in different stages of implementing ISDN.

An ISDN subscriber can establish two simultaneous independent calls (except when the terminal equipment is such that it occupies two 'B' channels for one call itself like in video conferencing etc.) on existing pair of wires of the telephone line (Basic rate ISDN) where as only one call is possible at present on the analog line /telephone connection. The two simultaneous calls in ISDN can be of any type like speech, data, image etc. The call setup time for a call between two ISDN subscribers is very short, of the order of 1 to 2 seconds. ISDN also supports a whole new set of additional facilities, called Supplementary Services.

Connectivity

The ISDN subscriber will have full connectivity,

nationally, to other analog telephone subscribers. At present ISDN services are available to and from India for the following countries:

Australia

Austria Belgium

Canada

Denmark

France

Germany

Ireland

Italy

Israel

Japan

Malaysia

Netherland

Norway

Phillipines

Singapore

Switzerland

Thailand

U.A.E

United Kingdom

U.S.A

Services Offered By ISDN

Normal Telephone & Fax (G3)

Digital Telephone -with a facility to identify the calling subscriber number and other facilities.

G4 Fax

Data Transmission at 64 Kbps with ISDN controller card

Video Conferencing at 128 Kbps

Video Conferencing at 384 Kbps (Possible with 3 ISDN lines)

ATM (Asynchronous Transfer Mode) or PVC (Permanent Virtual Circuit)

List of ISDN stations of BSNL in India

Variety of supplementary Services supported by ISDN.

Calling Line Identification Presentation(CLIP)

Calling Line Identification Restriction(CLIR)

Multiple Subscriber Number(MSN)

Terminal Portability(TP)

Call Hold(CH)

Call Waiting(CW)

User to User Signaling (UUSI)

Types of Accesses

There are two types of "accesses" (connections) for ISDN.

Basic Rate Access(BRA): 2B+D

2 Channels of 64 Kbps for Speech And Data.

1 Channel of 16 Kbps for Signalling

Primary Rate Access (PRA): 30 B+D

30 Channels of 64 Kbps for speech and data.

1 Channel of 64 Kbps for signalling.

Leased Line

To transmit data between computer and electronic information devices, BSNL provides data communication services to its subscribers. It offers a choice of high, medium and low speed leased data circuits as well as dial-up lines. Bandwidth is available on demand in most of the cities. Managed leased Line Network (MLLN) offers flexibility of providing circuits with speeds of n x 64 Kbps up to 2 Mbps. Useful for internet leased lines and international principle Leased Lines (IPLCs).

For dedicated point to point speech, private wire, teleprinter and data circuits are given on lease basis. Leased circuits are provided to subscribers for internal communication between their offices/factories at various sites within a city/town or different cities/town on point to point basis, or on a network basis interconnecting the various sites.

Managed Leased Line Service(MLLN): The MLLN is a Managed Leased Line Network system which is proposed to provide Leased line connectivity. The State-of-the-art technology equipment MLLN is designed mainly for having effective control, monitor on the leased line so that the down time is very much minimised.

Services

Speech Circuits (Hot Line or Private Wire) - Local or Long distance circuits within two locations in a city or between two different cities provided for the same applicant. The Terminating equipment at both ends is telephone without dialing facility. Both way signaling and speech is possible.

1. **Data Circuits** - Local or Long distance data circuits at different speeds viz. nx64 kbps and 2 mbps. Data Circuits are of different types:
2. **Point to Point Data Circuits** - Local and Long Distance
3. **Private Data Network** - More than one Local or Long Distance leased circuits converging on a location such that data from one leased circuit can be transferred automatically to another leased circuit for the same subscriber.
4. **Closed User Group** - Leased circuits can be used by more than one legal entity if they form closed user group. The following categories of user groups constitute closed user groups for the purpose of licensing Private Telecom Networks.
5. Producer of goods and his whole-sale traders /agents.

6. Provider of service (not being a telecommunication service) and his whole-sale traders/agents.
7. Producers of same categories of goods.
8. Providers of the same category of service.
9. Holding company and its subsidiaries.
10. Interconnected undertakings.
11. Companies under the same management
12. Travel agents issuing tickets on the member airlines, whose network they use including the network of a group of member airlines.
13. Computerized Reservations System (CRS) service providers owned by airlines.
14. Shared networks of banks for use of Automatic Teller Machines (ATMs), Electronic Points of Sale(EPOS)/credit authorization terminals.
15. Financial institutions registered primarily to deal in securities and their agents/dealers.
16. Financial institutions registered as Mutual funds and their agents.
17. Financial institutions which are registered as depositories and their agents/dealers.
18. Other non-banking financial institutions.

Intelligent Network

Recognizing the rising expectations and requirements of the customers, BSNL endeavors to harness the rewards of telecom revolution. Towards this, we have redefined the term 'telecom service' by introducing value added services in the form of intelligent network.

This technology makes possible, time and cost effective services, optimized solutions, meeting the exact needs of the customers, in additional business for you.

How it works ?

Intelligent Network provides a framework to create various services in a centralized place independent of the switch. In IN, calls generated by a subscribers are routed (Circuit Switched) to the nearest Service Switching Points, which in turn , consults, the Service Control Points (SCP) on high speed CCS 7 links to get the necessary information for further routing of the call. IN Services can be used by subscriber connected to any type of exchange using existing telephones.

Services Offered

Free-phone Service - Call charges paid by the called person. Ideal for service and Tourism industry.

Premium Rate Service - A great tool for professionals to sell priced information/consultation on phone.

Indian Telephone Card - A pre-paid facility for making local,STD or ISD calls from any telephone.

Virtual Private Network - Normal telephones programmed to work as cheaper and flexible - nationwide - private network.

Universal Number - A unique number nationwide.

Tele voting - for conducting opinion polls and surveys using BSNL network.

Account calling Card - For those who want to have a permanent account with BSNL can make use of this service. This is similar to India Telephone Card.

I-NET

It provides extremely cost effective and reliable solution to your High Speed Wide Area Networking needs. It can change the way of doing business by networking computers, data terminals, hosts and LANs in different offices and manufacturing units both within the country and outside, through Inet - an X.25 based packet switched Public Data Network of BSNL

Inet can be used in the following applications :

Electronic Mail Services

Corporate Communications

Information Retrieval

Database Services

Remote Job Applications

Credit Card Verifications

Travel Reservations

INTERNET connectivity

TELEX/TELEGRAPH

Telegram is a common man's communication need. The first telegraph message was transmitted live on Morse through electrical signals between Calcutta and Diamond Harbour on 5th November 1850.The Telegraph services were opened to public during February 1855. To implement modern technology in the telegraph network a National Message Switching Network Plan was prepared in 1986.

The growth of Telegraph services has been affected owing to the impact of other non-voice services and improvement in density of telephones, nevertheless the service has social relevance and historical importance.

Network

All the cities(300) and towns (4689) as per 1991 census and a large number of villages have access to Public Telegraph Services through Telegraph Offices.

Services

Telegraph services are being provided through Telegraph offices, Telecom Centers and Bureau FAX centers. A number of new types of telegraph services such as Store & forward message switching system, electronic key-board concentrator , electronic teleprinters and formatted terminals have been introduced.

Express Money Transfer Service

which aims at delivering money within few hours after rendering at the counter of a telegraph office was introduced in A.P. Telecom Circle on experimental basis. This service is being made available at many of the stations in Tamilnadu, Kerala, Karnataka, Maharashtra and metro cities of Delhi & Calcutta.

Apart from the facility of booking of telegrams, following services are also offered in some Telegraph Offices:

FAX Service is available at many selected telegraph offices for national and international outgoing and incoming messages

A new class of telegram "Fax Telegrams" is available for public.

Booking of telegrams on phone/Telex.

Delivery of telegram over Telex /Phone if the same is specified in the address of the telegram.

Delivery of telegrams through Fax, if the telegrams contain fax numbers in the address.

EPABX

BSNL permits telephone subscribers to use their own PABX/EPABX connected to the BSNL network under certain commercial/technical conditions :

The type of Subscriber owned EPABX should be approved by BSNL

External extensions outside subscriber's premises will be permitted only on the specific approval of the concerned authority and charged as per departmental tariff. In cases where external extensions from subscriber owned EPABX are provided within the premises of the subscribers using their own cables and wires without crossing any public road, no charge will be levied.

Subscriber is free to use the existing internal wiring of the internal extensions left at the premises after the closure of the PABX.

External extensions from subscriber owned PABX may be provided by the department and charged. Underground cables and lines may continue to be maintained by the department since the same may be required for provision of various telecom services the subscriber may require.

In cases where BSNL feels that the existing cables/ overhead wires are not be used/likely to be used by the company the same can be made over to the user after recovering the depreciated value of assets.

Where subscribers themselves provide and maintain external extensions from the EPABX, applicable license fee would be charged if the extensions are crossing a public road.

Cases where PBX/PABX facilities are surrendered before the expiry of the guarantee period will be regulated as per Company rules.

HVNET

HVNET the High Speed Satellite based VSAT network of Department of Telecom Services, provides high speed data transfers (up to 64 Kbps) and voice communication service covering the entire country.

Network

The network consists of a HUB station located near Thane(40 kms from Mumbai) **and** number of VSATs/Personal Earth Stations(PES) located throughout the country. The VSAT communicate to the HUB through the THAICOM III Satellite. All VSATs are connected in STAR topology and VSAT to VSAT communication is through the HUB at Mumbai.

VSAT Details

The VSAT which is required to be installed at subscribers premises consists of three units, namely an Outdoor Unit, an Indoor Unit and Inter Facility Link (IFL) Cable interconnecting the two Units. The Outdoor Unit contains the Antenna assembly & associated RF Equipments. The antenna is of 2.4 meter diameter parabolic type and can be installed easily in any open space and required a floor area of about 4 Mt. X 4Mt. The RF equipment includes an Up converter, Down converter, Solid state power amplifier which together comprise the ODU and Low noise amplifier which are installed on the Antenna. The ODU and DIU are connected by means of IFL cable which carries the telecom signals and power supply. The IFL cable can be up to 100 meter long. The Indoor Unit (DIU) also known as Personal Earth Station (PES) is a compact unit of size 44Cms X 11Cms X 18Cms contains mainly the following cards:

Intermediate Frequency Module (IFM) card.

Multiport card (MPC).

Voice & Data Port card (VDPC).

The IFM card is fixed in the lowermost slot of the Unit. This incorporates common functions such as frequency, modulation/demodulation, control & synchronization.

MPC provides up o eight user interface ports. Each port can be configured to process different protocol such as X .28 and X .25. Presently two protocols X 28 and X 25 are being provided one on each port.

VDPC is used to provide two wire telephone interface on RJ 11 interface.

Services on HVNET

Data communication at speeds up to 64kbps.

Aupport of X.28 and X.25 protocols for data communication.

Voice facility on the VSAT with connection to public telephone network(PSTN of BSNL)

Access to BSNL's RABMN network and Inet Phase I & II networks.

Access to International data networks through GPSS of VSNL.

Faster installation

Real time applications

Error free, accurate and reliable transmission.

Elimination of last mile problem of cable pair and overhead lines

Customer Status

Out of the network Capacity of 1000 VSATs, over 420 are in service

Major users of network are Department of Posts, Bharat Heavy Electricals Limited, Oil and Natural Gas Corporation Limited etc.

INSAT

Bharat Sanchar Nigam Limited is going to launch Mobile Satellite Service based on INSAT 3-B MSS pay load. The mobile satellite service will basically provide following types of services:-

(i) Encoded voice/data/fax service among Mobile terminals

(ii) Encoded voice/data/fax service between Mobile terminals and fixed users on PSTN for national and International calls

(iii) Reporting service from Mobile Terminals to User Head Office via PSTN data links or Telex Network. This service will be provided via PSTN or x.400 Mail Box with a maximum message length of 40 characters.

2. The existing earth station at Bangalore will also work as hub station for Type - A mobile service.

3. The subscribers will procure the BSNL approved Mobile Terminals

INMARSAT

Subscriber dialed INMARSAT services from Shore to Ship, Ship to Shore and Ship to Ship in Indian region are operational in the BSNL Network.

INMARSAT Calls from STD/ISD PCOs:

1. Subscriber dialed INMARSAT calls are also accessible to STD/ISD PCOs where these have been made available to ISD subscribers. Instances have been brought to the notice that STD PCO charge indicators are not able to record the pulses sent by exchange for these calls.
2. It is intimated that as per present specifications, STD PCO charge indicators are not equipped to record pulses of shorter durations as in the case of INMARSAT calls. The specifications of PCO Charge indicators are under review to incorporate the required software/hardware to recognize pulses of short durations. Some of the switches are also not yet able to send short duration pulses on PCO line due to technical constraints. These would also require up-gradation.
3. In view of above constraints, it has been decided to permit STD/ISD PCO franchisees to put through INMARSAT calls and charge the customers by manual computing based on the pulse rates applicable. The STD PCOs franchisees may be advised to prominently display the INMARSAT call pulse rates for information of public. The duration of the call displayed by charge indicator in use may be used for manual calculation of charges.
4. The above procedure will be permissible only for INMARSAT calls as a temporary measure.

Tariff

In accordance with TRAI, the new tariff for subscriber dialed INMARSAT services are given below:

1. INMARSAT has 4 access codes for telephones which are equivalent to country codes as per CCITT recommendations. These codes are

   Region Codes

   Indian Ocean Region (IOR) 873

Pacific Ocean Region (POR) 872

Atlantic (East) 871

Atlantic (West) 874

2. To record these calls in the subscriber meters, the duration of pulses required will be of 260 m. secs. for IOR calls and 150 m. secs. for AOR/POR calls. Introduction of this service in the shore to ship direction has a limitation that such short duration metering pulses cannot be transmitted over junction cables and mechanical meters in electro-mechanical exchanges cannot respond to these pulses as such this facility cannot be made available in electro-mechanical exchanges. However, in all other local electronic switches the pulses may be generated locally and services via INMARSAT opened. In C-DoT 256 Port RAX and ILT switches, these services cannot be implemented on account of technical constraints.

KU-Band

Space segment in Ku-Band in INSAT-3A Satellites

Transponder Lease Charges for Space Segment in Ku-band on INSAT-3B Satellite (with effect from 1.10.2001)

(a) Lease charges for 36 MHz bandwidth and satellite EIRP of 41.5 dBw primary coverage

   i. for period equal to one year Rs. 440.00 lakhs for every year and Rs. 110.00 lakhs for each quarter thereafter.

   ii. For periods equal to or in excess of 90 days Rs. 110.00 lakhs for every quarter (90 days) and Rs. 10.22 lakhs for every 7 days thereafter. Nevertheless the overall charges payable under this item shall be limited to Rs. 110.00 lakhs for each quarter or part thereof.

   iii. For periods less than 90 days Rs. 10.22 lakhs per week or part thereof, subject to an overall limit of Rs. 40.88 lakhs for a period of 30 days or part thereof.

(b) Lease charges for 31.5 MHz band width and satellite EIRP of 40.92 dBw at primary coverage:

i. for period equal to one year Rs. 395.68 lakhs for every year and Rs. 98.92 lakhs for each quarter thereafter.

ii. For periods equal to or in excess of 90 days Rs 98.92 lakhs for every quarter (90 days) and Rs. 9.19 lakhs for every 7 days thereafter. Nevertheless the overall charges payable under this item shall be limited to Rs. 98.92 lakhs for each quarter or part thereof.

iii. For periods less than 90 days Rs. 9.19 lakhs per week or part thereof, subject to an overall limit of Rs. 36.76 lakhs for a period of 30 days or part thereof.

(c) Lease charges for 27 MHz band width and satellite EIRP of 40.25 dBw at primary coverage:

i. for period equal to one year Rs. 350.04 lakhs for every year and Rs. 87.51 lakhs for each quarter thereafter.

ii. For periods equal to or in excess of 90 days Rs. 87.51 lakhs for every quarter (90 days) and Rs. 8.13 lakhs for every 7 days thereafter. Nevertheless the overall charges payable under this item shall be limited to Rs. 87.51 lakhs for each quarter or part thereof.

ii. For periods less than 90 days Rs. 8.13 lakhs per week or part thereof, subject to an overall limit of Rs. 32.52 lakhs for a period of 30 days or part thereof.

(d) Lease charges for 22.5 MHz band width and satellite EIRP of 39.46 dBw at primary coverage:

i. for period equal to one year Rs. 302.82 lakhs for every year and Rs. 75.71 lakhs for each quarter thereafter.

ii. For periods equal to or in excess of 90 days Rs. 75.71 lakhs for every quarter (90 days) and Rs. 7.03 lakhs for every 7 days thereafter. Nevertheless the overall charges payable under this item shall be limited to Rs. 75.71 lakhs for each quarter or part thereof.

iii. For periods less than 90 days Rs. 7.03 lakhs per week or part thereof, subject to an overall limit of Rs. 28.12 lakhs for a period of 30 days or part thereof.

Transponder

Space segments INSAT-II & 3B Satellites

Transponder lease charges for Normal C-Band, High/Low Power Extended C-Band in INSAT SYSTEM Effective from 1st October 2001.

(A) Normal C-Band

(a) Lease charges for 36 MHz bandwidth and satellite EIRP of 32 dBw and above (usable power 28 dBw or more) at primary coverage.

i. For periods equal to or in excess of 90 days Rs. 68.75 lakhs for every quarter (90 days) and Rs. 6.38 lakhs for every 7 days thereafter. Nevertheless the overall charges payable under this item shall be limited to Rs. 68.75 lakhs for each quarter or part thereof.

ii. For periods less than 90 days Rs. 6.38 lakhs per week or part thereof, subject to an overall limit of Rs. 25.5 lakhs for a period of 30 days or part thereof

(b) Lease charges for 31.5 MHz bandwidth and satellite EIRP of 27.42 dBw at primary coverage.

i. For periods equal to or in excess of 90 days Rs 61.83 lakhs for every quarter (90 days) and Rs. 5.74 lakhs for every 7 days thereafter. Nevertheless the overall charges payable under this item shall be limited to Rs. 61.83 lakhs for each quarter or part thereof.

ii. For periods less than 90 days Rs. 5.74 lakhs per week or part thereof, subject to an overall limit of Rs. 22.96 lakhs for a period of 30 days or part thereof

(c) Lease charges for 27 MHz bandwidth and satellite EIRP of 26.75 dBw at primary coverage.

i. For periods equal to or in excess of 90 days Rs. 54.70 lakhs for every quarter (90 days) and Rs.5.08 lakhs for every 7 days thereafter. Nevertheless the overall charges payable under this item shall be limited to Rs. 54.70 lakhs for each quarter or part thereof.

ii. For periods less than 90 days Rs. 5.08 lakhs per week or part thereof, subject to an overall limit of Rs. 20.32lakhs for a period of 30 days or part thereof.

(d) Lease charges for 22.5 MHz bandwidth and satellite EIRP of 25.96 dBw at primary coverage.

i. For periods equal to or in excess of 90 days Rs.47.32 lakhs for every quarter (90 days) and Rs.4.39 lakhs for every 7 days thereafter. Nevertheless the overall charges payable under this item shall be limited to Rs. 47.32 lakhs for each quarter or part thereof.

ii. For periods less than 90 days Rs. 4.39 lakhs per week or part thereof, subject to an overall limit of Rs. 17.56lakhs for a period of 30 days or part thereof.

INDIAN SPACE RESEARCH ORGANIZATION (ISRO)

The prime objective of ISRO has been to develop space technology and its application to various national tasks. Since 1969, when it was set up, ISRO has established space systems like the INSAT for telecommunication, television broadcasting and meteorological services, and the Indian Remote Sensing Satellites (IRS) for resources monitoring and management. ISRO has also developed the satellite launch vehicles PSLV and GSLV to place these satellites in the required orbits.

Indian space programme is driven by vision of Dr Vikram Sarabhai considered as the father of Indian Space Programme.

There are some who question the relevance of space activities in a developing nation. To us, there is no ambiguity of purpose. We do not have the fantasy of competing with the economically advanced nations in the exploration of the moon or the planets or manned space-flight. But we are convinced that

2002 2002-

2003 2003-

2004 2004-

2005 2005-

2006 2006-

2007

Programmes

Indian National Satellite System (INSAT)

Established in 1983 with commissioning of INSAT-1B.

A joint venture of Department of Space (DOS), Department of Telecommunications, India Meteorological Department, All India Radio and Doordarshan. DOS responsible for establishment and operation of INSAT space segment.

INSAT space segment at present consists of INSAT-1D, last of the INSAT-1 series launched in 1990 and three ISRO-built satellites, INSAT-2A launched in July 1992, INSAT-2B launched in July 1993 and INSAT-2C launched on December 7, 1995.

INSAT-2DT acquired from ARABSAT.

INSAT-2E launched on April 3,1999.

ISRO has leased eleven 36 MHz equivalent units of C-band capacity on board INSAT-2E to INTELSAT organisation

INSAT-3B launched on March 22nd 2000.

INSAT-3C launched on January 24th 2002.

INSAT-3A launched on April 10th 2003.

INSAT-3E launched on September 28th 2003.

Indian Remote Sensing Satellite (IRS) System

Commissioned with the launch of IRS-1A in March 1988

IRS system under National Natural Resources Management System (NNRMS) coordinated at national level by the Planning Committee of NNRMS (PC-NNRMS).

At present has four satellites, IRS-1B launched in August 1991, IRS-1C launched in December 1995 and IRS-1D launched on September 29,1997.

IRS-P3 and IRS-1D launched by India's Polar Satellite Launch Vehicle (PSLV).

IRS-P4 with an Ocean Colour Monitor (OCM) and a Multi-frequency Scanning Microwave Radiometer (MSMR) launched by PSLV-C2.

IRS-P6 for agricultural applications launched by PSLV-C5.

IRS-P5 with a Very High Resolution Panchromatic camera for cartographic applications planned for launch on board PSLV during 2003-2004.

Data from IRS satellites received and processed by the National Remote Sensing Agency, Hyderabad.

SI a US Company also receives and markets IRS data worldwide under a commercial contract with Antrix Corporation of the Department of Space.

Stretched Rohini Satellite Series (SROSS)

113 kg SROSS-C2 satellite, launched by ASLV-D4 on May 4, 1994 carries two scientific payloads, a Gamma-Ray Burst (GRB) experiment and a Retarding Potential Analyser (RPA). A similar satellite, SROSS-C had been launched by ASLV-D3 in May 1992. SROSS-C2 is in service.

Polar Satellite Launch Vehicle (PSLV)

Developmental flights completed with successful third developmental launch in March 1996.

Now available for launching 1,000-1,200 kg class of remote sensing satellites into polar sun-synchronous orbit. IRS-1D launched on September 29,1997.

IRS-P4(OCEANSAT) and two small satellites (KITSAT of Korea and TUBSAT of Germany) launched on on May 26,1999 by PSLV-C2.

PSLV-C3 launched three satellites — Technology Experiment Satellite (TES) of ISRO, BIRD of Germany and PROBA of Belgium - into their intended orbits on October 22, 2001.

ISRO's Polar Satellite Launch Vehicle, PSLV-C4 launched KALPANA-1 satellite on September 12, 2002.

ISRO's Polar Satellite Launch Vehicle, PSLV-C5 launched RESOURCESAT-1 (IRS-P6) satellite on October 17, 2003.

Geosynchronous Satellite Launch Vehicle (GSLV)

For launching 2,000 kg class of communication satellites into geosynchronous transfer orbit.

A three stage vehicle; first stage is a 129 tonne solid propellant core motor with four liquid propellant strap-ons with 40 tonne propellant each, second stage is a liquid propulsion system with 37.5 tonne propellant and a cryogenic upper stage with 12 tonne of liquid oxygen and liquid hydrogen.

First developmental flight GSLV-D1 completed with successful launch on April 18, 2001.

Second developmental flight GSLV-D2 launched GSAT-2 satellite on May 8, 2003.

Milestones

2003 ISRO's Polar Satellite Launch Vehicle, PSLV-C5, successfully launched RESOURCESAT-1 (IRS-P6) satellite from Sriharikota(October 17, 2003).

Successful launch of INSAT-3E by Ariane from Kourou French Guyana, (September 28, 2003).

The Second developmental launch of GSLV-D2 with GSAT-2 on board from Sriharikota (May 8, 2003).

Successful launch of INSAT-3A by Ariane from Kourou French Guyana, (April 10, 2003).

2002 ISRO's Polar Satellite Launch Vehicle, PSLV-C4, successfully launched KALPANA-1 satellite from Sriharikota(September 12, 2002).

Successful launch of INSAT-3C by Ariane from Kourou French Guyana, (January 24, 2002).

2001 ISRO's Polar Satellite Launch Vehicle, PSLV-C3, successfully launched three satellites — Technology Experiment Satellite (TES) of ISRO, BIRD of Germany and PROBA of Belgium - into their intended orbits (October 22, 2001).

The first developmental launch of GSLV-D1 with GSAT-1 on board from Sriharikota (April 18, 2001)

2000 INSAT-3B, the first satellite in the third generation INSAT-3 series, launched by Ariane from Kourou French Guyana, (March 22, 2000).

1999 Indian Remote Sensing Satellite, IRS-P4 (OCEANSAT), launched by Polar Satellite Launch Vehicle (PSLV-C2) along with Korean KITSAT-3 and German DLR-TUBSAT from Sriharikota

INSAT-2E, the last satellite in the multipurpose INSAT-2 series, launched by Ariane from Kourou French Guyana, (April 3, 1999).

1998 INSAT system capacity augmented with the readiness of INSAT-2DT acquired from ARABSAT (January 1998).

1997 INSAT-2D, fourth satellite in the INSAT series, launched (June 4, 1997). Becomes inoperable on October 4, 1997.

(An in-orbit satellite, ARABSAT-1C, since renamed INSAT-2DT, was acquired in November 1997 to partly augment the INSAT system).

First operational launch of PSLV with IRS-1D on board (September 29, 1997). Satellite placed in orbit.

1996 Third developmental launch of PSLV with IRS-P3 on board (March 21, 1996). Satellite placed in polar sunsynchronous orbit.

1995 Launch of third operational Indian Remote Sensing Satellite, IRS-1C (December 28, 1995).

INSAT-2C, the third satellite in the INSAT-2 series, launched (December 7, 1995).

1994 Second developmental launch of PSLV with IRS-P2 on board (October 15, 1994). Satellite successfully placed in polar sunsynchronous orbit.

Fourth developmental launch of ASLV with SROSS-C2 on board (May 4, 1994). Satellite placed in orbit.

1993 First developmental launch of PSLV with IRS-1E on board (September 20, 1993). Satellite could not be placed in orbit.

INSAT-2B, the second satellite in the INSAT-2 series, launched (July 23, 1993).

1992 INSAT-2A, the first satellite of the indigenously-built second-generation INSAT series, launched (July 10, 1992).

Third developmental launch of ASLV with SROSS-C on board (May 20, 1992). Satellite placed in orbit.

1991 Second operational Remote Sensing satellite, IRS-1B, launched (August 29, 1991).

1990 INSAT-1D launched (June 12, 1990).

1988 INSAT-1C launched (July 21, 1988). Abandoned in November 1989.

Second developmental launch of ASLV with SROSS-2 on board (July 13, 1988). Satellite could not be placed in orbit.

Launch of first operational Indian Remote Sensing Satellite, IRS-1A (March 17, 1988).

1987 First developmental launch of ASLV with SROSS-1 satellite on board (March 24, 1987). Satellite could not be placed in orbit.

1984 Indo-Soviet manned space mission (April 1984).

1983 INSAT-1B, launched (August 30, 1983).

Second developmental launch of SLV-3. RS-D2 placed in orbit (April 17, 1983).

1982 INSAT-1A launched (April 10, 1982).

Deactivated on September 6, 1982.

1981 Bhaskara-II launched (November 20, 1981).

APPLE, an experimental geo-stationary communication satellite successfully launched (June 19, 1981).

RS-D1 placed in orbit (May 31, 1981)

1980 Second Experimental launch of SLV-3, Rohini satellite successfully placed in orbit. (July 18, 1980).

1979 First Experimental launch of SLV-3 with Rohini Technology Payload on board (August 10, 1979). Satellite could not be placed in orbit.

Bhaskara-I, an experimental satellite for earth observations, launched (June 7, 1979).

1977 Satellite Telecommunication Experiments Project (STEP) carried out.

1975-1976 Satellite Instructional Television Experiment (SITE) conducted.

1975 ISRO First Indian Satellite, Aryabhata, launched (April 19, 1975).

Becomes Government Organisation (April 1, 1975).

1972-1976 Air-borne remote sensing experiments.

1972 Space Commission and Department of Space set up (June 1, 1972). ISRO brought under DOS.

1969 Indian Space Research Organisation (ISRO) formed under Department of Atomic Energy (August 15, 1969).

1968 TERLS dedicated to the United Nations (February 2, 1968).

1967 Satellite Telecommunication Earth Station set up at Ahmedabad.

1965 Space Science & Technology Centre (SSTC) established in Thumba.

1963 First sounding rocket launched from TERLS (November 21, 1963).

1962 Indian National Committee for Space Research (INCOSPAR) formed by the Department of Atomic Energy and work on establishing Thumba Equatorial Rocket Launching Station (TERLS) started.

8
Glossary

Abstract : a brief set of statements that summarize, classifies, evaluates, or describes the important points of a text, particularly a journal article. An abstract is typically found on the first page of a scholarly article. Because an abstract summarizes an article, it is very useful for either browsing or keyword searching.

Abstracting journal: a periodical devoted to publishing abstracts, usually in a specific field of research. For example, Chemical Abstracts or Psychological Abstracts. Abstract journals enable researchers to peruse recent work in their area of interest, and serve as an archive of bibliographic information. Many important abstracting journals are now available in electronic format. (See the Marriott Databases & Indexes page.) Many indexes which formerly provided only citation information are now providing abstracts as they convert to electronic formats.

Access point: in a catalog or index, a heading that may be used to find information on an item; common access points include author, title, and assigned subject headings.

Accession number: a number assigned to an item when it is added to a databse, such as a periodical index or library catalog; it indicates only the chronological order in which materials were added to the database.

ACLIS: Academic Computing and Library Information Services; the department of Marriott Library responsible for: library information systems; campus computing services such as e-mail, test scanning, and student access computing labs; the Faculty Assistance Center; the Help Desk (581-6494), etc.

ACM: Association for Computing Machines; a professional society for computer scientists, and a major publisher in the field. Marriott subscribes to virtually all of the ACM journals and special interest group (SIG) conference proceedings in full-text electronic format.

Acquisitions: the Marriott Library department responsible for the actual ordering and purchase of materials being added to the Library's collection, including gifts.

ACS: American Chemical Society; a professional society and major publisher in all areas of chemistry. Marriott subscribes to most ACS journals in both print and full-text electronic format; the electronic access is being provided through UALC.

Added entry: in a card catalog, cards other than the main entry, providing access to an item by such things as joint author, title, subject, series, etc., but with less complete bibliographic information than given on the main entry (to save typing).

Add-ons: programs that provide extra facilities for a WWW browser (e.g. sound, video) (see helper application, plug-in, viewer)

Adds: items which are a part of a monograph or serial series and are added to the library collection automatically.

Adobe Acrobat Reader: a program for viewing PDF files, used in many full-text electronic journals. The reader program is free, and if you do not have it on your machine when it is needed to access an article, instructions for downloading it will usually appear on your screen.

AIChE: American Institute of Chemical Engineers; a professional society and major publisher in chemical engineering.

AIP: American Institute of Physics; a professional society and major publisher in the field of physics; Marriott subscribes to most AIP journals in both print and full-text electronic format.

Almanac: a volume containing a collection of miscellaneous facts and statistics on many subjects.

AMS: American Mathematical Society; a professional society and major publisher in mathematics.

Annotation: an explanatory or critical note or commentary. Annotation is also the process of adding an explanatory or critical note or commentary to a text. Reference lists are often annotated with comments about what each resource covered and how useful it was.

Annual: a serial publication issued regularly once a year.

Anonym: 1. an anonymous publication; 2. a person or author whose name is not known; 3. a pseudonym.

Anonymous ftp: a means of retrieving publicly available files from a host computer. The user logs in as an unnamed guest with limited privileges.

ANSI: American National Standards Institute; an umbrella organization which publishes standards, as well as approving standards prepared by other U.S. organizations. Marriott does not have a standing subscription to ANSI standards, but will purchase them on demand for UU faculty.

Appendix: a group of supplementary material appended to a text. It is usually related to the material in the main part of the text but not so closely related to it that it should be put into the main text. Put background information and supporting facts in the appendices. An example of a file that should be put in an appendix is a file of detailed charts and graphs of resent research closely related to the paper's main topic.

Applet :A small *Java* program that can be embedded in an *HTML* page. Applets differ from full-fledged Java applications in that they are not allowed to access certain resources on the local computer, such as files and serial devices (modems, printers, etc.), and are prohibited from communicating with most other computers across a network. The common rule is that an applet can only make an Internet connection to the computer from which the applet was sent.

Archie: A tool (software) for finding files stored on *anonymous FTP* sites. You need to know the exact file name or a substring of it. By 1999 *Archie* had been almost completely replaced by web-based search engines.

ARPANet — (Advanced Research Projects Agency Network) : The precursor to the *Internet*. Developed in the late 60's and early 70's by the US Department of Defense as an experiment in wide-area-networking to connect together computers that were each running different system so that people at one location could use computing resources from another location.

Archive: a place in which historical documents and other records are preserved. Usually operated by large organizations, they may or may not be open to the public. The University of Toronto, for example has an archive that requires a five story building and contains several climate controlled vaults. A virtual archive is similar except the documents have no physical presence and seldom have historical value.

Archives Information Center: integrated Web site designed to guide users to materials related to the history of the IPFW campus.

Article: 1. a contribution, by one or more authors, published in a periodical.

ASCE: American Society of Civil Engineers; a professional society and major publisher in all areas of civil engineering.

ASCII — (American Standard Code for Information Interchange) : This is the defacto world-wide standard for the code numbers used by computers to represent all the upper and lower-case Latin letters, numbers, punctuation, etc. There are 128 standard ASCII codes each of which can be represented by a 7 digit binary number: 0000000 through 1111111.

ASME: American Society of Mechanical Engineers; a professional society and major publisher in mechanical engineering. ASME is a major publisher of standards; Marriott does not have a standing subscription to ASME standards, but will purchase them on demand by UU faculty.

ASTM: American Society for Testing and Materials; a major publisher of standards in the area of materials and engineering. Marriott purchases a full set of ASTM standards every 3 years which is kept at the Science & Engineering Desk. b UNIX has built-in TCP/IP and is the most commonly used operating system for servers on the Internet.

Atlas: usually, a volume of maps; also used for a volume of plates illustrating any subject, particularly in anatomy.

Audio-Visual: non-book materials such as various formats of audio and video recordings, which require equipment to be usable. Marriott's collection of audio-visual materials is housed in the Multimedia Center.

Author entry: in a card catalog, a card filed by the author; the card for the first author is generally considered the main entry

Author search: in an electronic catalog or index, to search for an article or book by a particular author. "Author" may include persons responsible for the work, such as composers, artists, actors, directors, etc., and organizations may also be authors ("corporate author" in library parlance).

Author: is an originator of a creative work, particularly a writer of a text. Searching by author can be an effective form of information gathering.

Autotron: a device which keeps track of the number of copies made on a photocopying machine. No longer used in Marriott's copy centers.

back number: synonymous with back issue; any issue of a periodical older than the most recent issue.

Backbone: A high-speed line or series of connections that forms a major pathway within a network. The term is relative as a backbone in a small *network* will likely be much smaller than many non-backbone lines in a large network.

Backlist: items still available for sale from a given publisher, though they are not on the publisher's "new" or "current" list. Since most books go out of print within a year or two of publication, backlists generally consist of works of long-standing value or demand.

Bandwidth: How much stuff you can send through a connection. Usually measured in bits-per-second. A full page of English text is about 16,000 bits. A fast modem can move about 57,000 bits in one second. Full-motion full-screen video would require roughly 10,000,000 bits-per-second, depending on compression.

Bar code label: a small label comprised of vertical lines which contain machine-readable data; each item acquired by the Library receives a bar code label with a unique number.

Baud: In common usage the baud rate of a *modem* is how many bitsit can send or receive per second. Technically, baud is the number of times per second that the carrier signal shifts value - for example a 1200 bit-per-second modem actually runs at 300 baud, but it moves 4 bits per baud (4 x 300= 1200 bits per second).

BBS -- (Bulletin Board System) : A computerized meeting and announcement system that allows people to carry on discussions, upload and download files, and make announcements without the people being connected to the computer at the same time. In the early 1990's there were many thousands (millions?) of BBS?s around the world, most are very small, running on a single IBM clone PC with 1 or 2 phone lines. Some are very large and the line between a BBS and a system like AOL gets crossed at some point, but it is not clearly drawn.

Beilstein a massive compendium of data on organic chemical compounds. The actual title is Handbuch der Organischen Chemie, and its call number is QD251 .B4.

Bi-annual: a publication (e.g. a magazine) which is issued twice a year. Because of confusion with the term biennial (a publication issued every two years), the terms "half-yearly," "twice yearly" or "semi-annual" are more commonly used.

Bibliographic citation: (synonym for bibliographic reference) identifying information about a publication, used in catalogs and indexes as well as in lists of "literature cited" or "references" in scholarly publications. Formats vary, but a book citation generally includes at least information on the author, title, publisher, and date of publication; an article citation includes author, title, date, and information on the periodical in which it was published.

Bibliographic database: an electronic version of a catalog or index. A bibliographic database allows the user to identify publications by author, subject, title, or other search terms. It generally provides at least a full citation to the item, and often other information such as abstracts and assigned subject headings.

Bibliography: 1) a list of books or articles which are related in some way, for example, about a particular subject (such as Guide to the Literature of the Zoological Sciences) or written by a specific author (such as a Bibliographical Checklist and Index to the Published Writings of Albert Einstein).2) the study of books as physical entities.

Biennial: a serial publication issued every two years.

Bi-monthly: a serial publication issued every two months.

Binary: Information consisting entirely of ones and zeros. Also, commonly used to refer to files that are not simply text files, e.g. images.

Bindery: department responsible for binding periodicals between hard covers and repair of items with damaged bindings. At Marriott, periodicals are sent to an off-campus commercial bindery. Items are generally inaccessible for approximately 2 weeks while being bound.

Binhex — (BINary HEXadecimal): A method for converting non-text files (non-ASCII) into *ASCII*. This is needed because Internet e-mail can only handle ASCII.

Bit — (Binary DigIT): A single digit number in base-2, in other words, either a 1 or a zero. The smallest unit of computerized data. *Bandwidth*is usually measured in bits-per-second.

BITNET : Because It's Time NETwork or Because It's There NETwork, A *network* of educational sites separate from the Internet, but e-mail is freely exchanged between BITNET and the Internet. ***Listservs***®, a popular form of e-mail discussion groups, originated on BITNET. At its peak (the late 1980's and early 1990's) BITNET machines were usually mainframes, often running IBM's MVS operating system. BITNET is probably the only international network that is shrinking.

Bi-weekly: serial publication issued every two weeks (similar to a semi-monthly).

Blogs: are typically updated daily using software that allows people with little or no technical background to update and maintain the blog.

Postings on a blog are almost always arranged in chronological order with the most recent additions featured most prominently.

Blurb: a brief summary or description of a work printed on the book jacket, publisher's catalog or advertisement to entice potential purchasers.

Bone box: a plastic model of a human skeleton, in two boxes housed in General Reserve.

Book jobber: a book supplier.

Book number: the part of a call number which distinguishes an item from all others in that subject class. Book numbers may be author numbers and/or work numbers, and are assigned to place materials in the desired order on the shelves. (See Cutter number .) Example in the call number HM206 .D48 1997, D48 is the book number, and is an author number, for author Jared Diamond.

Book Sale: items weeded from the collection and donated materials not needed for the collection, which are offered for sale to the public. In general, hardback books are $1 and paperbacks are 50 cents. Funds raised are used for purchase of needed materials. The Book Sale is managed by the Gifts department, and the sale shelves are located on Level 3 in the Duplication Center.

Bookmark: a saved link to a Web page that allows the user to return to it later.

Boolean logic: the algebraic system, developed by George Boole that is applied to Boolean expressions that contain Boolean operators such as AND, OR, NOT AND, and XOR (exclusive OR). This binary algebraic system is used primarily in switching circuits and database searches. Boolean operators are not to be confused with proximity operators such as NEAR..

Boolean operator: conjunctions AND, OR, and NOT in logical expressions; named for mathematician George Boole (1815-1864). In library usage, refers to these conjunctions in electronic search criteria.AND retrieves items in which both terms are found wolves and Yellowstone OR retrieves items in which either term is found woman or women NOT retrieves items in which the first term is present but the second term is not AIDS not United States

BPS: (Bits-Per-Second) A measurement of how fast data is moved from one place to another. A 56K *modem* can move about 57,000 bits per second.

Browse: to inspect something casually, particularly to use an internet browser to casually inspect Web pages. This involves following links from page to page (also called surfing) rather than searching directly. The main difference between browsing and searching is that with browsing you have very little advance knowledge of what will be on the next page.

BTW: "By the way" - an acronym frequently encountered in e-mail correspondence.

Bulletin board system (BBS): the electronic equivalent of a notice board, generally subject-specific. A BBS is a form of electronic mail in which users post messages to a common receiver (the bulletin board) and have access to all messages posted.

Bus: the electronic pathway along which signals travel from one part of the computer to another: address bus allocates memory addresses data bus moves data between the processor and memory control bus carries signals from the control unit

Byte: A set of Bits that represent a single character. Usually there are 8 Bits in a Byte, sometimes more, depending on how the measurement is being made.

Call Number: A combination of letters and numbers that identifies the broad subject and shelf location of items in the library collection. The call number appears in IUCAT and on the item itself. The two types of call numbers used in the IPFW library include the Library of Congress (LC) and Superintendent of

Card catalog: a descriptive record of library holdings printed on cards and arranged in cabinets in a definite order. Marriott no longer has a card catalog.

Card reader: the device on a photocopier, printer or other machine that reads a card's barcode, smart chip or magnetic strip, enables the service, and deducts the appropriate amount of credit as the card is used.

Card set: in a card catalog, the group of cards relating to each bibliographical item. Includes author card (main entry), title card, subject card, series (if applicable), etc.

Carrel: a table for one reader, providing a somewhat secluded study area by means of front and side screening.

CAS Registry Number: a unique identifying number assigned to a chemical by the **Chemical Abstracts Service.** Useful for searching for a particular chemical in some databases, including Chemical Abstracts and the spectra databases, and in many physical property reference works.

CASSI: Chemical Abstracts Service Source Index. A 3-volume reference listing all titles cited in Chemical Abstracts, arranged alphabetically by abbreviation; very useful for identifying sources cited, and housed at the Science & Engineering desk.

Catalog: a complete and systematically organized enumeration of items, particularly the complete enumeration of a libraries' resources on a set of paper cards (card catalog) or in an electronic database (bibliographic database).

Cataloging: the process of making entries for a library's catalog. This includes recording of descriptive information about the work (author, title, physical characteristics, any notes deemed necessary, etc.) as well as assignment of approved subject headings and assignment of call numbers to place the item in the desired order on the shelves.

CATP — (Caffeine Access Transport Protocol): Common method of moving caffeine across *Wide Area Networks* such as the *Internet*, CATP was first used at the Binary Cafe in Cybertown and quickly spread world-wide. There are reported problems with short-circuits and rust and decaffinated beverages were not supprted until version 1.5.3

CD-ROM: Compact Disk - Read-Only Memory; a high-capacity optical (laser) information storage device in the form of a plastic disk. A CD-ROM disk holds approximately 600 MB of information, (about 300,000 pages of text). In the library, many databases and reference works are physically in CD-ROM format, housed on servers, and it is increasingly common for books, particularly in science and engineering fields, to be published with accompanying CD-ROMs containing supplemental information and programs.

Certificate Authority : An issuer of *Security Certificates* used in *SSL* connections.

CEU Continuing Education Unit: One CEU is equal to one hour of instruction or contact time. CEUs are required for public school educators, including Library Media Specialists. (LINK)

CGI — (Common Gateway Interface): A set of rules that describe how a *Web Server* communicates with another piece of software on the same machine, and how the other piece of software (the ?CGI program?) talks to the web server. Any piece of software can be a CGI program if it handles input and output according to the CGI standard.

CIP Cataloging in Publication: Cataloging information located on the verso of the title page of a book (or other type of material). Provides call number, main entry, subject headings, etc.

Circulation Services: Steps involved in lending library materials, including check out and renewal, recalls for overdue items, holds for items needed by another user, and fines for lost materials.

Circulation: the library department responsible for activities connected with the lending and return of library materials, including re-shelving, searching, rush requests for material in process, etc.

Citation index: a bibliographic index which allows the user to trace research forward in time by searching for articles that have cited a known relevant article.

Citation search: a search, by name, of all references to an individual. Some databases have a specific citation search option, otherwise you use a full-text search. For an example of a database that has a specific citation search option go to the University of Michigan Library Database.

Citation: the pertinent information needed to find the full text of a publication. Citations are provided in bibliographies, indexes, and the lists of references in scholarly works. Citation formats vary according to field of study and/or requirements of particular publications (see style guide).A book citation generally includes: author(s), title, publisher, date. A citation of an article in a periodical generally includes: author(s), article title, source journal title, volume, pages, and date. book Ramsay, J.A. The Experimental Basis of Modern Biology. Cambridge: University Press, 1965. article Rodbard, S. "Vascular Caliber." Cardiology 60 (1975): 4-49.

Cited article: an article referenced in another scholarly publication. In a citation search, the known relevant article - the user is looking for later papers that have cited that item.

Cited author: an author whose publication has been referenced in a scholarly work. In a citation search, users are often trying to determine the frequency with which a particular author (perhaps themselves) has been cited in later publications.

Citrix: a program that allows our DOS and Windows programs and databases to be run in a World Wide Web environment; this enables users to access such programs from outside the library.

Class number: The first part of a call number, which corresponds to the item's primary subject, and indicates its place in the classification system and its physical location on the shelves. All books with the same class number will be about the same subject. EXAMPLE: TK 2842 (TK=electrical engineering; 2842=circuit breakers)

Classification: the arrangement of knowledge into specific groups or systems. The main classification systems used at Marriott are: Library of Congress (LC) QH45.5 .G68 1991 used for most of the collection Dewey Decimal (DCC) 813.4 A355 M512s for juvenile and older works Superintendent of Documents (SuDocs) A 57.38/26: G13 for U.S. Government publications

Client : A software program that is used to contact and obtain data from a *Server* software program on another computer, often across a great distance. Each*Client* program is designed to work with one or more specific kinds of *Server* programs, and each *Server* requires a specific kind of *Client*. A Web *Browser* is a specific kind of *Client*.

Closed Collection; A library collection, such as university archives or rare books, not open to the public but accessible by appointment only. Ask at the Service Desk for assistance. Course Reserves Supplementary reading materials assigned by faculty, available in physical and/or electronic format.

Closed stacks: collections in which library staff retrieve requested items for users rather than allowing users to browse the shelves and retrieve items on their own. Closed stacks are generally for materials that require special protection or handling, such as archival and rare materials.

Coden: a unique alphanumeric code assigned to titles of serial publications; can be used for searching in some catalogs and indexes.

Collation: in a catalog record, the physical description (e.g. number of pages, size, etc.) of an item EXAMPLE: xviii, 359 p., 49 plates : ill. (some col.), facsims., plans, ports. (some col.) ; 26 cm.

Collective title: the over-all (conventional) title for an item which is made up of several works.

Co-location : Most often used to refer to having a *server* that belongs to one person or group physically located on an *Internet*-connected *network* that belongs to another person or group. Usually this is done because the server owner wants their machine to be on a high-speed Internet connection and/or they do not want the security risks of having the server on thier own network.

Compendium: a work which treats a subject in brief "digest" form, such as a handbook or an encyclopedia.

Compound surname: a surname composed of two or more proper names, usually connected by a hyphen or preposition. Usually filed after single surnames, for example: Henderson, Judith, Henderson, Theodore, Henderson-Sellers, Anna

Compression: a method (e.g. zipping) for reducing the

size of files to save space or transmission time; compressed files must be uncompressed before use.

Computerized Archives; an indexing tool that helps in finding gopher files.

Conference: in library terms, a gathering in which scholars report their recent research findings to peers in the same field. Papers presented at a conference are often published in volumes known as "conference proceedings," which are therefore important sources for current information. The work presented may or may not later be revised and published in a refereed journal.

Consultation Service: in-depth reference assistance from a librarian, available by appointment.

Controlled vocabulary: IT refers to limiting ones searches to the exact subject headings contained in the Library of Congress. An example would be "History - Bibliography etc". Some indexes, like Wilson Indexes, have their own system of headings and hence their own controlled vocabulary.

Cookie: The most common meaning of "Cookie" on the Internet refers to a piece of information sent by a Web *Server* to a Web *Browser* that the Browser software is expected to save and to send back to the Server whenever the browser makes additional requests from the Server. Depending on the type of Cookie used, and the Browsers' settings, the Browser may accept or not accept the Cookie, and may save the Cookie for either a short time or a long time. Cookies might contain information such as login or registration information, online "shopping cart" information, user preferences, etc. When a Server receives a request from a Browser that includes a Cookie, the Server is able to use the information stored in the Cookie. For example, the Server might customize what is sent back to the user, or keep a log of particular users' requests. Cookies are usually set to expire after a predetermined amount of time and are usually saved in memory until the Browser software is closed down, at which time they may be saved to disk if their "expire time" has not been reached. Cookies do not read your hard drive and send your life story to the CIA, but they can be used to gather more information about a user than would be possible without them.

Copyright: the legal right granted to a copyright holder for the exclusive sale, distribution or reproduction of a creative work. It is a form of intellectual property that prevents others from using a creative work without consent of the owner. For example, Thomas Mann holds the copyright on the book The Oxford Guide to Library Research.

Corporate author: an organization (e.g., a business, government agency, institution, etc.) considered to be the author of a work. EXAMPLE: Albany Institute of History and Art. Hudson Valley painting, 1700-1750, in the Albany Institute of History and Art. [Albany, 1959]

Coverage: in indexes, the range of years and number and type of publications included.

CRC Chemical Rubber Company, a publisher of a large number of reference works in physical sciences and engineering. A patron requesting "the CRC" is probably asking for the CRC Handbook of Chemistry and Physics; the most recent several copies are kept at the Science & Engineering Desk, and a copy is kept on Reserve.

Cross reference database: a collection of records that have one or more fields that reference other related records. These connections (for example between "marketing" and "promotion") make browsing very productive and allow related-items searches.

CSS: (Cascading Style Sheet). A standard for specifying the appearance of text and other elements. CSS was developed for use with *HTML* in *Web pages* but is also used in other situations, notably in applications built using *XPFE*. CSS is typically used to provide a single "library" of styles that are used over and over throughout a large number of related documents, as in a web site. A CSS file might specify that all numbered lists are to appear in *italics*. By changing that single specification the look of a large number of documents can be easily changed.

Cumulative index: a compilation (usually annually) of previously published indexes. The cumulation includes all the information in the prior, individual indexes, which can then be discarded.

Current awareness publications: an index which provides information (usually the tables-of-contents) on the very latest issues of periodicals. Since it may take several months after publication for citations and abstracts to appear in standard indexes, these provide the most timely information available on a topic. Example: Current Contents, UnCover.

Current periodical: the most recent issues of journals and magazines, not yet bound between hard covers; since current periodicals are in high demand, they are non-circulating.

Cursor: on the display screen of a computer, the small lighted rectangle, arrow, or other symbol which indicates where the next character will appear.

Cutter number: in the call number, a unique alphanumeric code which makes books within a given subject class fall into alphabetical order by author. (= book number

Cyberpunk: Cyberpunk was originally a cultural sub-genre of science fiction taking place in a not-so-distant, dystopian, over-industrialized society. The term grew out of the work of William Gibson and Bruce Sterling and has evolved into a cultural label encompassing many different kinds of human, machine, and punk attitudes. It includes clothing and lifestyle choices as well.

Cyberspace; Term originated by author William Gibson in his novel *Neuromancer* the word Cyberspace is currently used to describe the whole range of information resources available through computer networks.

Data bank: the actual, substantive, factual information which goes into a database.

Database: a standardized collection of information in computerized format, searchable by various parameters; in libraries often refers to electronic catalogs and indexes.

Depository library: a library designated as a recipient and citizens' access point for government publications (federal or state). Synonymous with repository library. Marriott is a depository library.

Descriptor: an index term used to identify a record in a database. It can consist of a word, phrase, or alphanumerical term. It can describe the content of the record or be an arbitrary code. When a descriptor is descriptive, it can be an effective search parameter.

DHTML — (Dynamic HyperText Markup Language) DHTML refers to *web pages* that use a combination of *HTML*, *JavaScript*, and *CSS* to create features such as letting the user drag items around on the web page, some simple kinds of animation, and many more.

Dialog box: in a graphical user interface, a box that opens for the user to supply additional information before the program continues.

Dialog: a supplier of computer databases for online bibliographic searching.

Dictionary catalog: a catalog with all entries (author, title, subject, and added entries) arranged in a single alphabetical sequence. Compare with divided catalog.

Digerati: The digital version of literati, it is a reference to a vague cloud of people seen to be knowledgeable, hip, or otherwise in-the-know in regardsto the digital revolution.

Directional question: one relating to location of sources, floor plan of library, hours, etc. EXAMPLE: "Where are the periodical indexes located?" (Compare with reference question.)

Dissertation: a written treatise or thesis, usually lengthy, usually authored by a doctoral candidate, usually directed by a faculty advisor, and usually intended to advance the state of the art in a given discipline. There can be an oral component to the process, in which the dissertation must be defended in front of critical judges. Dissertation searches are valuable because of their currency.

DNS (Domain Name System)**:** The Domain Name System is the system that translates Internet *domain names* into *IP numbers*. A "DNS Server" is a *server* that performs this kind of translation.

Document Delivery Services: An electronic library system for requesting books and photocopies of articles that IPFW library does not own.

Document delivery: refers to the transfer of a database record, or other information resource, to the end user. It can involve direct internet or email transfers, CD delivery via mail, paper delivery via mail, or delivery via interlibrary loan.

Document: a physical entity of any printed work, such as a book, manuscript etc.

Documents: the division of the library that collects, catalogs, and provides reference assistance for government publications. At Marriott, Documents is located on Level 1 ("old" building) and includes U.S. Government and U.N. publications. (State and local government publications will be found in Special Collections.)

Domain name server (DNS): dns translates between a machine name (e.g. Journals@elsevier.co.uk) and that machine's numerical IP internet address.

Domain Name: The unique name that identifies an Internet site. Domain Names always have 2 or more parts, separated by dots. The part on the left is the most specific, and the part on the right is the most general. A given machine may have more than one Domain Name but a given Domain Name points to only one machine. For example, the domain names: matisse.net, mail.matisse.net, workshop.matisse.net. Usually, all of the machines on a given Network will have the same thing as the right-hand portion of their Domain Names (matisse.net in the examples above). It is also possible for a Domain Name to exist but not be connected to an actual machine. This is often done so that a group or business can have an Internet e-mail address without having to establish a real Internet site. In these cases, some real Internet machine must handle the mail on behalf of the listed Domain Name.

Download: Transferring data (usually a file) from a another computer to the computer your are using. The opposite of *upload*.

DSL — (Digital Subscriber Line). A method for moving data over regular phone lines. A DSL circuit is much faster than a regular phone connection, and the wires coming into the subscriber's premises are the same (copper) wires used for regular phone service. A DSL circuit must be configured to connect two specific locations, similar to a leased line (howeverr a DSL circuit is not a *leased line*. A common configuration of DSL allows downloads at speeds of up to 1.544 megabits (not megabytes) per second, and uploads at speeds of 128 kilobits per second. This arrangement is called *ADSL*: Asymmetric Digital Subscriber Line. Another common configuration is symmetrical: 384 Kilobits per second in both directions. In theory ADSL allows download speeds of up to 9 megabits per second and upload speeds of up to 640 kilobits per second. DSL is now a popular alternative to Leased Lines and ISDN, being faster than ISDN and less costly than traditional Leased Lines.

Dummy: a block, usually of wood, used when a book has been re-located from the site where a patron would expect to find it according to the catalog. The dummy is placed on the shelf, and is labelled with the name and actual present location of the item it has replaced.

Duplication Center: the library's photocopy service center. Marriott's main

Eccles Library: The University of Utah Health Sciences Library, located near the University Hospital.

Edition: 1) all copies of a bibliographic item produced from the same master copy. A citation will not usually indicate a "first edition," but will note later editions: "revised edition," "fifth edition," etc. 2) one of the various editions of a newspaper or magazine printed at different times of the day, etc.; for example: " daily edition," "evening edition" or "special. edition."

Email — (Electronic Mail), Messages, usually text, sent from one person to another via computer. E-mail can also be sent automatically to a large number of addresses.

Enliven: a multimedia player from Narrative that provides interactive streaming video, sound and animation (see Quicktime and Shockwave).

Entry: any record, or a field in a record, that has been included, or entered, into a **database**. An entry word is the headword in a dictionary, encyclopedia, or glossary.

Errata: errors discovered after publication. Corrections are printed on a separate sheet and "tipped in" or otherwise attached to the book.

Ethernet: a common protocol for networking computers.

Ethernet: A very common method of networking computers in a *LAN*. There is more than one type of Ethernet. By 2001 the standard type was "100-BaseT" which can handle up to about 100,000,000 bits-per-second and can be used with almost any kind of computer.

Example: Call numbers for Dinosaurs of Utah by Frank DeCourten LC DDC QE862.D5 567.9 Class number, D42 DeC book number (author number) 1998 1998 publication year

Exchange Department: the library division which handles exchanges of publications among cooperating institutions. Marriott no longer has an Exchange department; our only exchanges are for periodicals, which are handled by the Serials division.

Exit permit: the printed form used to issue otherwise non-circulating material to authorized faculty and graduate students, generally for a few hours or overnight, and sometimes only with the consent of the librarian responsible for the subject area.

Extranet: An *intranet* that is accesible to computers that are not hysically part of a companys' own private *network*, but that is not accessible to the general public, for example to allow vendors and business partners to access a company web site. Often an intranet will make use of a Virtual Private Network. (*VPN*.)

Faculty Assistance Center: a service division of ACLIS which assists faculty in classroom uses of technology, such as putting course materials on the web; using the internet for course-related communication; general training in technological literacy, etc.

Faculty library representative: a faculty member who serves as the department's contact for library matters; faculty representatives often funnel requests from their colleagues to the appropriate selector librarian, transmit library announcements to the department, and consult on major purchases and cancellations.

FAQ: Frequently Asked Questions; many Internet sites, such as organizations' websites and USENET discussion lists, provide a FAQ; newcomers are encouraged to read the FAQ before posting questions to avoid unnecessarily repetitious discussion.

FDDI — (Fiber Distributed Data Interface), A standard for transmitting data on optical fiber cables at a rate of around 100,000,000 bits-per-second (10 times as fast as 10-BaseT*Ethernet*, about twice as fast as *T-3*).

Ffacsimile: an exact replica of a bibliographic item, both in text and physical appearance. Some of the items in Special Collections are facsimiles of rare editions.

Fiche: short for microfiche. A small sheet (4" x 6") containing microfilmed images of pages, read with a microfilm reader. Many pages of text fit onto a single fiche, and their major advantage is in saving shelf space.

Field: in a database, the part of a record reserved for a particular type of data; for example, in a library catalog, author, title, ISBN, subject headings, etc. would all be fields.

Field: an element of a database record. It contains one type of information and has a unique address. All or most other records in the database have a similar field. An example is the field "name".

Fill-in form: a document of a WWW page in which you can enter information

Finger: An Internet software tool for locating people on other Internet sites. Finger is also sometimes used to give access to non-personal information, but the most common use is to see if a person has an account at a particular Internet site. Many sites do not allow incoming Finger requests, but many do.

Firewall: a combination of software and hardware that limits access to a WWW site and provides a degree of security

Firm order books: books ordered directly by a selector librarian, rather than arriving by default on an approval plan. At Marriott, funds available to selectors to purchase materials for their subjects are split into "approval" and "firm order" accounts. Any amount left over from the approval plan at the end of the fiscal year may be used for firm orders.

Flame War: When an online discussion degenerates into a series of personal attacks against the debators, rather than discussion of their positions. A heated exchange.

Flame: Originally, "flame" meant to carry forth in a passionate manner in the spirit of honorable debate. Flames most often involved the use of flowery language and flaming well was an art form. More recently flame has come to refer to any kind of derogatory comment no matter how witless or crude.

Flexible binding: temporary cardboard binding; often used for binding incomplete runs of a periodical - in hopes that the missing item(s) will be obtained, at which time the volume will be re-bound. Also called tie-bound.

Free-text search:a simple word or character search, usually with very few Boolean, proximity, or scope limiting options. It is simple and fast. A free-text search(2) is a search in which all the entries are freed from their original format of presentation. Text that originated in a journal article looks much the same as text that originated in a glossary or chat room. A free-text search(3) refers to the deliberate limiting of the scope of the search parameters to include only records that are available free of charge.

Freeware: software provided free of charge by its creator.

Frequency: the interval at which a serial is published;

FTP — (File Transfer Protocol), A very common method of moving files between two Internet sites. FTP is a way to *login* to another Internet site for the purposes of retrieving and/or sending files. There are many Internet sites that have established publicly accessible repositories of material that can be obtained using FTP, by logging in using the account name "anonymous", thus these sites are called "anonymous ftp servers". FTP was invented and in wide use long before the advent of the *World Wide Web* and originally was always used from a text-only interface.

Full text: when the entire content of an item, such as an article, book, or encyclopedia, is available in electronic format. Marriott has a large number of

Full-text electronic journals; see "Electronic Journals" on the Marriott homepage.

Full-text Journals Online: The library's link to thousands of periodicals, scholarly journals, popular magazines, newspapers, and other serials, all available in convenient full text.

Gateway: The technical meaning is a hardware or software set-up that translates between two dissimilar protocols, for example America Online has a gateway that translates between its internal, proprietary e-mail format and Internet e-mail format. Another, sloppier meaning of gateway is to describe any mechanism for providing access to another system, e.g. AOL might be called a gateway to the Internet.

Gazetteer: a geographical dictionary (place names, geographical features such as mountains, rivers, etc.); may also provide historical and statistical information about places.

Generic searching: in searching computerized catalogs or indexes, to search under broader subject headings than the most specific ones relating to one's topic, in order to retrieve more material.

Geologic map: a map showing the geological structure of an area. These very often have "geologic map" in the title, and the subject heading will always include "geology" and "maps" (for example, Geology—Utah—Rich County—Maps); to find them in UNIS, try a keyword search including geology and maps.

GIF — (Graphic Interchange Format), A common format for image files, especially suitable for images containing large areas of the same color. GIF format files of simple images are often smaller than the same file would be if stored in *JPEG* format, but GIF format does not store photographic images as well as JPEG.

Gifts: the library department responsible for handling materials received as gifts from individuals and other institutions. Marriott's Gifts department is located in the Storage facility, and also runs the book sale.

Gigabyte : 1000 or 1024 *Megabytes*, depending on who is measuring.

Glossary: an alphabetical list, with definitions, of terms specific to a particular subject field.

Gmelin: a massive compendium of data on inorganic compounds; the full title is Gmelins Handbuch der Anorganischen Chemie, call number QD151.G521.

Gopher: Invented at the University of Minnesota in 1993 just before the *Web*, gopher was a widely successful method of making menus of material available over the Internet. Gopher was designed to be much easier to use than *FTP*, while still using a text-only interface. Gopher is a *Client* and *Server* style program, whichrequires that the user have a Gopher *Client* program. Although Gopher spread rapidly across the globe in only a couple of years, it has been largely supplanted by Hypertext, also known as *WWW (World Wide Web)*. There are still thousands of Gopher *Servers* on the Internet and we can expect they will remain for a while.

Gopherspace: a term that describes the collection of files accessible through gopher servers.

Graphical browser: a browser capable of displaying pictures.

Grid: a pattern of squares used to locate specific points or items on a sheet; in libraries, used in reference to microfiche and maps.

GUI: (pronounced "gooey") graphical user interface; a program in which the user executes commands, selects files, etc. by using a mouse or other pointer device to select items (such as program icons, commands in a drop-down menu or options in a dialog box) rather than by typing in text commands.

Hard copy: data printed on paper, in human-readable form, usually by a computer. Compare with soft copy, which is an image on a computer screen.

Heading: the name, work, or phrase used as an access point to a bibliographic record, determined by a prescribed set of rules; the word or phrase by which you search for an item in a catalog or index.

Helmke Library Homepage: Find us on the Web at http:/ /www.lib.ipfw.edu/.

Help Desk an ACLIS service desk providing assistance to

users of the campus modems, e-mail, web and other ACLIS services. The Help Desk is located at 464

Helper application: an add-on program that plays or displays a file (e.g. sound, video) in a separate window to the browser.

Hit: an item identified or retrieved in a catalog or index search; many indexes will show the number of hits for a search on the screen before actually displaying the citations or documents retrieved, to allow the user to revise the search. A false hit is an item retrieved by the search statement which is not actually relevant or useful to the user.

Hold: a request that an item be kept for a patron until they can pick it up. A patron may place a hold on an item currently on loan to another patron, or on an item that is on order or being processed; they will then be in line to use the item as soon as it becomes available. Hold items are kept at the main Circulation Desk on Level 3.

Holdings :The statement in IUCAT that identifies the volumes, issues, and years of a periodical (journal, magazine, newspaper, or other serial publication) owned by each campus in the Indiana University Libraries system.

Home page: 1) the World Wide Web document displayed first when one's browser starts up (for example, the Marriott Reference machines are set up to load to the Marriott home page); 2) the main web page for an individual or organization.

Horizon: a Web-based, graphical-interface library catalog system which will be used by all academic institutions in Utah except BYU; Marriott's catalog will move to a Horizon system in March 1999.

Host: Any computer on a *network* that is a repository for services available to other computers on the *network*. It is quite common to have one host machine provide several services, such as *SMTP* (email) and *HTTP* (web).

HTML: Hyper Text Markup Language; the coding syntax used to write WWW documents, which are read by browsers.

HTTP: Hyper Text Transfer Protocol; the WWW protocol that performs the request and retrieve functions of a server. Commonly seen as the first part of a website address.

Hyperlink: a hypertext link; a graphic or text string which, when clicked, opens a new web page or jumps to a new location in the current page.

Hypertext: The basic concept behind the WWW, whereby one resource can be linked to other relevant information elsewhere on the WWW. The user can view information non-sequentially; the idea is that the information is available in much the way that humans think - by association rather than linear sequence.

Ibid.: abbreviation for Latin ibidem, "in the same place." Used in references and citations to refer to the last work cited, saving re-typing the author and title. EXAMPLE: 1. Wessel, Janet A. Fitness for the Modern Teenager. New York. The Ronald Press, 1963. p.70. 2. Ibid., p.87.

Icon: a pictorial image used in a graphical user interface to represent a program, a command, a link to a Web page, etc. ;

IEE: often called "I double E." The Institution of Electrical Engineers, the major British professional society for electrical engineers. IEE produces the INSPEC database as well as a number of journals.

IEEE: often called "I triple E." The Institute of Electrical and Electronics Engineers, the major American professional society for electrical engineers as well as computer engineers. IEEE publishes a large number of journals, magazines and conference proceedings; Marriott Library subscribes to essentially all of them. Their conferences change names constantly and are best found in UNIS with a keyword search.

Imagemap: an image in a Web browser in which different areas act as hyperlinks.

IMAP — (Internet Message Access Protocol). IMAP is gradually replacing *POP* as the main protocol used by email *clients* in communicating with email *servers*. Using IMAP an email client program can not only retrieve email but can also manipulate message stored on the server, without having to actually retrieve the messages. So messages can be deleted, have their status changed, multiple mail boxes can be managed, etc.IMAP is defined in RFC 2060

IMHO: In My Humble Opinion - acronym often included in e-mail or other online discussion, to show that the writer is aware of expressing a debatable opinion. A number of such acronyms are used for politeness in electronic discussions, since statements can easily seem excessively strong or offensive.

Imprint: information about the publication of a book;

In print: still being published, and therefore available for purchase from the publisher or dealer.

Index: a list or systematic guide to the contents of a set of data, such as a periodical index or an index in a book. See periodical index.

indexes that require them.

Information Literacy: Information literacy enables an IPFW student to recognize an information need, develop a strategy to locate, evaluate, and synthesize information, and cite sources of information accurately.

In-process material: newly acquired items in a library which are undergoing technical processing such as cataloging, marking, etc. Patrons who need an in-process item can place a rush request for it with Circulation; it will usually be available within a day.

Instruction: library department responsible for coordinating and conducting the library's orientation and instruction efforts, including: building tours; credit classes in research; short courses on databases, programs, and specific subject areas; and course-specific sessions

Interlibrary loan: when patrons of a library arrange for resources from other libraries to be sent to their library. This resource sharing system is being promoted by the International Federation of Library Associations.

Internet: A collection of data networks, bibliographic databases, electronic bulletin boards, library catalogs, and many other resources, accessed by computers over high-speed lines.

internet (Lower case i) Any time you connect 2 or more *networks* together, you have an internet - as in inter-national or inter-state.

Internet (Upper case I) The vast collection of inter-connected networks that are connected using the *TCP/IP* protocols and that evolved from the *ARPANET* of the late 60's and early 70's. The Internet connects tens of thousands of independent networks into a vast global *internet* and is probably the largest *Wide Area Network* in the world.

Internet Explorer: a WWW browser developed by Microsoft.

Internet Service Provider (ISP): a commercial company that sells Internet

Internet Society: an international nonprofit organization that governs such issues as the assignment of IP addresses.

Intranet: A private *network* inside a company or organization that uses the same kinds of software that you would find on the public *Internet*, but that is only for internal use. Compare with *extranet*.

IOP: Institute of Physics; a British professional society and major publisher in physics and some areas of engineering.

IP Number — (Internet Protocol Number) Sometimes called a dotted quad. A unique number consisting of 4 parts separated by dots, e.g. 165.113.245.2, Every machine that is on the Internet has a unique IP number - if a machine does not have an IP number, it is not really on the Internet. Many machines (especially servers) also have one or more Domain Names that are easier for people to remember.

IRC — (Internet Relay Chat) Basically a huge multi-user live chat facility. There are a number of major IRC *servers* around the world which are linked to each other. Anyone can create a channel and anything that anyone types in a given channel is seen by all others in the channel. Private channels can (and are) created for multi-person conference calls.

Irregular serial: a serial publication which is not issued on a regular, predictable schedule; there may be several issues in one year, or only one every several years.

ISBN International Standard Book Number: A unique number assigned to every book published in this country, and many in other countries. The ISBN system is recognized internationally. An ISBN has nine or ten digits; the first digit denotes country of publication, the next several the publisher, the remainder identify the item.

ISDN — (Integrated Services Digital Network) Basically a way to move more dataover existing regular phone lines. ISDN is available to much of the USA and in most markets it is priced very comparably to standard analog phone circuits. It can provide speeds of roughly 128,000 bits-per-second over regular phone lines. In practice, most people will be limited to 56,000or 64,000 bits-per-second. Unlike *DSL*, ISDN can be used to connect to many different locations, one at a time, just like a regular telephone call, as long the other location also has ISDN.

ISP — (Internet Service Provider) An institution that provides access to the Internet in some form, usually for money.

ISSN International Standard Serial Number: A unique eight-digit number, in two groups of four, assigned to a periodical by the International Serials Data System.

IUCAT: Indiana University Libraries' online catalog, containing more than 5 million entries for books, edited volumes, periodical titles, videos, sound recordings, and other library materials.

Java: Java is a network-friendly programming language invented by Sun Microsystems. Java is often used to build large, complex systems that involve several different computers interacting across networks, for example transaction processing systems. Java is also becoming popular for creating programs that run in small electronic devicws, such as mobile telephones. A very common use of Java is to create programs that can be safely downloaded to your computer through the Internet and immediately run without fear of viruses or other harm to your computer or files. Using small Java programs (called "*Applets*"), Web pages can include functions such as animations,calculators, and other fancy tricks.

JavaScript: JavaScript is a programming language that is mostly used in web pages, usually to add features that make the web page more interactive. When JavaScript is included in an *HTML* file it relies upon the browser to interpret the JavaScript. When JavaScript is combined with *Cascading Style Sheets*(CSS), and later versions of HTML (4.0 and later) the result is often called *DHTML*.

JDK — (Java Development Kit) A software development package from Sun Microsystems that implements the basic set of tools needed to write, test and debug*Java* applications and *applets*

Jobber: a book supplier (a.k.a book jobber)

Journal: a periodical publication in which researchers report the results of their work to their peer community; compare with magazine. Articles are reviewed by an editorial board of scholars in the field prior to acceptance for publication (see also refereed journal), and generally include an abstract and numerous citations to previous work. The writing style in journals is formal rather than engaging, and journals generally have little or no advertising or glossy, catchy graphics and illustrations. Journals often have pages numbered continuously through the several issues of a given volume (for example, v.15 #1 has pages 1-223; v.15 #2 runs from p.224-587, and so forth to the last issue of the volume).

JPEG — (Joint Photographic Experts Group) JPEG is most commonly mentioned as a format for image files. JPEG format is preferred to the *GIF* format for photographic images as opposed to line art or simple logo art.

Keyword searching: is the searching of a database using a significant word from the title, abstract, or descriptor of a record as a point of reference to the article's overall content. This type of search is usually the best type to start with.

Keyword: a significant word in the title, abstract or text of a work; some periodical indexes identify keywords in a separate data field, so that they can be searched without searching the full text of the document. Some indexes use such keywords in place of assigning standard subject headings to items.

Kilobyte: A thousand bytes. Actually, usually 1024 (2^{10}) bytes.

LAN: Local Area Network; a group of computers networked to share resources, confined to a small geographic area (often a single building).

LANDSAT maps: high-altitude satellite photograph-like

Leased Line : Refers to line such as a telephone line or fiber-optic cable that is rented for exclusive 24-hour, 7-days-a-week use from your location to another location. The highest speed data connections require a leased line.

Library classes: a variety of courses and one-shot classes and workshops offered by the **Library of Congress (LC) Classification:** The call number system that uses a combination of letters and numbers to identify the broad subject and shelf location of items in the library collection.

Library Workstations: Computers in the library that

provide access to the IUCAT online catalog, Helmke Library's homepage, and other Web resources.

Linux A widely used Open Source Unix-like operating system. Linux was first released by its inventor Linus Torvalds in 1991. There are versions of Linux for almost every available type of computer hardware from desktop machines to IBM mainframes. The inner workings of Linux are open and available for anyone to examine and change as long as they make their changes available to the public. This has resulted in thousands of people working on various aspects of Linux and adaptation of Linux for a huge variety of purposes, from servers to TV-recording boxes.

List server: a program that sends and receives messages for subscribers of an e-mail discussion list.

Listserv ®: The most common kind of *maillist*, "Listserv" is a registered trademark of L-Soft international, Inc. Listservs originated on *BITNET* but they are now common on the *Internet*.

Literature guide: a reference work that describes special features of the scholarly literature in a given discipline, including important standard reference materials and serials.

Literature search: the search of traditional resources including books, catalogs, encyclopedias, dictionaries, atlases, bibliographies, handbooks, manuals, periodicals, indexes, yearbooks, gazetteers, directories, chronologies, almanacs, and guides. It is useful because it opens up a vast world of pre-1995 information that is not available online.

Literature: (collections, reviews, popularizations, textbooks, encyclopedias, handbooks, etc.), and tools which point the user to primary sources (abstracts, indexes, bibliographies). Secondary literature provides broader dissemination of information that has already appeared in another form.

Llocked case books: books shelved in a locked room due to high vulnerability to theft or vandalism; some are entirely non-circulating, others may circulate on an exit permit. There are locked case materials in the Science, Fine Arts, and Middle East collections; ask for them at the respective desks.

Loan period: the length of time for which a library patron may borrow an item.

Loc.cit.: Latin, abbreviation for loco citato: "in the place cited." In a footnote, used with the author's last name; stands for the title of a work, and the page, cited in an earlier footnote. EXAMPLE: 41 Gross, loc.cit.

Login: Noun or a verb. **Noun:** The account name used to gain access to a computer system. Not a secret (contrast with *Password*). **Verb:** the act of connecting to a computer system by giving your credentials (usually your "username" and "password")

Logon script: a small program that executes a set of commands when a user logs on to the system; at Marriott, Systems sometimes uses logon scripts to automatically provide user ID and password information when users access

Logon, logoff: to begin or to end operation of a computer or program.

Mac: Short for "Macintosh" - a range of personal computers from the Apple company which use a graphical user interface. In Marriott, teaching lab 1745 is equipped with Macs, and there are Macs available for student use in the Multimedia Center.

Magazine: a periodical, generally with a more "popular" style and presentation than a research journal. Usually, magazine articles are authored by staff writers for an audience of the general public or interested amateurs in a given field (rather than by researchers for their peers), and edited by a magazine employee rather than an independent board of scholars. Style tends to be engaging and eye-catching, and magazines often include substantial advertising. Pagination usually starts over at "1" with each issue. Compare with journal.

Maillist: (or Mailing List) A (usually automated) system that allows people to send *e-mail* to one address, whereupon their message is copied and sent to all of the other subscribers to the maillist. In this way, people who have many different kinds of e-mail access can participate in discussions together.

Main entry: in a card catalog, the card with the most complete bibliographic information on an item, listing subject headings and tracings such as other authors; usually the main entry is filed by first author.

Manuscripts: the division responsible for the collection, cataloging, and maintenance of the Library's unpublished historical collections, including diaries, autobiographies, correspondence, business and personal records. Subject areas covered in Marriott's Manuscripts collections include Politics; Communications; Architecture; Ethnic groups; Science, Engineering and Medicine; History, Philosophy, and Religion; Outdoor Recreation; Mining; Visual and

Map projection: an arrangement of the longitude and latitude grid to enable part or all of the globe's curved surface to be represented on a flat surface. (For example, Mercator's Projection.)

MARC MAchine Readable Cataloging: MARC records contain data in standardized format and allow conversion to automated cataloging and circulation systems.

Media Viewing & Music Listening Equipment: Check out headphones and cartridges, along with music CDs and videos at the Service Desk. The third floor offers a viewing and listening area, or use headphones for some applications in the student-access computer lab.

Megabyte: A million *bytes*. Actually, technically, 1024 *kilobytes*.

Menu: a list of options from which a computer user can choose. This saves the user from having to memorize a set of commands. It also reduces the decision down to the basic information required (note the etymology from the French word minuet meaning small).

Meta Tag: A specific kind of *HTML* tag that contains information not normally displayed to the user. Meta tags contan information about the page itself, hence the name ("meta" means "about this subject") Typical uses of Meta tags are to include information for *search engines* to help them better categorize a page. You can see the Meta tags in a page if you view the pages' source code.

Microfiche: A small sheet (4" x 6") containing microfilmed images of pages, read with a microfilm reader. Many pages of text fit onto a single fiche, and their major advantage is in saving shelf space. Many government documents are issued in fiche format.

Microfilm: microphotographs of printed material, on a reel of cellulose film, viewed using a microfilm reader/printer (in Marriott, located on Level 1, in the Documents area). Items in awkward or frail formats (such as newsprint) and popular magazines subject to damage from heavy use are often purchased in microfilm format rather than being bound between hard covers.

Microforms: all forms of microreproduction, e.g.

Microprint: an obsolete form of microphotograph which can hold many pages of text on a 9"x6" card, viewed with the aid of a microprint reader. It is similar to a microfiche, but has positive images of the pages printed on an opaque card. Marriott's materials in microprint are not actually accessible at present, as there are no functional readers and the machines are no longer being manufactured.

MIME: Multipurpose Internet Mail Extensions. A standard for attaching non-text files (images, audio, video, programs, spreadsheets, formatted word-processor documents, etc.) to standard Internet mail messages. A "MIME-compliant" email program can both send and receive files using the MIME standard. The non-text files are encoded into text for transmission: the

MIME standard specifies the type of file being sent and the method to be used to convert it back to its original form. The MIME standard is also used for transferring files between Web Servers and Clients

Mirror sites: web sites that keep exact copies of material from another site, to provide improved access.

Mirror: Generally speaking, "to mirror" is to maintain an exact copy of something. Probably the most common use of the term on the Internet refers to "mirror sites" which are *web* sites, or *FTP* sites that maintain copies of material originated at another location, usually in order to provide more widespread access to the resource. For example, one site might create a library of software, and 5 other sites might maintain mirrors of that library.

Modem — (MOdulator, DEModulator) A device that connects a computer to a phone line. A telephone for a computer. A modem allows a computer to talk to other computers through the phone system. Basically, modems do for computers what a telephone does for humans.

Monograph: a written document (i.e., graph) on a single subject (i.e., mono). It is usually scholarly in nature and of approximately book length. They are valuable information sources because of their depth in a limited subject area.

Monographic series: monographs issued as part of a titled series, at either regular or irregular intervals. For example, the Cambridge Nonlinear Science Series. Each item in the series is separately titled, but is also identified by the series title and often a number within the series.

MOO — (Mud, Object Oriented) One of several kinds of multi-user role-playing environments.

MUD, Object-Oriented: a multi-user role-playing environment (MUD) with an object-based environment (e.g. BioMOO).

Mosaic: The first *WWW browser* that was available for the Macintosh, Windows,and UNIX all with the same interface.

Mosaic really started the popularity of the Web. The source-code to Mosaic was licensed by several companies and used to create many other web browsers. Mosaic was developed at the National Center for Supercomputing Applications (NCSA), at the Univeristy of Urbana-Champange in Illinois, USA. The first version was released in late 1993.

MPEG: Moving Picture Expert Group; a standard for digital encoding of video.

MUD — (Multi-User Dungeon or Dimension) (usually text-based) multi-user simulation environment. Some are purely for fun and flirting, others are used for serious software development, or education purposes and all thatlies in between. A significant feature of most MUDs is that users can create things that stay after they leave and which other users can interact within their absence, thus allowing a world to be built gradually and collectively.

Multimedia Center (MMC): the facility which houses and provides access to

Multimedia: a document or program that integrates text, graphics, audio and video.

MUSE — (Multi-User Simulated Environment) One kind of MUD - usually with little or no violence.

NAPs Network Access Points; these interconnect the commercial ISPs.

Nautical chart: a map for use in navigation of waterways, which includes such features as depth contours, loran lines, and beacon locations. To find these in

Netiquette The etiquette on the *Internet*.

Netiquette: Internet etiquette; unwritten rules of conduct governing communication over the Internet.

Netizen: Derived from the term citizen, referring to a citizen of the *Internet*,or someone who uses networked resources. The term connotes civic responsibility and participation.

Netscape: A *WWW Browser* and the name of a company. The Netscape (tm) browser was originally based on the *Mosaic* program developed at the National Center for Supercomputing Applications (NCSA).

Network: Any time you connect 2 or more computers together so that they can share resources, you have a computer network. Connect 2 or more networks together and you have an *internet*.

Newsgroup: The name for discussion groups on *USENET*.

NIC — (Network Information Center) Generally, any office that handles information for a network. The most famous of these on the Internet was the InterNIC, which was where most new domain names were registered until that process was decentralized to a number of private companies. Also means "Network Interface card", which is the card in a computer that you plug a network cable into.

NNTP — (Network News Transport Protocol) The protocol used by *client*and *server* software to carry *USENET* postings back and forth over a *TCP/IP network*. If you are using any of the more common software such as *Netscape*, Nuntius, Internet Explorer, etc. to participate in *newsgroups* then you are benefiting from an NNTP connection.

Node: Any single computer connected to a *network*.

Non-circulating items: include archival material, rare books, reference material, current periodicals and other items which must remain accessible within the library at all times.

Non-circulating: library materials which may not be checked out by patrons.

Oacket: the basic unit of data transmitted over the Internet; packets are transmitted independently and then reassembled at their destination.

OCLC: Online Computer Library Center. A nonprofit library computer service and research organization with the stated goals of helping libraries further access to information and reduce information costs. Thousands of libraries around the world participate in the OCLC system. OCLC offers a large number of databases through their FirstSearch online system, including WorldCat, a combined catalog of participating libraries with links to facilitate interlibrary loans, and many special subject periodical indexes. OCLC is also used extensively by libraries for obtaining cataloging information for processing materials.

Official University ID card: Get your picture ID card at the Walb Student Union Information Desk to use as your official IPFW identification, library card, and photocopy debit card.

Online cataloging: generally, preparing catalog entries with the use of a machine-readable database. In library usage, often refers to obtaining cataloging information by purchasing and downloading from another source, such as OCLC or publisher information, rather than starting from scratch ("original cataloging").

Online searching: in general, searching a computerized database. In libraries, may refer to a paid, librarian- mediated search of databases from a vendor such as STN (for Chemical Abstracts) or Dialog, in contrast to databases available for end-users to search on CD-ROM or Web-based subscriptions. At Marriott, there is very little demand any more for such paid searches because of the extensive availability of subscription databases.

Online: any capability available or work done directly on a computer. For example, online help or online cataloging .

OPAC: Online Public Access Catalog; a computerized library catalog, or the portion of the catalog available for patron use. UNIS is Marriott's OPAC.

Open access: refers to book stacks to which users have free access to browse and retrieve items on their own, as opposed to closed stacks. Most of the Marriott Library is open access.

Open Content: Copyrighted information (such as this

Glossary) that is made available by the copyright owner to the general public under license terms that allow reuse of the material, often with the requirement (as with this Glossary) that the re-user grant the public the same rights to the modified version that the re-user received from the copyright owner. Information that is in the Public Domain might also be considered a form of Open Content.

Open Source Software: Open Source Software is software for which the underlying programming code is available to the users so that they may read it, make changes to it, and build new versions of the software incorporating their changes. There are many types of Open Source Software, mainly differing in the licensing term under which (altered) copies of the source code may (or must be) redistributed.

Operating system: the program that manages all the applications on a computer. For example, DOS and UNIX are operating systems.

Operators: symbols that represent operations. In computer science there are binary and unary operators depending on the number of elements or records an operator acts on. In database searching there are Boolean and Proximity operators. Boolean operators are a subclass of logical operators (Logical operators are binary operators that manipulate data at the bit level.). A Boolean operator manipulates the binary value "true/false".

Original cataloging: preparing catalog information directly from the item in hand, rather than obtaining the data from another source (see online cataloging). Original cataloging is labor-intensive and generally used only when the information is not otherwise available.

Overdue: an item still charged to a patron after the due date (end of the loan period). Fines may be assessed on overdue items, and books that remain overdue for four weeks are declared lost and the responsible patron will be charged for the replacement cost of the item plus a $25.00 processing fee.

Oversized books: books too large to fit in the regular shelving. At Marriott, these are housed in a special Oversize stacks area on Level 2.

Packet Switching: The method used to move data around on the *Internet*. In packet switching,all the data coming out of a machine is broken up into chunks, each chunk has the address of where it came from and where it is going. This enables chunks of data from many different sources to co-mingle on the same lines, and be sorted and directed along different routes by special machines along the way. This way many people can use the same lines at the same time. You might think of several caravans of trucks all using the same road system to carry materials.

Password: A code used to gain access (*login*) to a locked system. Good passwords contain letters and non-letters and are not simple combinations such as *virtue7*. A good password might be: 5%df(29) But don't use that one!

PC: Personal Computer; a personal computer conforming to the IBM (as opposed to Macintosh) standard.

PDF: Portable Document Format; a document-encoding process developed by Adobe that maintains page layout, fonts and graphics and can include many other features, e.g. hyperlinks.

Performing Arts: Skiing; Women's organizations; and Ranching.

Periodical index: a work which lists, by subject (and often author), the articles which appear in a prescribed group of periodicals. Some periodical indexes are general (Reader's Guide, General Science Index) and some treat specific fields (Engineering Index). Provides citations and sometimes abstracts or even full-text of the articles.

Periodical: a serial (journal, magazine) which is published at regular intervals, is numbered, contains separate articles, and has no pre-determined end date. Does not include newspapers or conference proceedings.

Permuterm: a type of subject index generated by computer and showing paired combinations of the significant words in titles. Used in some major print indexes, notably Science Citation Index and Biological Abstracts.

Photocopiers: Photocopy machines located on the first, second, and fourth floors accept coins or bills to make copies at $0.10 per page, or $0.08 using a debit card. A color copier is available on campus at Printing Services.

Ping: To check if a server is running. From the sound that a sonar systems makes in movies, you know, when they are searching for a submarine.

Pixel: short for "picture element"; one of the dots that make up a digitized image. A pixel may be binary (black and white) or multivalued for colored displays. The number of pixels in a display determines resolution, more pixels providing higher resolution.

Plagiarism: the passing off as your own, the work of others'. Original sources are not given credit.

Plug-in: a software module that adds a specific feature to a larger system, for example plug-ins for the Netscape Navigator that enable it to display audio and video files. Plug-ins display the files within the browser window, without having to open a separate window as helper applications do. (see Enliven,

PNG — (Portable Network Graphics) PNG is a graphics format specifically designed for use on the World Wide Web. PNG enable compression of images without any loss of quality, including high-resolution images. Another important feature of PNG is that anyone may create software that works with PNG images without paying any fees - the PNG standard is free of any licensing costs.

POP — (Point of Presence, also Post Office Protocol) Two commonly used meanings:

Point of Presence and Post Office Protocol. A Point of Presence usually means a city or location where a network can be connected to, often with dial up phone lines. So if an Internet company says they will soon have a POP in Belgrade, it means that they will soon have a local phone number in Belgrade and/ or a place where leased lines can connect to their network. A second meaning, Post Office Protocol refers to a way that e-mail *client* software such as Eudora gets mail from a mail *server*. When you obtain an account from an Internet Service Provider (*ISP*) you almost always get a POP account with it, and it is this POP account that you tell your e-mail software to use to get your mail. Another protocol called IMAP is replacing POP for email.

Port: 3 meanings. First and most generally, a place where information goes into or out of a computer, or both. E.g. the serial port on a personal computer is where a *modem* would be connected. On the Internet port often refers to a number that is part of a URL, appearing after a colon (:) right after the domain name. Every service on an Internet server listens on a particular port number on that server. Most services have standard port numbers, e.g. Web servers normally listen on port 80. Services can also listen on non-standard ports, in which case the port number must be specified in a URL when accessing the server, so you might see a URL of the form: gopher:// peg.cwis.uci.edu:7000/ This shows a gopher server running on a non-standard port (the standard gopher port is 70). Finally, port also refers to translating a piece of software to bring it from one type of computer system to another, e.g. to translate a Windows program so that is will run on a Macintosh.

Portal: Usually used as a marketing term to described a Web site that is or is intended to be the first place people see when using the Web. Typically a "Portal site" has a catalog of web sites, a search engine, or both. A Portal site may also offer email and other service to entice people to use that site as their main "point of entry" (hence "portal") to the Web.

Posting: A single message entered into a network communications system.

PPP — (Point to Point Protocol) The most common protocol used to connect home computers to the Internet over regular phone lines. Most well known as a protocol that allows a computer to use a regular telephone line and a *modem* to make *TCP/IP*connections and thus be really and truly on the *Internet*.

Preprint: 1. a portion of a work printed and issued before the publication of the complete work; for example, a copy of an article issued before the journal is published.2. a conference paper issued prior to the holding of the conference.

Primary literature: the original research or writings on a subject. Includes technical reports, conference literature, patents, theses, and journals (the main medium for the dissemination of new knowledge). See secondary literature.

Primary record: a resource created by the same people that initially experienced or used it. They create the records for their own purposes, records that often remain unpublished. Sometimes they witness an event, sometimes they are involved in an event, and sometimes the record is directly created by the event.

Primary source: the originator of a primary record. A

Proper names: personal and geographical names.

Protocol: On the Internet "protocol" usually refers to a set of rules that define an exact format for communication between systems. For example the *HTTP* protocol defines the format for communication between web browsers and web servers, the *IMAP* protocol defines the format for communication between IMAP email servers and clients, and the *SSL* protocol defines a format for encrypted communications over the Internet. Virtually all Internet protocls are defined in *RFC* documents.

Proxy Server: A Proxy Server sits in between a *Client* and the "real" *Server* that a Client is trying to use. Client's are sometimes configured to use a Proxy Server, usually an *HTTP* server. The clients makes all of it's requests from the Proxy Server, which then makes requests from the "real" server and passes the result back to the Client. Sometimes the Proxy server will store the results and give a stored result instead of making a new one (to reduce use of a *Network*). Proxy servers are commonly established on *Local Area Networks*

PSTN — (Public Switched Telephone Network): The regular old-fashioned telephone system.

Public domain software: uncopyrighted software, freely accessible to all users.

Public Information Reference Service (PIRS): An integrated set of Web pages that guides users to selected local, state, U.S., and international government documents, statistical compendia, and other resources.

Publication date: 1. in a book — the date appears at the bottom of the title page (as opposed to the copyright date which is on the verso of the title page). 2. in a periodical — the day or month, etc., it was issued.

Publisher: the person, company or organization responsible for placing a book, journal, or other publication on the market (as opposed to the printer or bookseller).

Push: an information-delivery technology whereby users are 'pushed' information by the server rather than 'pulling' it themselves (e.g. news delivery by PointCast); in fact, the user has already requested the information by first downloading a client program, which records details of the user, and requests information on their behalf.

Quads: nickname for USGS topographical maps, or "quadrangle" maps, so named because of the grid pattern they are based on.

Quarterly: periodical published at regular intervals four times a year.

QuickTime: a multimedia player from Apple, combining audio, video, animation and text (see Enliven, Shockwave).

RDF — (Resource Definition Framework) A set of rules

(a sort of language) for creating descriptions of information, especially information available on the *World Wide Web*. RDF could be used to describe a collection of books, or artists, or a collection of *web pages* as in the *RSS* data format which uses RDF to create machine-readable summaries of web sites. RDF is also used in *XPFE* applications to define the relationships between different collections of elements, for example RDF could be used to define the relationship between the data in a database and the way that data is displayed to a user.

Reader-copiers: Machines in the microform reading room that project and enlarge images for reading, and produce photocopies. The cost is $0.10 per page, payable at the Service Desk.

RealAudio: client-server software from Progressive Networks, for selecting and playing back audio files; RealAudio has a very short download time, allowing use in "real time" as opposed to previous technology which took many minutes to download one minute of audio material.

Recall: to request an item that is currently checked out to another patron. (The first patron is entitled to have the item for at least two weeks; after that it is subject to recall.) Recalls may be placed electronically (see the Marriott homepage) or at the Marriott Circulation desk.

Record: an individual entry in a database and simultaneously a collection of related data fields. Each field , although related, is of a different type to all the other fields in the record (and this is what differentiates a record from an array).

Recto: the right-hand page of a book, usually with odd-numbered pages. Opposite of verso.

Refereed journal: a journal in which articles have been evaluated by an independent expert in the field of research before acceptance for publication.

Reference Assistance: Services designed to teach skills

and concepts that help you use and evaluate a variety of information resources best suited to your needs.

Reference Collection: A selection of general and specialized encyclopedias, dictionaries, almanacs, atlases, handbooks, bibliographies, periodical indexes, databases, and other library materials to help you find information and do research.

Reference Consulting Area: A place equipped with library workstations and printers for librarians to work with you one-on-one, located on the first floor near the Service Desk and the reference collection.

Reference Desk: a service point in the library, generally staffed by reference librarians, where patrons can obtain assistance in finding materials and information.

Reference Interview: Communication between you and a librarian with the goal of selecting the best information for your needs.

Reference question: a request for information which requires staff member's knowledge of bibliographic and reference skills. For example, "In which periodical index will I find articles on civil engineering?"

Reference: an indication of where to find specific information, for example the references cited in scholarly work, or reference assistance from library staff.

Reissue: re-publication of an item, often at a new price or in a new form, but with the main text unaltered, so that it is not a new edition.

Remote sensing image: image made by sensors, usually form an aircraft or spacecraft, which records features on the earth's surface. For example, LANDSAT maps.

Renewal: an extension of the loan period on an item, granted to the current borrower. Renewals may be requested from the Marriott homepage or by e-mail to renewal@library.utah.edu.

Repository: synonymous with depository.

Reserve: a collection of material in very high demand due to use in the curriculum. Instructors may request that library materials (or, in some cases, their own materials) be placed on reserve for students to borrow on short loan periods (generally from one hour to two weeks) for the duration of a course.

Reserves EXpress: Digitized course reserves accessible on and off campus via the Web. Copyright restrictions require passwords so that only those students enrolled in the course have access.

Reshelve area: stacks in which materials that have just been gathered up after use are rough-sorted and held until shelvers return them to their homes. Marriott's reshelve area **is located on Level 2 in the former auditorium.**

Review article: a periodical article that describes, analyses', and criticizes a book, journal article, movie, or other creative or academic work.

RFC — (Request For Comments) The name of the result and the process for creating a standard on the *Internet*. New standards are proposed and published on the Internet, as a Request For Comments. The proposal is reviewed by the Internet Engineering Task Force (http://www.ietf.org/), a consensus-building body that facilitates discussion, and eventually a new standard is established, but the reference number/name for the standard retains the acronym RFC, e.g. the official standard for *e-mail* message formats is RFC 822.

Root: The first directory in a hierachy of directories and subdirectories.

Router: A special-purpose computer (or software package) that handles the connection between 2 or more Packet-Switched *networks*. Routers spend all their time looking at the source and destination addresses of the *packets* passing through them and deciding which route to send them on.

RSS — (Rich Site Summary or RDF Site Summary or Real

Simple Syndication) XML-based summary of a web site, used for syndication, etc.

Rush: to expedite the availability of a new item; patrons may place a rush request for an item that is presently on order or in process, and it will be obtained, processed and held for them as quickly as possible, often within a day or two. Selector librarians may place a rush order for urgently-needed items.

Scale (maps): the ratio of the distance on a map to the actual distance represented; for example, 1:100,000.

Schedule: a classification schedule; a printed list (in a hierarchial order) of all the main classes and divisions of the system, such as the Library of Congress Classification Schedule.

Scholarly article: an article, usually in a scholarly journal, that deals with academic subject matter at an advanced level.

Science Information Center: This library-within-a-library reference service and collection on the fourth floor delivers specialized science, technology, and health science information.

SDSL — (Symmetric Digital Subscriber Line) A version of *DSL* where the upload speeds and download speeds are the same.

Search engine: A (usually web-based) system for searching the information available on the *Web*. Some search engines work by automatically searching the contents of other systems and creating a database of the results. other search engines contains only material manually approved for inclusion in a database, and some combine the two approaches.

Search strategy: a generalized set of technique used in the process of determining what information you currently have, determining what information you need, and determining how to get it. Some possible strategies include; controlled vocabulary searches, specific entry searches, browsing, general scanning, broad to narrow searches, adjacent item browsing, subject tracings searches, keyword searches, citation searches, literature searches, cross reference searches, and chat room questions and other direct people contact searches.

Secondary literature: material published about the primary

Security Certificate: A chunk of information (often stored as a text file) that is used by the *SSL* protocol to establish a secure connection.

See also" reference: in a catalog, indicates that other headings may also be used, in addition to the one the user is searching under. Extends the limit of the search.

SEO — (Search Engine Optimization) The practice of designing web pages so that they rank as high as possible in search results from *search engines*.

There is "good" SEO and "bad" SEO. Good SEO involves making the web page clearly describe its subject, making sure it contains truly useful information, including accurate information in *Meta tags*, and arranging for other web sites to make links to the page. Bad SEO involves attempting to deceive people into believing the page is more relevant than it truly is by doing things like adding inaccurate Meta tags to the page.

Serials: any publication issued in successive parts, usually (though not always) at regular intervals, and intended to be continued indefinitely.

Series: group of separate items issued under a collective title, as well as under individual titles.

Server: A computer, or a software package, that provides a specific kind of service to *client* software running on other computers. The term can refer to a particular piece of software, such as a *WWW* server, or to the machine on which the software is running, e.g. "Our mail server is down today, that's why e-mail isn't getting out." A single server machine can (and often does) have several different server software packages running on it, thus providing many different servers to *clients* on the *network*. Sometimes server software is designed so that additional capabilities can be added to the main program by adding small programs known as *servlets*.

Service Desk: The service point on the first floor where staff will help you check out library materials and course reserves, use equipment, and get started on library research.

Servlet: A small computer program designed to be add capabilities to a larger piece of *server* software. Common examples are "Java servlets", which are small programs written in the *Java* language and which are added to a *web* server. Typically a web server that uses Java servlets will have many of them, each one designed to handle a very specific situation, for example one servlet will handle adding items to a "shopping cart", while a different servlet will handle deleting items from the "shopping cart."

Set: two or more separate items which are treated as a single entity in a bibliographic description; for example, a multi-volume encyclopedia, or a textbook with an accompanying cd-rom.

Shareware: software provided free by its creator for a trial period, after which the user is expected to send a stated price to continue to use the software.

Shelflist: a catalog (list) of holdings arranged in call number order (that is, in the same order items are found on the shelf).

Shockwave: a group of interactive multimedia players from Macromedia that provide streaming audio and animation (see Enliven, QuickTime).

Site: a collective term covering all the Internet facilities offered by one organization.

SLIP — (Serial Line Internet Protocol) A standard for using a regular telephone line (a serial line) and a *modem* to connect a computer as a real*Internet* site. SLIP has largely been replaced by *PPP*.

SMDS — (Switched Multimegabit Data Service) A standard for very high-speed data transfer.

SMTP — (Simple Mail Transfer Protocol) The main protocol used to send electronic mail from *server* to server on the Internet. SMTP is defined in *RFC* 821 and modified by many later RFC's.

SNMP — (Simple Network Management Protocol) A set of standards for communication with devices connected to a TCP/IP *network*. Examples of these devices include *routers*, hubs, and switches. SNMP is defined in *RFC* 1089

Spam (or Spamming) An inappropriate attempt to use a *mailing list*, or *USENET* or other networked communications facility as if it was a broadcast medium (which it is not) by sending the same message to a large number of people who didn?t ask for it. The term probably comes from a famous Monty Python skit which featured the word spam repeated over and over. The term may also have come from someone?s low opinion of the food product with the same name, which is generally perceived as a generic content-free waste of resources. (Spam® is a registered trademark of Hormel Corporation, for its processed meat product.)

Special Collections: the division in Marriott Library responsible for collecting, organizing, maintaining, and providing reference assistance for our archival and Special-purpose collections, including: Manuscripts, Middle East, Photograph Archives, Rare Books and Maps,University Archives, University Records Center, Western Americana.

SQL — (Structured Query Language) A specialized language for sending queries to databases. Most industrial-strength and many smaller database applications can be addressed using SQL. Each specific application will have its own slightly different version of SQL implementing features unique to that application, but all SQL-capable databases support a common subset of SQL.

Ssearch: a systematic examination of data make in order to locate specific information; can be done, "manually" or on a computer.

SSL — (Secure Socket Layer) A protocol designed by Netscape Communications to enable encrypted, authenticated communications across the Internet.

Stacks: rows of bookshelves in a library.

Standards (specifications): detailed descriptions used in industry to specify how something should be built, installed or manufactured. A large number of agencies produce standards, including ANSI, ASTM, ASME, IEEE, API.... Marriott Library periodically purchases a complete set of ASTM standards, which are the most frequently requested standards. Faculty and students may request that a librarian purchase other individual standards as needed.

Standing order: a book order placed with a dealer who will automatically supply the parts of a continuing item as they are published until instructed not to.

Statistical abstracts: a compilation summarizing social, political, economic or other statistics for a given geographic, political, or other entity. For example, the indispensable Statistical Abstract of the United States.

Storage: a facility on Guardsman Way where infrequently used materials are kept in order to free up shelf space in the library stacks. Items in storage are listed in UNIS. Patrons may request retrieval of materials in storage at the Circulation desk; items are retrieved once a day.

Streaming: audio/video that plays as it arrives, rather than waiting until the whole file has downloaded (see RealAudio and Shockwave).

Student Lab Account: These accounts insure that only valid IPFW students use the computing resources paid for by their technology fees. Students with active accounts may also acquire personal Web space for non-commercial academic purposes. Contact a student-access computer lab consultant or call the Help Desk (481-6030) to activate your account.

Style guide: a publication which specifies details of writing style required by a particular publishing house or professional organization, including such matters as punctuation, capitalization, and rules for citing references. For example, the ACS Style Guide : a Manual for Authors and Editors.

Subject directory: an hierarchical grouping of related subject headings. The tree structure shows relationships between subject headings. They can be found either inside a database or separate from a data base. Generally a thesaurus is a book of synonyms, often also containing antonyms. An example is Roget's Thesaurus. In database searching, a thesaurus strategy is to use multiple iterations to search for related words and generate **results. The database will often suggest synonyms and related words to try.**

Subject heading: a term, name, or phrase used as an access point in a catalog or index which is arranged by topic. Generally, any particular index will use a standardized set of subject headings, which improves search precision once the user determines the "approved" headings being used for their topic.

Subject search: to seek information by topic (as opposed to author or title). In many indexes and catalogs, a "subject" search implies searching by the use of standardized subject headings assigned by the indexers, as opposed to keyword searching, where the user essentially guesses at words included in titles or abstracts of relevant items.

Subtitle: an explanatory phrase following a main.

Superintendent of Documents (SUDOC) Classification: The call number system that uses a combination of letters and numbers to identify the issuing agency and shelf location of items in the library's U.S. Government Publications collection.

Syndetic structure: in a catalog or index, the system of "see" and "see also" cross references to other headings. TCP/IP:

Transmission Control Protocol/Internet Protocol; the communication program common to most connected

Sysop — (System Operator) Anyone responsible for the physical operations of a computer system or network resource. For example, a System Administrator decides how often backups and maintenance should be performed and the System Operator performs those tasks.

T-1 A *leased-line* connection capable of carrying data at 1,544,000 *bits*-per-second. At maximum theoretical capacity, a T-1 line could move a *megabyte* in less than 10 seconds. That is still not fast enough for full-screen, full-motion video, for which you need at least 10,000,000 bits-per-second. T-1 lines are commonly used to connect large *LAN*s to the*Internet*.

T-3 : A *leased-line* connection capable of carrying data at 44,736,000 bits-per-second. This is more than enough to do full-screen, full-motionvideo.

TCP/IP — (Transmission Control Protocol/Internet Protocol) This is the suiteof protocols that defines the *Internet*. Originally designed for the *UNIX* operating system, TCP/IP software is now included with every major kind of computer operating system. To be truly on the *Internet*, your computer must have TCP/IP software.

Technical Services: the departments which handle acquisition, cataloging, processing, and maintenance of the materials in the library.

Tellus: Marriott's suggestion box - patrons may give us their questions and suggestions either physically by dropping them off in the Tellus box on level 3, or by e-mail; comments and responses are posted on the Tellus board by the level 3 entrance.

Telnet: The command and program used to *login* from one *Internet* siteto another. The telnet command/program gets you to the login: prompt of another *host*.

Temporary control number: a number that appears in the "status" line in UNIS for items that are on order or in process, but not yet available on the shelves. Patrons may request rush ordering or processing of such items by giving the temporary control number to the circulation desk.

Terabyte: 1000 *gigabytes*.

Terminal Server: A special purpose computer that has places to plug in many *modems*on one side, and a connection to a *LAN* or *host* machine onthe other side. Thus the terminal server does the work of answering thecalls and passes the connections on to the appropriate *node*. Mostterminal servers can provide *PPP* or *SLIP* services if connectedto the *Internet*.

Terminal: A device that allows you to send commands to a computer somewhere else. At a minimum, this usually means a keyboard and a display screen and some simple circuitry. Usually you will use terminal software in a personal computer - the software pretends to be (emulates) a physical terminal and allows you to type commands to a computer somewhere else.

Textbook: a limited edition, or a book club item. The "hyper" in Hypertext comes from the fact that in HTML you can specify that a block of text, or an image, is linked to another file on the Internet. HTML files are meant to be viewed using a "Web Browser". The coding language used to create *Hypertext* documents for use on the *World Wide Web*. HTML looks a lot like old-fashioned typesetting code, where you surround a block of text with codes that indicate how it should appear. The protocol for moving *hypertext*files across the *Internet*. Requires a HTTP *client* program on one end, and an HTTP *server* program on the other end. HTTP is the most important protocol used in the *World Wide Web (WWW)*. These indexes are very commonly used by faculty in their tenure process to indicate the impact of their publications on others' research. Citation indexes can also be used for standard author/subject searching.

Theses: often refers to the treatises written by candidates for the Master's Degree, as distinct from doctoral dissertations. Marriott has 2 copies of theses completed at the University of Utah, a circulating copy and an archival copy kept in Special Collections. We do not generally own copies of theses completed at other institutions; these must be obtained by interlibrary loan or purchase.

Thesis statement: a one or two sentence description of the main point you intent to make in the paper or dissertation. It is usually found very near the beginning of the work. An example is "In this paper I will provide evidence that...".

Tie-bound periodicals: volumes loosely bound in cardboard covers because one or more issues of the "run" are missing.

Title search: to search for an item by its title, generally in an alphabetical listing.

TLD — (Top Level Domain) The last (right-hand) part of a complete *Domain Name*. For example in the domain name www.matisse.net ".net" is the Top Level Domain.There are a large number of TLD's, for example .biz, .com, .edu, .gov, .info, .int, .mil, .net, .org, and a collection of two-letter TLD's corresponding to the standard two-letter country codes, for example, .us, .ca, .jp, etc.

Topo: short for topographic map (below)

Topographic map: a map showing physical or natural features of an area, generally including altitude contours. "Maps, topographic" is a standard LC sub-heading which can be used to help find these in UNIS; for example, one could search k=utah and beaver and maps topographic.

Tracings: a list at the bottom of a catalog card showing the other headings under which the item is listed.

Trade book: produced for sale through a bookstore, rather than being a

Trade magazine: a periodical dedicated to the interests

institution is supposed to make a commitment to keep the resource available at that address.

USENET: a world-wide system of electronic discussion groups with over 10,000 discussion areas, referred to as Newsgroups.

UUENCODE — (Unix to Unix Encoding) A method for converting files from *Binary*to *ASCII* (text) so that they can be sent across the Internet via *email*.

Uuncompression: expanding files that have been compressed.

Verification: confirmation of the accuracy of bibliographical data. A common task at the reference desk; a user having difficulty finding an item may need to verify the citation they are working from.

Veronica — (Very Easy Rodent Oriented Net-wide Index to Computerized Archives) Developed at the University of Nevada, Veronica was a constantly updated database of the names of almost every menu item on thousands of *gopher*servers. The Veronica database could be searched from most major *gopher*menus. Now made obsolete by web-bases search engines.

Verso: the left-hand page of a book, usually with even-numbered pages. Opposite of recto (and much more commonly-used term). The copyright date of a book is found on **the verso (back) of the title page.**

Viewer: another name for helper application.

Virus: A chunk of computer programming code that makes copies of itself without any concious human intervention. Some viruses do more than simply replicate themselves, they might display messages, install other software or files, delete software of files, etc. A virus requires the presence of some other program to replicate itself. Typically viruses spread by attaching themselves to programs and in some cases files, for example the file formats for Microsoft word processor and spreadsheet programs allow the inclusion of programs called "macros" which can in some cases be a breeding ground for viruses.

Volume: 1. a unit in a set or series. 2. a single bibliographic unit, i.e. a book. 3. a bound periodical containing several issues.

VPN — (Virtual Private Network) Usually refers to a *network* in which some of the parts are connected using the public *Internet*, but the data sent across the Internet is encrypted, so the entire network is "virtually" private.

WAIS — (Wide Area Information Servers) A commercial software package that allows the indexing of huge quantities of information, and then making those indices searchable across *networks* such as the *Internet*. A prominent feature of WAIS is that the search results are ranked (scored) accordingto how relevant the hits are, and that subsequent searches can find more stuff like that last batch and thus refine the search process.

WAN: Wide Area Network; any computer network over an area larger than a single building or campus.

Web page: A document designed for viewing in a *web browser*. Typically written in *HTML*. A *web site* is made of one or more web pages.

Web search: to use one of the hierarchical subject guides or search engines available from a Web browser to identify and retrieve information housed on the

Web: short for World Wide Web.

Website: The entire collection of *web pages* and other information (such as images, sound, and video files, etc.) that are made available through what appears to users as a single web server. Typically all the of pages in a web site share the same basic *URL*, for example the following URLs are all for pages within the same web site: http://www.baytherapy.com/, http://www.baytherapy.com/whatis/, The term has a somewhat informal nature since a large organization might have separate "web sites" for each division, but someone might talk informally about the organizations' "web site" when speaking of all of them.

Wi-Fi — (Wireless Fidelity) A popular term for a form of wireless data communication, basically Wi-Fi is "Wireless Ethernet".

World Wide Web: A variety of search engines are available by clicking the browser's "Search" button; note that the search syntax used, the set of data being searched, and the retrieval parameters are different for each search

World Wide Web: the set of information resources (or of the hypertext servers which house them) that can be accessed through tools such as Gopher, FTP, HTTP, telnet, USENET, WAIS, etc.

Worm: A worm is a *virus* that does not infect other programs. It makes copies of itself, and infects additional computers (typically by making use of network connections) but does not attach itself to additional programs; however a worm might alter, install, or destroy files and programs.

WWW — (World Wide Web): World Wide Web (or simply Web for short) is a term frequently used (incorrectly) when referring to "The Internet", WWW has two major meanings:First, loosely used: the whole constellation of resources that can be accessed using *Gopher, FTP, HTTP, telnet, USENET, WAIS* and some other tools. Second, the universe of hypertext *servers (HTTP servers)*, more commonly called "web servers", which are the servers that serve *web pages* to web *browsers*.

XML — (eXtensible Markup Language) A widely used system for defining data formats. XML provides a very rich system to define complex documents and data structures such as invoices, molecular data, news feeds, glossaries, inventory descriptions, real estate properties, etc. As long as a programmer has the XML definition for a collection of data (often called a "schema") then they can create a program to reliably process any data formatted according to those rules.

XPFE — (Cross Platform Front End) A suite of technologies used to create applications that will work and look the same on different computer operating systems. A widely used XPFE application; is the Netscape web browser in version 7 and later. The primary technologies used in creating XPFE applications are *Javascript*, *Cascading Style Sheets*, and *XUL*.

XUL — (eXtensible User-interface Language) A markup language similar to *HTML* and based on *XML*. XUL used to define what the user interface will look like for a particular piece of software. XUL is used to define what buttons, scrollbars, text boxes, and other user-interface items will appear, but it is not used to define how those item will look (e.g. what color they are). The most widely used example of XUL use is probably in theMozilla web browser, where the entire user interface is defined using the XUL language.

Yahoo!: one of a number of Web search engines; allows both direct searching and a hierarchical directory organized by subject classification.

Zebra number: number from barcode label used by Circulation.

ZIP: A method of compressing large files for transfer and storage, which can be expanded back for use with.

INDEX